MW00827542

THE NEW COMMON\
OF CONSTITUTIONALISM
Theory and Practice

Stephen Gardbaum argues that recent bills of rights in Canada, New Zealand, the United Kingdom and Australia are an experiment in a new third way of organizing basic institutional arrangements in a democracy. This 'new Commonwealth model of constitutionalism' promises both an alternative to the conventional dichotomy of legislative versus judicial supremacy and innovative techniques for protecting rights. As such, it is an intriguing and important development in constitutional design of relevance to drafters of bills of rights everywhere. In developing the theory and exploring the practice of this new model, the book analyses its novelty and normative appeal as a third general model of constitutionalism before presenting individual and comparative assessments of the operational stability, distinctness and success of its different versions in the various jurisdictions. It closes by proposing a set of general and specific reforms aimed at enhancing these practical outcomes.

STEPHEN GARDBAUM is the MacArthur Foundation Professor of International Justice and Human Rights at the University of California, Los Angeles (UCLA) School of Law. His research focuses on comparative constitutional law, constitutional theory, and federalism.

CAMBRIDGE STUDIES IN CONSTITUTIONAL LAW

The aim of this series is to produce leading monographs in constitutional law. All areas of constitutional law and public law fall within the ambit of the series, including human rights and civil liberties law, administrative law, as well as constitutional theory and the history of constitutional law. A wide variety of scholarly approaches is encouraged, with the governing criterion being simply that the work is of interest to an international audience. Thus, works concerned with only one jurisdiction will be included in the series as appropriate, while, at the same time, the series will include works which are explicitly comparative or theoretical – or both. The series editors likewise welcome proposals that work at the intersection of constitutional and international law, or that seek to bridge the gaps between civil law systems, the US, and the common law jurisdictions of the Commonwealth.

Series Editors

David Dyzenhaus, *Professor of Law and Philosophy,*
University of Toronto, Canada
Adam Tomkins, *John Millar Professor of Public Law,*
University of Glasgow, UK

Editorial Advisory Board

T. R. S. Allan, Cambridge, UK
Damian Chalmers, LSE, UK
Sujit Choudhry, Toronto, Canada
Monica Claes, Maastricht, Netherlands
David Cole, Georgetown, USA
K. D. Ewing, King's College London, UK
David Feldman, Cambridge, UK
Cora Hoexter, Witwatersrand, South Africa
Christoph Moellers, Goettingen, Germany
Adrienne Stone, Melbourne, Australia
Adrian Vermeule, Harvard, USA

THE NEW COMMONWEALTH MODEL OF CONSTITUTIONALISM

Theory and Practice

STEPHEN GARDBAUM

CAMBRIDGE
UNIVERSITY PRESS

CAMBRIDGE UNIVERSITY PRESS
Cambridge, New York, Melbourne, Madrid, Cape Town,
Singapore, São Paulo, Delhi, Mexico City

Cambridge University Press
The Edinburgh Building, Cambridge CB2 8RU, UK

Published in the United States of America by Cambridge University Press, New York

www.cambridge.org
Information on this title: www.cambridge.org/9781107009288

© Stephen Gardbaum 2013

This publication is in copyright. Subject to statutory exception
and to the provisions of relevant collective licensing agreements,
no reproduction of any part may take place without the written
permission of Cambridge University Press.

First published 2013

Printed and bound in the United Kingdom by the MPG Books Group

A catalogue record for this publication is available from the British Library

Library of Congress Cataloguing in Publication data
Gardbaum, Stephen
The new Commonwealth model of constitutionalism : theory and
practice / Stephen Gardbaum.
p.   cm.
Includes bibliographical references.
ISBN 978-1-107-00928-8
1. Constitutional law – Commonwealth countries.   I. Title.
KD5025.G37   2012
342′.11241001–dc23
2012024809

ISBN 978-1-107-00928-8 Hardback
ISBN 978-1-107-40199-0 Paperback

Cambridge University Press has no responsibility for the persistence or
accuracy of URLs for external or third-party internet websites referred to
in this publication, and does not guarantee that any content on such
websites is, or will remain, accurate or appropriate.

For Laura

CONTENTS

ACKNOWLEDGEMENTS

This book grows out of, but substantially develops, my previous thinking and writing on 'the new Commonwealth model of constitutionalism'. Its immediate origins were three invitations I received during the course of 2009. In February, Hilary Charlesworth of the Australian National University invited me to deliver a presentation on how the new Commonwealth model was working in Canada, New Zealand and the United Kingdom at the Protecting Human Rights Conference to be held that October in Sydney in the midst of the national debate on whether Australia should enact a federal human rights act. As it turned out, the conference took place the day before the National Consultation Committee, established by the Labor Government of Kevin Rudd and chaired by the attending Father Frank Brennan, was expected to release its eagerly awaited recommendation and report. In response to the second invitation, issued by Lorraine Weinrib, I presented the resulting paper at the University of Toronto Law Faculty's Constitutional Round Table in December, where David Dyzenhaus encouraged me to think about writing a book on the topic and submitting a proposal for his new Cambridge Studies in Constitutional Law series, co-edited with Adam Tomkins. I am very grateful to all three.

I should also like to express my gratitude to the John Simon Guggenheim Foundation for appointing me as the 2011 Fellow in Constitutional Studies and to the Dorothy Tapper Goldman Foundation for supporting this fellowship, which made it possible for me to complete this book. Equally essential was the moral and financial support of my Dean at UCLA School of Law, Rachel Moran, enabling me to take a research leave during the Fall 2011 semester. For part of this time, New York University School of Law was kind enough to provide me with an office. Also at UCLA, the superb library and research infrastructure was, as ever, invaluable. Thanks, in particular, to Terry Stedman for excellent and painstaking research assistance.

Many of the arguments made in the book were improved as a result of responding to, and thinking further about, questions and comments from audiences during my presentations at the Regulatory Networks Faculty seminar at ANU, the University of Melbourne Centre for Comparative Constitutional Studies, the above-mentioned Constitutional Round Table at Toronto, the Cardozo/NYU I·CON Colloquium on Global and Public Law Theory, the University of Chicago Law School Constitutional Law Workshop, the 2010 Law and Society Association Annual Meeting, the UCLA School of Law International Human Rights Programme workshop, the Comparative Constitutional Law Round Table at George Washington University Law School and Indiana University's Center for Constitutional Democracy. Thanks to the following for organising these events: Hilary Charlesworth, Carolyn Evans, David Fontana, David Kaye, Mattias Kumm, Michel Rosenfeld, Ed Santow, Miguel Schor, Adrienne Stone, David Strauss, Joseph Weiler, Lorraine Weinrib and Susan Williams.

Over the period of time I have been working on this book, I have benefited from wonderful conversations and discussions with, and suggestions about both substance and sources from, Bruce Ackerman, Aharon Barak, Samantha Besson, Sujit Choudhry, Rosalind Dixon, Janet Hiebert, Bruce Howard, Grant Huscroft, Máximo Langer, Paul Rishworth, Seana Shiffrin, Kent Roach, John Tobin, Adam Tomkins, Mark Tushnet and Alison Young.

Finally, I should like to acknowledge those friends and colleagues who took the time and trouble to provide such helpful and valuable feedback on previous drafts of the book, in part or whole: Petra Butler, Lawrence Douglas, Jeremy Gans, Grant Huscroft, Vicki Jackson, Tsvi Kahana, Chris McCrudden, Michael Perry, Seana Shiffrin, John Tobin and Alison Young. To each, my heartfelt thanks.

1

Introduction

As a recent and ongoing experiment in constitutional design, the new Commonwealth model of constitutionalism may be something new under the sun. It represents a third approach to structuring and institutionalizing basic constitutional arrangements that occupies the intermediate ground in between the two traditional and previously mutually exclusive options of legislative and judicial supremacy. It also provides novel, and arguably more optimal techniques for protecting rights within a democracy through a reallocation of powers between courts and legislatures that brings them into greater balance than under either of these two lopsided existing models. In this way, the new Commonwealth model promises to be to forms of constitutionalism what the mixed economy is to forms of economic organization: a distinct and appealing third way in between two purer, but flawed, extremes. Or, it may prove to be, as some have claimed, more like a comet that shone brightly and beguilingly in the constitutional firmament for a brief moment but quickly burned up, a victim of the inexorable law of the excluded middle. In developing the theory and exploring the practice of the new Commonwealth model, this book assesses whether ink or eraser is the better response to its current pencilled-in status on the shortlist of alternatives from which constitutional drafters everywhere make their momentous decisions.

'The new Commonwealth model of constitutionalism' – 'the new model' for short – refers to a common general structure or approach underlying the bills of rights introduced in recent years in Canada (1982), New Zealand (1990), the United Kingdom (1998), the Australian Capital Territory (2004) and state of Victoria (2006). This approach self-consciously departs from the *old* or traditional Commonwealth model of legislative supremacy, in which there is no general, codified bill of rights. Rather, particular rights are created and changed by the legislature through ordinary statutes on an ad hoc basis. Under this traditional model, courts have no power to review legislation for infringing rights, as rights are not limits on legislation but its product, and are changeable by it. In this way, legislatures are supreme because they determine what legal rights there are and how rights issues are resolved. The judicial function is limited to faithfully interpreting and applying whatever laws the legislature enacts.

At the same time, however, the new model also contrasts with the alternative standard option for institutionalizing basic constitutional arrangements: namely, judicial or constitutional supremacy. Here, there is a general, codified bill of rights, which imposes constitutional limits on legislative power. These limits are enforced by authorising courts to review legislation for consistency with the bill of rights and to invalidate statutes that, in their final view, infringe its provisions. As a result, courts are supreme because they have the last word on the validity of legislation and the resolution of rights issues, at least within the existing bill of rights.

As we shall see in detail in the following chapter, the new model's novel third approach calls for the enactment of a bill of rights – although not necessarily one that imposes constitutional limits on the legislature – and its enforcement through the twin mechanisms of judicial *and* political rights review of legislation, but with the legal power of the final word going to the politically accountable branch of government, rather than the courts. In this way, the new model treats legislatures and courts as joint or supplementary rather than alternative exclusive protectors and promoters of rights, as under the two traditional models, and decouples the power of judicial review of legislation from judicial supremacy or finality.

I

If comparative constitutional law, as a recently revived and dynamic academic subject, is a child of the 'rights revolution'[1] that has taken place domestically and internationally since the end of the Second World War, then the new Commonwealth model is a second-generation product – a grandchild – of that revolution in two senses.

First, at the domestic level, the rights revolution was manifested and institutionalized in a massive switch from legislative to judicial supremacy in many parts of the world between 1945 and the late 1970s. Entrenched constitutional bills of rights, enforced through the judicial power to invalidate conflicting legislation against which parliaments were powerless to act by ordinary majority vote, became a central pillar of the 'post-war

---

[1] For this term, see M. Ignatieff, *The Rights Revolution* (Toronto: House of Anansi Press, 2000); S. Choudhry, 'After the Rights Revolution: Bills of Rights in the Post-Conflict State' (2010) *Annual Review of Law and Social Science* 301.

paradigm'[2] of constitutionalism. By contrast, the new model is, in many ways, a second-generation response on the part of certain countries that, starting in the 1980s, embraced the spirit of the revolution but resisted this aspect of the new paradigm as its necessary institutional means.

Prior to World War II, the general model of legislative supremacy, as exemplified not only by the British/Commonwealth doctrine of parliamentary sovereignty but also by the French doctrine that acts of the legislature are the supreme expression of the people's general will,[3] was the dominant model of constitutionalism throughout the world, especially in Europe and with respect to the issue of individual rights and civil liberties.[4] Outside of the United States and a group of newly independent Latin American countries which viewed it as the inspiration for their own revolutionary wars against colonial rule, the very few courts that had the power to review the constitutionality of national legislation for violations of fundamental rights fell into one or more of three categories: they were recent or brief experiments; their claims to such power were heavily contested; or they exercised it in theory but not in practice. Thus, Ireland expressly established judicial review of legislation under its 1937 Constitution,[5] which included protection of fundamental rights. The first two specialized constitutional courts were established in the new republics of Czechoslovakia (1920–38) and Austria (1920–34), but the jurisdiction of the latter was limited until 1929 to petitions from the other branches of government and in practice dealt only with separation of powers issues.[6] Its founder's opposition to

---

[2] L. Weinrib, 'The Postwar Paradigm and American Exceptionalism' in S. Choudhry (ed.), *The Migration of Constitutional Ideas* (Cambridge University Press, 2005).

[3] Article 6 of the Declaration of the Rights of Man, 1789, states that statutes (*lois*) are the supreme expression of the general will. This was interpreted as meaning that Parliament's enactments enjoyed the status appropriate to the expression of the will of the sovereign. See J. Bell, *French Constitutional Law* (Oxford: Clarendon Press, 1992), p. 225.

[4] The fact that the model of legislative supremacy has sometimes been the vehicle for absolutist or authoritarian regimes should not mislead one into denying that it is a form of constitutionalism. Many Latin American countries adopted the model of constitutional supremacy during the nineteenth century, but this did not prevent some of them descending into dictatorship in. See A. Brewer-Carias, *Judicial Review in Comparative Law* (Cambridge University Press, 1989), p. 156. What both of these facts suggest is that constitutionalism is not a matter of form alone. In Canada, Australia, Germany and Switzerland, some form of judicial review of the federalism boundaries between central and provincial governments appeared before 1945, but not with respect to individual rights.

[5] Irish Constitution, Article 34.

[6] Discussing the work of the Austrian Constitutional Court, Cappelletti and Cohen observe that 'laws which curtailed individual liberties remained practically speaking outside the

a bill of rights is famous.[7] In Spain, a specialized court, the Court of Constitutional Guarantees, operated from 1933 to 1936 under the ill-fated Second Republic.[8] In Weimar Germany, the two highest general courts on occasion claimed for themselves the power to review legislation despite silence on this issue in the Constitution, but in practice rarely exercised it, and never with respect to individual rights.[9]

Once the rights revolution was underway, the obvious and catastrophic failure of the legislative supremacy model of constitutionalism to prevent totalitarian takeovers, and the sheer scale of human rights violations before and during World War II, meant that, almost without exception, when the occasion arose for a country to make a fresh start and enact a new constitution, the essentials of the only other available model of constitutionalism were adopted.[10] This is the model of judicial or constitutional supremacy first established in the United States in deliberate and direct rejection of the fundamental British principle of parliamentary sovereignty which, whatever the general merits of its claims to adequately protect liberty, was adjudged by its former American colonial subjects to have utterly failed to protect their common law rights and freedoms. This then-new model inverted the twin principles of the sovereignty of Parliament so that legislative power is legally limited and courts are empowered to enforce these limits.[11]

ambit of [court] control'. M. Cappelletti and W. Cohen, *Comparative Constitutional Law* (Indianapolis: Bobbs-Merrill, 1979), p. 87.

[7] H. Kelsen, 'La Garantie Juridictionnelle de la Constitution' (1928) 4 *Revue du Droit Public* 197.

[8] On the structure and jurisdiction of this court, see Brewer-Carias, *Judicial Review in Comparative Law*, pp. 225–6.

[9] The decision of the *Reichsgericht* of 4 November 1925 asserted the power of judicial review most clearly. But as one commentator describes the situation, German courts 'did not [use the power] to protect fundamental rights': L. Favoreu, 'Constitutional Review in Europe', in L. Henkin and A. Rosenthal (eds.), *Constitutionalism and Rights: The Influence of the United States Constitution Abroad* (New York: Columbia University Press, 1990). See also Brewer-Carias, *Judicial Review in Comparative Law*, p. 204 ('nevertheless, the situation of the system of judicial review [in Germany] up to 1933 was not completely clear so that judicial review of federal laws by all courts was not always accepted and was frequently criticized').

[10] On the 'fresh start' as one of several paradigms explaining the growth of constitutional supremacy after 1945, see B. Ackerman, 'The Rise of World Constitutionalism' (1997) 83 *Virginia Law Review* 771.

[11] These limits were first that a few legislative powers are denied to both federal and state governments, then the total remaining legislative powers were divided between nation and states in the federal system under the doctrine of enumerated powers. Federal legislative power was further limited by the doctrine of separation of powers, and

Accordingly, in order effectively to protect, and express their new commitment to, fundamental human rights and liberties, country after country abandoned legislative supremacy and switched to an entrenched, supreme law constitution with a bill of rights that was judicially, or quasi-judicially, enforced. These included the three former Axis powers, Germany (1949), Italy (1948) and Japan (1947); Spain (1978), Portugal (1982) and Greece (1975) when they emerged from authoritarian dictatorship; France under the current Fifth Republic (1958),[12] as well as Cyprus (1960) and Turkey (1961). Currently, within Western Europe, only the Netherlands and Switzerland do not permit any form of judicial review of national legislation.[13] Until 2000, Finland was a fellow member of this exclusive group, but under its new Basic Law, a limited power of constitutional review is granted to the courts.[14] This brings it more or less into line with the three other Nordic countries of Sweden, Denmark, and Norway, which essentially share a tradition in which an ultimate, residual power of constitutional review is acknowledged in theory, but in practice gives way to *de facto* legislative supremacy.[15] A second concentrated burst of constitutionalization took place in central and eastern Europe after the break-up of the Soviet system

from 1791 also by the Bill of Rights. The Fourteenth Amendment was ultimately interpreted to incorporate almost all of the limits contained in the Bill of Rights against the states. Of course, the US Constitution itself contains no clear grant of the power of judicial review to the courts, but was inferred by Chief Justice Marshall from the status of the Constitution as supreme law, itself (with respect to federal legislation) a structural inference from its written nature: *Marbury* v. *Madison* (1803) 5 US 137.

[12] In France, the *conseil constitutionnel* has exercised review powers with respect to individual rights only since 1971, when it interpreted the preamble to the 1958 Constitution as incorporating both the 1789 Declaration of the Rights of Man and the rights contained in the preamble to the 1946 Constitution of the Fourth Republic. CC decision no. 71–44 DC of 16 July 1971. Its powers were extended from abstract *a priori* review only to include concrete review from the *Conseil d'État* and the *Cour de cassation* under the 2008 constitutional amendments.

[13] 'The constitutionality of Acts of Parliament and treaties shall not be reviewed by the courts', Netherlands Constitution, Article 120. 'Federal statutes and public international law are authoritative for the Federal Supreme Court and the other judicial authorities', Swiss Constitution, Article 190. Luxembourg (1997) and Belgium (1988 and extended in 2003) made the change relatively recently.

[14] Section 106 of Finland's Basic Law 2000 provides that 'if in a matter being tried by a court, the application of an Act would be in evident conflict with the Constitution, the court shall give primacy to the provision in the Constitution.' This innovation complements the existing *ex ante* review conducted by the Constitutional law Committee of the legislature. See J. Husa, 'Guarding the Constitutionality of Laws in the Nordic Countries: A Comparative Perspective' (2000) 48 *American Journal of Comparative Law* 345; K. Tuori, 'Judicial Constitutional Review as a Last Resort' in T. Campbell, K. Ewing and A. Tomkins, *The Legal Protection of Human Rights: Sceptical Essays* (Oxford University Press, 2011).

[15] Husa, 'Guarding the Constitutionality of Laws in the Nordic Countries', p. 365.

in 1989. Here, the creation of constitutional courts has been a universal phenomenon, alongside new constitutions and entrenched bills of rights, extending to Poland (1986),[16] Hungary (1990), Russia (1991), Bulgaria (1991), Czech Republic (1992), Slovak Republic (1992), Romania (1992) and Slovenia (1993).[17] Outside Europe, the same phenomenon has occurred in Asia,[18] in post-junta Latin America[19] and in several African countries, most notably South Africa (1994).

To be sure, both the contents of the fundamental rights protected and the forms of constitutional review adopted in Western Europe after 1945, and again in the former Soviet bloc, Latin America, Africa and Asia since the late 1980s, differ in interesting and well-known ways from the situation in the United States.[20] Notwithstanding these important differences – differences which are central objects of study in comparative constitutional law courses and texts – they ultimately constitute variations within, not from, the American model of constitutional or judicial supremacy as they all share its essential structural features. A specific set of fundamental rights and liberties has the status of supreme law, is entrenched against amendment or repeal by ordinary legislative majorities, and is enforced by an independent institution (usually though not necessarily a 'court'), which has the power to strike down legislation that it finds in conflict with these rights and against whose decisions the legislature is legally powerless to act by ordinary majority. These essentials once again define a constitutional arrangement that is in each respect the polar opposite of the situation in which legislative

---

[16] Poland was the only country in the former Soviet bloc to have a constitutional court, which was established in 1986 with very limited powers to try and head off opposition to the regime. After the fall of the Communists, the court's powers of judicial review were enlarged in 1989. Until 1997, parliament could override a court decision invalidating a statute by a two-thirds majority, but the override power was abolished in the 1997 Constitution.

[17] On the general developments in constitutionalism in central and eastern Europe, see H. Schwartz, *The Struggle for Constitutional Justice in Post-Communist Europe* (Chicago: University of Chicago Press, 2000).

[18] For example, new constitutional courts were created in South Korea (1988), Mongolia (1992) and Thailand (1997). See T. Ginsburg, *Judicial Review in New Democracies: Constitutional Courts in Asian Cases* (Cambridge University Press, 2003).

[19] For example, in Colombia (1991) and Argentina, where the Supreme Court has become independent of the executive and more prominent since the constitutional reforms of 1994 and 2003.

[20] As to forms of constitutional review, most notably the differences are between (1) centralized or concentrated and decentralized or diffuse judicial review; (2) abstract and concrete-only review; (3) *a priori* and *a posteriori* review; and (4) anonymous and unanimous judgments of the court versus individual, dissenting and concurring judgments.

supremacy reigns. The terms legislative and judicial supremacy thus describe not only which institution has the final word on any constitutional issue, but also which institution is primarily entrusted with the tasks of declaring and protecting citizens' rights and liberties.

Like the other countries just discussed, Canada, New Zealand and the United Kingdom, as well as the sub-national entities of the Australian Capital Territory (ACT) and the state of Victoria, have in recent years sought to create greater legal protection for fundamental rights than under their traditional systems of legislative supremacy. But unlike the others, these five jurisdictions have attempted to do so while deliberately refusing to embrace the opposite model of constitutionalism, with its perceived excesses of judicial power. In its place, they have sought to create greater institutional balance and joint responsibility for rights, and thereby to establish a new third model of constitutionalism in between a fully constitutionalized bill of rights and full legislative supremacy, the only two pre-existing options.

There is a second way in which the new Commonwealth model is a less direct, more distant product of the post-1945 rights revolution. Although this revolution was constituted by developments at both the domestic (constitutional bills of rights) and international (international human rights law) levels, for the most part these were parallel developments that took place separately. Comparative constitutional law emerged as an academic subject in significant part to study these domestic developments, comparing the contents of the new bills of rights and their judicial interpretation and application by new constitutional courts – among themselves and with older systems, such as the United States. In both substantive and methodological respects, however, the new model is characterized by more recent trends in the theory and practice of human rights, and is more deeply influenced by international and comparative constitutional law.

Like the bills of rights in several new or extensively amended post-military junta constitutions in Latin America,[21] but unlike the first generation of post-1945 bills of rights, the new model, especially in its most recent instantiations, employs international human rights law to provide much of its content. The preamble to the New Zealand Bill of Rights Act 1990 (NZBORA) states that one of its two purposes is 'to affirm New Zealand's commitment to the International Covenant on Civil and Political Rights

---

[21] Argentina is perhaps the leading example, giving ten specific international human right treaties and instruments domestic constitutional status. Constitution of Argentina, section 75(22).

(ICCPR)', and most of the included rights correspond to ones contained in that treaty. The UK's Human Rights Act 1998 (HRA) declares that its purpose is 'to give further effect to rights and freedoms guaranteed under the European Convention on Human Rights',[22] and the wording of the included rights is identical to those in this treaty.[23] Indeed, the content of these rights is given only by reference to the text of the European Convention on Human Rights (ECHR), which is appended to the HRA as Schedule 1. The Australian Capital Territory's Human Rights Act 2004 (ACTHRA) states that 'the primary source of these rights is the International Covenant on Civil and Political Rights'[24] and the content of the rights in the state of Victoria's Charter of Human Rights and Responsibilities Act 2006 (VCHRR) is similarly largely drawn from the ICCPR.

Methodologically, the new model has also increasingly taken a self-consciously comparative approach by looking at, and learning from, jurisdictions deemed most similar and relevant. Not only, to be sure, in the subsequent interpretation of the document, as we shall see on many occasions, but also in its creation. This is part of what gives it the sense of being a shared work in progress. Thus, once the constitutional strategy had been rejected, framers of the NZBORA were highly conscious of, and keen to avoid, what Paul Rishworth has referred to as the 'anti-precedent' of the statutory Canadian Bill of Rights 1960 (CBOR), with its implied judicial power to invalidate inconsistent legislation.[25] The finished product was well-known and discussed at the time the UK's HRA was enacted,[26] and the two Australian bills have self-consciously attempted to improve on what are perceived as some of the weaknesses of the latter. In this way, as a leading example of comparative rights jurisprudence in action, the new model has helped to move comparative constitutional law out of the study.

II

On the general politics of the new model, all five bills of rights were enacted by left-of-centre governments – Liberals in Canada and Labour

---

[22] HRA, preamble.

[23] A few provisions of the ECHR are omitted from the HRA, namely Articles 1 and 13.

[24] ACTHRA, Part 3, note.

[25] P. Rishworth, 'The Inevitability of Judicial Review under "Interpretive" Bills of Rights: Canada's Legacy to New Zealand and Commonwealth Constitutionalism?' (2004) 23 *Supreme Court Law Review* (second series) 233, 266.

[26] See, for example, A. Butler, 'The Bill of Rights Debate: Why the New Zealand Bill of Rights Act 1990 is a Bad Model for Britain' (1997) 17 *Oxford Journal of Legal Studies* 323.

elsewhere – and opposed by right-of-centre opposition parties. This political alignment itself reflects a realignment of sorts, as traditionally, left-of-centre parties in these countries had been deeply suspicious of judicial power as a conservative, if not reactionary, check on their electoral mandates for democratic reform. What significantly prompted this paradigm shift was the impact of the rights revolution, with its generally progressive aura and sense of constituting the new norm, together with the growing perception that civil liberties were under serious threat and needed greater protection.[27] In addition, there were certain country-specific factors at play, including the more idealistic fresh start of 'repatriating' the constitution in Canada and the more pragmatic concerns in the UK about the country's embarrassingly poor record before the European Court of Human Rights (ECtHR).[28]

The opposition of the centre-right parties in each jurisdiction has continued since initial enactment, with the exception of the currently governing National Party in New Zealand. This opposition took the form of an overt promise to repeal the statutory bill of rights in the UK, and somewhat more veiled and ambiguous threats in Victoria and the ACT. In Canada, faced with the hugely popular[29] – not to mention entrenched and constitutionalized – Canadian Charter of Rights and Freedoms 1982 (the Charter), the governing Conservative Party maintains a studied hostility to it and periodically reaffirms its option of employing the distinctive section 33 legislative override mechanism.[30] By contrast, at least two Liberal Prime Ministers have declared section 33 a mistake and vowed never to use it.[31] Accordingly,

---

[27] In the UK, this was the result of the perceived erosion of civil liberties during the Thatcher era, see K. Ewing and C. Gearty, *Freedom Under Thatcher* (Oxford University Press, 1990); in Canada, the sense of a need for greater protection arose because of the ineffectiveness and dilution of the Canadian Bill of Rights, 1960.

[28] For a detailed study of the origins of each of the bills of rights, see D. Erdos, *Delegating Rights Protection: The Rise of Bills of Rights in the Westminster World* (Oxford University Press, 2010).

[29] In two public opinion polls, the latest in 1999, 82 per cent of respondents rated the Charter 'a good thing'. F. L. Morton (ed.), *Law, Politics and the Judicial Process in Canada*, 3rd edition (Calgary: University of Calgary Press, 2002), at 490.

[30] 'Parliament or the legislature of a province may expressly declare in an Act of Parliament or of the legislature, as the case may be, that the Act or a provision thereof shall operate notwithstanding a provision included in section 2 or sections 7 to 15 of this Charter.' Canadian Charter of Rights and Freedoms 1982, section 33(1). For detailed discussion of section 33, see Chapters 2 and 5 below.

[31] Jean Chrétien and Paul Martin. In addition, Conservative Prime Minister Brian Mulroney, whose proposed Meech Lake and Charlottetown Accords were undermined

although the Charter provokes deeply divided partisan politics, its future does not appear to be seriously at stake.

With the most recent electoral victories of the Conservatives in the UK and the Liberal-Nationals in Victoria, the same is not true of the HRA and VCHRR. Fuelled by a combination of enhanced national security concerns post 9/11 and 7/7, media-induced perception of the HRA as a 'rogues' charter' and growing hostility to European interference in domestic affairs, Conservative plans to repeal it have been thwarted by their Liberal-Democratic coalition partners. Currently, the whole issue has been delegated to an independent commission that is scheduled to report by the end of 2012,[32] and so remains up in the air. The situation is somewhat similar with the VCHRR. The Liberal-National majority on the parliamentary committee conducting its mandatory four-year review recently recommended stripping the courts of their limited enforcement powers, and it is uncertain whether the Baillieu government will take up this recommendation in its response to the review.[33] The ACTHRA appears safe as long as the current Labor government remains in office, whereas at the national level the wafer-thin Labor majority's political fear of bill of rights scepticism has mostly resulted in a stand-off on the issue.[34] Only in New Zealand is the bill of rights generally supported by both of the major political parties.

III

At this point, a few clarifying words on nomenclature and associated matters are in order. I first employed the term 'the new Commonwealth model of constitutionalism' in an article published in 2001[35] and, as already mentioned, intended by it to identify and distinguish a new model of constitutionalism adopted in these Commonwealth jurisdictions for the protection of basic rights that self-consciously departed from the *old* or traditional Commonwealth model of parliamentary sovereignty. To avoid possible confusion, I was not and am not using the term in the sense of 'the new' versus 'the old Commonwealth'; that is,

---

in part by the backlash caused by Quebec's use of section 33, also expressed public opposition to section 33.

[32] For more details, see Chapter 7.   [33] For details, see Chapter 8.

[34] Although, as detailed in Chapter 8, there has been one recent legislative development at the national level: enactment of the Human Rights (Parliamentary Scrutiny) Act 2011.

[35] S. Gardbaum, 'The New Commonwealth Model of Constitutionalism' (2001) 49 *American Journal of Comparative Law* 707.

the later British colonies, mostly in Africa and Asia, which were not significantly settled but only ruled – administratively and militarily – by the British until gaining independence after 1945, versus the earlier colonies populated by settlers from the United Kingdom and granted dominion or self-governing status before 1945.[36] Clearly, within this dichotomy, the jurisdictions I am discussing are all part of the old Commonwealth.[37]

I initially used my term because the Commonwealth was where this new model originated and spread, and is still, with a few relatively minor or partial exceptions,[38] the only place where it has been adopted. In so doing, I was employing a fairly standard practice in comparative law, where historical place of origin is often used for labelling purposes to distinguish different general models of a given concept or practice. Think of the 'Austrian' or 'European' model of judicial review versus the 'American', to distinguish centralized and decentralized systems of constitutional review.[39] It is certainly no part of my claim in employing the term that the new model is necessarily or conceptually connected, and so limited, to the Commonwealth. After all, only three out of fifty-four Commonwealth jurisdictions have adopted it at the national level and, as I just mentioned, the 'few relatively minor or partial exceptions' suggest that it is capable of

---

[36] Perhaps the major source of this informal distinction is S. A. de Smith, *The New Commonwealth and its Constitutions* (London: Stevens, 1964).

[37] Accordingly, perhaps it would be more accurate for me to refer to the 'new old Commonwealth model of constitutionalism' but, apart from likely causing its own confusion, this term might have an (even greater) undesired limiting connotation that undercuts the claimed generality of the model.

[38] In Israel, the Basic Law: Freedom of Occupation, one of 11 Basic Laws, was re-enacted in 1994 with a 'notwithstanding' provision (in section 8) permitting the Knesset to immunize a statute from the Basic Law by a vote of a majority of its members if expressly so stated when enacted. From 1989 until 1997, the Polish legislature was empowered to override a court decision invalidating a statute by a two-thirds majority. Under Article 145(1) of the Romanian Constitution, the legislature may override a constitutional court decision on abstract review before promulgation of a statute by re-enacting the statute with a two-thirds majority vote in each of the two chambers. Finally, in enacting the European Convention on Human Rights Act 2003, Ireland borrowed much of the structure of the UK's Human Rights Act 1998, including the judicial declaration of incompatibility mechanism. However, within the Irish legal system this amounts to a supplementary set of statutory rights (incorporating those under the European Convention on Human Rights (ECHR)) to the ones already contained in its supreme law constitution, and so reflects only partial rather than general adoption of the new model.

[39] See M. Cappelletti, P. J. Kollmer and J. M. Olson, *The Judicial Process in Comparative Perspective* (Oxford: Clarendon Press, 1989); Favoreu, 'Constitutional Review in Europe'.

adoption outside the Commonwealth. Nor even is my claim that the new model is so connected and limited to common law or previously legislative supremacy jurisdictions,[40] or indeed to parliamentary versus presidential systems of government. On the contrary, it is a quite general model, like the two traditional ones. In my view, there is nothing conceptually to prevent a previously judicial supremacy jurisdiction, such as the United States (presidential) or Germany (parliamentary), from adopting or adapting the new model – although in the case of these two particular countries the obvious historical, institutional and cultural obstacles are such that this change is hard to imagine. I have been told by academics in Brazil and Turkey, who approached me because they wanted to make articles on it accessible to their legal communities, that in their view the new model would be particularly suitable for these countries, and I could even more easily conceive the model operating in one or more Nordic countries, with their histories of ultra-minimalist judicial review.[41] And, of course, it already operates in both federal (Canada) and unitary systems (New Zealand, United Kingdom), and came close to being adopted in a second federal system, at the national level in Australia, two years ago.[42]

Indeed, somewhat ironically, in one way it may be common law jurisdictions that are least suited to the new model. Arguably, it was precisely because of the high prestige and overt law-making powers of judges within this legal tradition that a strong doctrine of parliamentary sovereignty, with its clear and categorical limits on judicial power, was deemed most necessary. Once that strong version of the doctrine is weakened, as we shall see it is under the new model, the continuing cultural prestige and power of the judiciary may make it relatively more difficult for the legislature to challenge their expressed views than it might in the civil law world, with its less powerful and grandiose general conception of the judicial role. Once human or fundamental rights become a legal and not only a political issue, it may prove harder to maintain a balance between these two, as the new model attempts to do, than it might elsewhere.

As to why the new model has in fact so far been more or less limited to the Commonwealth, I think this is mostly for a combination of historical-cultural and practical-structural reasons. It is, first of all, early days in its

---

[40] For what it is worth, although the 'relatively minor or partial exceptions' are all outside the Commonwealth, both Israel (in part) and Ireland are common law jurisdictions with historical connections to British law.

[41] See, for example, Husa, 'Guarding Constitutionality of Laws in the Nordic Countries'.

[42] See Chapter 8.

history and news has mostly spread, as it were, to family members only. There is a commonality of legal culture among the sub-family of Commonwealth common law jurisdictions,[43] as evidenced by the practice of parliaments and courts in citing the legislation and judicial opinions of these jurisdictions far more readily and frequently than others. There are also at least three Commonwealth law journals,[44] a series of Commonwealth law reports,[45] a Commonwealth Lawyers' Association, and an Oxford chair in Commonwealth (and United States) law.[46] When seeking to institutionalize change in their rights regimes, but in the relatively incremental and non-revolutionary mode that characterizes their general political and legal systems, these countries first looked to each other. Secondly, although (as just stated) by no means necessarily limited to previously legislative supremacy jurisdictions, the observed phenomenon that it is generally easier to let the genie of judicial power out of the bottle than to get it back in – to increase rather than reduce it – suggests that in practice the movement is more likely to be in this direction. Also, the most common version of the new model, a statutory or interpretative bill of rights, only really works where the constitution has the legal status of ordinary law, where there is no existing big-C constitution.[47] Since the Commonwealth contains the greatest remaining cluster of countries which have not formally adopted constitutional supremacy, it is not surprising that the first candidates for the new model should emerge there.

To address a second source of possible terminological confusion (the new versus the old Commonwealth being the first), the model of constitutionalism that is the subject matter of this book has also come to be known by several other names. These are: (1) 'weak-form judicial review'[48] or just 'weak judicial review';[49] (2) 'the parliamentary bill of

---

[43] A little over half of the 54 members of the Commonwealth have common law legal systems.

[44] These are the *Oxford University Commonwealth Law Journal*, the *Journal of Commonwealth Law and Legal Education*, and the *Commonwealth Law Bulletin*.

[45] *Law Reports of the Commonwealth* (Butterworth).

[46] Rhodes Professorship of the Laws of the Commonwealth and the United States.

[47] M. Elliott, 'Interpretative Bills of Rights and the Mystery of the Unwritten Constitution' (2011) *New Zealand Law Review* 591. This is also why Ireland has only partially adopted the new model, see n. 38.

[48] M. Tushnet, 'Alternative Forms of Judicial Review' (2003) 101 *Michigan Law Review* 2781.

[49] J. Waldron, 'The Core of the Case Against Judicial Review' (2006) 115 *Yale Law Journal* 1348, 1354.

rights model';[50] and (3) 'the dialogue model', 'the model of democratic dialogue'[51] or 'dialogic judicial review'.[52] For the most part, these are simply alternative terms for the same phenomenon and can be thought of synonymously, as interchangeable with the new Commonwealth model of constitutionalism.

Although I do not hold strong views on the matter, I continue to prefer this latter term because on balance it seems to me to have the best overall fit. The concept of 'weak-form judicial review' is extremely helpful in distinguishing the intermediate powers of courts under the new model from both the 'strong-form judicial review' of constitutional or judicial supremacy and the absence of any powers of constitutional review of (primary) legislation under traditional parliamentary sovereignty or legislative supremacy. This is why I shall be employing this term myself throughout the book to refer to this feature of the new model. As a general term for the new model as a whole, however, it is under-inclusive because weak-form judicial review is one (important) component of the new model, but not the only one. The model is not limited to these differences among the constitutional review powers of courts, but also includes other specific and essential features that will be explained in the following chapter, including, most importantly, mandatory pre-enactment political rights review. It is this entire package that defines and distinguishes the new model. Focusing only on the courts' powers of review is not only descriptively under-inclusive, but also risks distorting assessment of the new model's overall distinctness and success, as arguably already witnessed in discussions of whether the power of courts in the UK or Canada is 'really' weak.[53] The term may also be over-inclusive, insofar as it could also be used to describe other, different and currently fashionable constitutional theories that grant more limited powers to courts than under standard versions of judicial supremacy, such as 'popular constitutionalism' and 'departmentalism' in the United States.[54] As a

---

[50] J. Hiebert, 'Parliamentary Bills of Rights: An Alternative Model?' (2006) 69 *Modern Law Review* 7.

[51] A. L. Young, *Parliamentary Sovereignty and the Human Rights Act* (Oxford: Hart Publishing, 2009), ch. 5.

[52] K. Roach, 'Dialogic Judicial Review and its Critics' (2004) 23 *Supreme Court Law Review* (second series) 49.

[53] See A. Kavanagh, *Constitutional Review under the UK Human Rights Act* (Cambridge University Press, 2009), pp. 416–19 (UK); G. Huscroft, 'Constitutionalism from the Top Down' (2007) 45 *Osgoode Hall Law Journal* 91, 95–8 (Canada).

[54] See L. Kramer, *The People Themselves: Popular Constitutionalism and Judicial Review* (New York: Oxford University Press, 2004); R. Post and R. Siegel, 'Popular Constitutionalism, Departmentalism, and Judicial Supremacy' (2004) 92 *California*

general label, weak-form judicial review does not distinguish the new model from (at least certain versions of) these two other theories, as its defining feature of judicial non-finality is common to all three.[55]

By contrast, 'the parliamentary bill of rights model' very helpfully emphasizes the other half of the new model: its dispersion of rights responsibilities from the courts to the elected institutions, and particularly the legislature, as compared with judicial supremacy. As an overall label, however, it too is under-inclusive in a way that potentially detracts from the generality of the new model on a par with the two traditional ones. First, if 'parliamentary' means or comes to be equated with 'statutory', it would seem to exclude, or only awkwardly include, a constitutional bill of rights, such as the Canadian Charter, which is not only *an* instance of the new model but, along with the Canadian Bill of Rights 1960 (the CBOR),[56] its founding one. Secondly, in focusing on the major component of the new model omitted by the previous term, it overcompensates by de-emphasizing the role and distinctive form of judicial review. Thirdly, it also seems to exclude, or include only awkwardly, non-parliamentary systems, which (unlike the case of constitutional bills of rights) is accurate if the label is a descriptive-only one. If it has a more conceptual or general connotation, then it is preferable if the term used does not exclude what in principle could be within the scope of the new model's operation.

Although I initially used the term 'dialogue' in my 2001 article to describe one of several potential normative benefits of the new model,[57] I have since become somewhat sceptical of the term, and largely try to avoid it for reasons explained more fully in Chapter 5. For now, let me just say that as either a label for, or primary goal of, the new model, I think that 'democratic dialogue' or 'the dialogue model' or 'dialogic judicial review' is somewhat vague and over-inclusive. It does not

---

Law Review 1027; M. S. Paulsen, 'The Most Dangerous Branch: Executive Power to Say What the Law Is' (1994) 83 *Georgetown Law Review* 217.

[55] Indeed, Mark Tushnet suggests that at least one version of departmentalism (the one held by Thomas Jefferson) has a similar structure to weak-form judicial review in Canada, New Zealand and the UK. See M. Tushnet, *Weak Courts, Strong Rights: Judicial Review and Social Welfare Rights in Comparative Constitutional Law* (Princeton: Princeton University Press, 2008), p. 16. Alon Harel and Adam Shinar refer to all three theories collectively as 'theories of constrained judicial review'. See Harel and Shinar, 'Between Judicial and Legislative Supremacy' (forthcoming).

[56] The Canadian Bill of Rights Act 1960, a statutory bill of rights applying only to the federal government, is still in force. As mentioned below, it remains as a distinct version of the new model with its (implied) power of judicial invalidation of statutes. For more detail, see Chapter 5.

[57] Gardbaum, 'The New Commonwealth Model of Constitutionalism', 746–7.

sufficiently distinguish the new model as a distinct institutional form of constitutionalism from constitutional or judicial supremacy, but rather blurs the differences between the two. If limitations clauses in constitutions trigger dialogue between courts and legislators,[58] if even the constitutional system in the United States produces and embraces dialogue between the courts and Congress[59] or between the Supreme Court and public opinion,[60] as we are told, then there would appear to be virtually no such thing as non-dialogic judicial review. At most, any distinction on this score between the new model and the traditional model of judicial supremacy would be quantitative only; that is, how dialogic.

A final word on terminology. Unless otherwise stated, I shall be using the following sets of terms more or less synonymously: (1) constitutional supremacy, judicial supremacy and legal constitutionalism; (2) parliamentary sovereignty, legislative supremacy and political constitutionalism; (3) judicial review (in the American sense) and constitutional review.[61]

IV

The aims of this book are twofold: (1) to present the new model as a novel and general model of constitutionalism in a more systematic and comprehensive way than before, and (2) to assess whether and to what extent it is operating distinctly and successfully. To fulfil these twin aims, the book is divided into two parts, exploring respectively the theory and practice of the new model. Chapter 2 is analytical in focus and has the goal of explaining what the new model is and what distinguishes it from the two traditional, and previously mutually exclusive, institutional forms of constitutionalism. As part of this task, it identifies the new model's novel and distinctive techniques for protecting rights in a democracy, and its suggestion that the conceptual map of constitutionalism should be drawn on a larger scale, revealing more of a continuum

---

[58] P. Hogg and A. Bushell, 'The Charter Dialogue Between Courts and Legislatures (Or Perhaps The Charter of Rights Isn't Such A Bad Thing After All)' (1997) 35 *Osgoode Hall Law Journal* 75.

[59] N. Devins and L. Fisher, *The Democratic Constitution* (Oxford University Press, 2004), pp. 238–9.

[60] B. Friedman, 'Dialogue and Judicial Review' (1993) 91 *Michigan Law Review* 577; B. Friedman, *The Will of the People: How Public Opinion has Influenced the Supreme Court and Shaped the Meaning of the Constitution* (New York: Farrar, Straus and Giroux, 2009).

[61] I shall be saying more about legal and political constitutionalism, and explaining my 'more or less' synonymous usage with the other terms, at the beginning of the next chapter.

than a bipolar universe. Chapter 3, by contrast, is normative and presents the general case for the new model as a third and intermediate form of constitutionalism. In so doing, this chapter engages with the latest theoretical contributions to the debate about the merits of judicial or constitutional review, and argues that the new model radically and compellingly permits a form of proportional representation among the best arguments for and against the practice rather than the 'warts and all' of the traditional either/or approach. If Chapter 3 can be said to present the 'external' normative case for the new model as against the other two standard forms of constitutionalism, Chapter 4 develops the 'internal' normative case for it, in the sense of articulating an ideal theory of how the model ought to work. In particular, it will explore the norms that should govern each of the three characteristic stages of the new model which institutionalize its deliberate sequence of political and legal rights review, and also the question of when should a legislature act on its independent judgement and exercise its distinctive legal power of the final word where protected rights are at stake.

In Part II, the book changes gear, from the theoretical to the practical. Chapters 5 to 8 describe the different versions of the new model adopted in Canada, New Zealand, the United Kingdom and Australia respectively, assess how successfully they are working as instantiations of the new model and in delivering its theoretical benefits presented in Part I, and identify any major practical problems or weaknesses that have emerged. Chapter 9 pulls all this material together by presenting an overall assessment of the new model and an answer to the ink or eraser question. It evaluates the general success and distinctness of the new model in practice and, in the process, critically examines sceptical claims of inherent instability and insufficient difference from judicial supremacy. It concludes with a series of general and specific reforms that may help the new model to better achieve its normative goals in practice.

PART I

Theory

What is the new Commonwealth model and what is new about it?

I Legal and political constitutionalism

At the risk of over-simplification, constitutional democracies share the two basic concepts from which this form of government derives, but differ in how they are institutionalized. Emerging from seventeenth-century battles of sword and mind against political absolutism, the basic concept of constitutionalism at its core is about the *scope* and modes of governmental power and, in particular, the constraints that are placed on it to protect the individual and collective liberties of its subjects. By contrast, the basic concept of democracy, invented (so far as we know) in ancient Greece and rediscovered mostly in the nineteenth century, is centrally about the *source* and legitimation of governmental power and, at a minimum, in its modern retooling, about the need for this power to be electorally accountable to its citizens as the key mechanism of their self-government and political equality. Because at root the two concepts have somewhat different objects or functions, it is possible to have alternative forms of government to a constitutional democracy that conform to one but not the other, such as a ruling, or 'efficient',[1] hereditary constitutional monarch and a democratically elected and maintained dictatorship.[2]

Accordingly, a fundamental issue concerning constitutionalism – and especially within a democracy – is how should constraints on governmental

---

[1] The reference is to Bagehot's distinction between the dignified ('those which excite and preserve the reverence of the population') and efficient ('those by which it, in fact, works and rules') parts of a constitution and the British monarch's position as exemplifying the former. W. Bagehot, *The English Constitution*, The Fontana Library (London: Collins, 1963), p. 61.

[2] For an excellent recent account that does not risk over-simplifying the relationship between constitutionalism and democracy but rather analyses its rich complexity, see N. Walker, 'Constitutionalism and the Incompleteness of Democracy: An Iterative Relationship' (2010) 39 *Rechtsfilosofie & Rechtstheorie* 206. For another that emphasizes the opposition between the two concepts, see J. Waldron, 'Constitutionalism – A Skeptical View' in T. Christiano and J. Christman (eds.), *Contemporary Debates in Political Philosophy* (London: Wiley-Blackwell, 2009).

power be institutionalized, what institutional form should they take? Constitutional democracies have historically provided two major answers to this question, two institutional forms of constitutionalism from which to choose. These two options go by various names – legislative supremacy or parliamentary sovereignty and judicial or constitutional supremacy, as we have seen – but perhaps the most helpful for immediate purposes are the currently fashionable labels, at least in certain places: political and legal constitutionalism.[3] Roughly speaking, political constitutionalism stands for the proposition that the limits on governmental power inherent in the concept of constitutionalism – limits that qualify the noun in the term 'constitutional democracy' – and especially those that are expressed in terms of individual rights and liberties, are or should be predominantly political in nature, enforced through the ordinary mechanisms of Madisonian-style structural constraints[4] and, especially, through electoral accountability.[5] In other words, to a significant extent the representative nature of modern democracy provides it own built-in check on the scope of governmental power, thereby fusing the two constitutive concepts. By contrast, legal constitutionalists believe that these limits in general, and rights in particular, are or should be predominantly legal in nature and enforced through the power of courts to disapply acts that exceed them. Although in the English-speaking world, legal constitutionalism is usually traced back to Coke, it was first clearly adopted in the United States, and discussion of the relative merits of these two models goes back at least as far as Chief Justice Marshall's opinion in *Marbury* v. *Madison* and his rebuttal of the arguments against constitutional supremacy,[6] if not to *The Federalist Papers.*[7]

---

[3] For an explanation and defence, as well as the limits of, my synonymous use of these three terms, see section IV below.

[4] That is, by creating checks and balances within the ordinary operation of the political system itself, such as legislative oversight of the executive.

[5] Two leading manifestos of political constitutionalism are A. Tomkins, *Our Republican Constitution* (Oxford: Hart Publishing, 2005) and R. Bellamy, *Political Constitutionalism: A Republican Defence of the Constitutionality of Democracy* (Cambridge University Press, 2007).

[6] Note that Chief Justice Marshall's argument, that leaving limits to the legislature rather than the courts would be an absurd and toothless exercise in self-checking, overlooks political constitutionalism's major argument that the external check on governmental power comes from its political accountability to the electorate. Although, to be sure, Congress's direct political accountability to the electorate was significantly less in 1803 than now.

[7] Proto-arguments for both legal and political constitutionalism can be found in *The Federalist Papers*. Compare Madison's reliance on structural/political limits on governmental power in Nos. 10 and 51 with Hamilton's arguments for legal constitutionalism and judicial review in No. 78.

Within the bounds of political constitutionalism, it is possible for rights and liberties to be legalized in the common law or by statute, as long as they are politically changeable and controllable through ordinary, politically accountable decision-making of the legislature. Within legal constitutionalism, by contrast, at least some rights are enforceable by the courts as higher, not ordinary, law and are therefore not changeable by normal political means.

In recent years, public law theory in the United Kingdom has been dominated by the discourse and competing models of political and legal constitutionalism. This dominance has emerged as a result of mutually reinforcing developments in both practice and theory that in combination have created the strong impression that the country is moving away from the political constitutionalism associated with its traditional model of parliamentary sovereignty, in which the legislative power of Parliament is legally unlimited and courts have no power to call into question the validity of statutes on substantive grounds. On the practical side, these well-known developments include the legal consequences of membership of the European Union and the ECHR, the expansion and strengthening of judicial review of administrative actions,[8] judicial fashioning of the principle of 'legality',[9] and the enactment and application of the HRA. On the theory side, legal constitutionalists have helped to 'incite'[10] this shift and wish to see it further extended. In particular, they have provided and refined a form of legal constitutionalism that is more immediately relevant to the UK than the traditional rival and polar opposite of parliamentary sovereignty: the American model of constitutional supremacy. This second form of legal constitutionalism is common law constitutionalism.[11] If legal constitutionalism in general posits a higher form of law than ordinary statute that courts have the power to

---

[8] See C. Forsyth (ed.), *Judicial Review and the Constitution* (Oxford: Hart Publishing, 2000).

[9] S. Lakin, 'Debunking the Idea of Parliamentary Sovereignty: the Controlling Factor of Legality in the British Constitution' (2008) 28 *Oxford Journal of Legal Studies* 28; *R. v. Secretary of State for the Home Department ex parte Simms* [2000] 2 AC 115 at 131, per Lord Hoffman.

[10] J. Goldsworthy, *Parliamentary Sovereignty: Contemporary Debates* (Cambridge University Press, 2010), p. 12.

[11] See T. R. S. Allan, *Law, Liberty, and Justice: The Legal Foundations of British Constitutionalism* (Oxford University Press, 1993); T. R. S. Allan, *Constitutional Justice: A Liberal Theory of the Rule of Law* (Oxford University Press, 2001); J. Laws, 'Law and Democracy' (1995) *Public Law* 72–93; J. Laws, 'The Constitution, Morals and Rights' (1996) *Public Law* 622–35.

enforce against conflicting government acts, then these two versions of it rely on different sources of that higher law: the written constitution in the case of the American model, and judicially recognized common law principles in the case of common law constitutionalism. Both are thus forms of constitutional supremacy, in theory at least they differ only as to the source of the higher law constitution that courts are empowered to enforce.[12] Political constitutionalists are deeply concerned by this apparent trend and have developed a well-theorized and articulated response to it in the last few years in the hope of halting or reversing it. In Australia, the recent active consideration but ultimate political rejection of a statutory bill of rights at the national level was largely conducted in terms of the debate between legal and political constitutionalism.[13]

Accordingly, by adding a second form of legal constitutionalism, the contemporary debate between legal and political constitutionalists has recast – and enriched – the standard dichotomy between the models of judicial and legislative supremacy, but not transcended it. To the contrary, the work of common law constitutionalists has deepened the divide by providing a form of legal constitutionalism – a form of judicial supremacy – particularly suited to the traditions of Westminster-based systems. It claims the existence of judicially enforceable higher law even absent a switch to a formal written constitution, including the power of courts to disapply conflicting statutes.

Elsewhere, the opposition between political and legal constitutionalism has mostly taken the more purely academic form of an ongoing debate over the merits and demerits of judicial/constitutional review.[14] This similarly dichotomous debate has also flared back into life independently of these particular developments, with several notable and innovative contributions on either side in recent years.[15] Although of course a central component of the discourse taking place within traditionally Westminster-style systems,

---

[12] Although some versions of common law constitutionalism posit that common law principles inherently form a higher law constitution regardless of the absence or existence – and so even in the presence – of a written constitution.

[13] See Chapter 8.

[14] It is more purely academic because, as a practical matter, the real world debate has been decisively won by legal constitutionalism. As Mark Tushnet memorably put it, prior to the rise of the new experiments, the Westminster model of legislative supremacy had been withdrawn from sale. M. Tushnet, 'New Forms of Judicial Review and the Persistence of Rights- and Democracy-Based Worries' (2003) 38 *Wake Forest Law Review* 813, 814.

[15] These include R. Fallon, 'The Core of an Uneasy Case for Judicial Review' (2008) 121 *Harvard Law Review* 1693; A. Harel and T. Kahana, 'The Easy Core Case for Judicial

this currently lively and increasingly global academic debate about judicial review ranges well beyond its jurisdictional confines to countries such as the United States, with deeply rooted systems of constitutional supremacy (and deeply rooted academic concerns about the practice), as well as to the newer democracies of eastern Europe.[16]

What is new and exciting about the new Commonwealth model is that it promises to transcend the either/or nature of the existing choice, to offer a third institutional form of constitutionalism in between the two traditional and dichotomous ones of legal or political constitutionalism, constitutional or legislative supremacy, judicial review or no judicial review. As part and parcel of this new intermediate form, the new model pushes beyond the outer limits of political constitutionalism's toleration of legal forms of rights protection but stops short of legal constitutionalism's near-exclusive focus on them. By mixing political and legal limits, political and legal modes of accountability, the new model carves out a distinct third answer to the general question of how constitutionalism's core limits on governmental power should be institutionalized in a democracy.

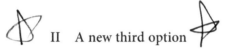

II   A new third option

In essence, the new Commonwealth model of constitutionalism consists in the combination of two novel techniques for protecting rights. These are mandatory pre-enactment political rights review and weak-form judicial review.

The first technique requires both of the elective branches of government to engage in rights review of a proposed statute before and during the bill's legislative process. The formalized, mandatory and deliberate nature of political rights review under the new model distinguishes it from characteristic practices under both other forms of constitutionalism, where if any such review occurs it tends to be ad hoc, voluntary and

---

Review' (2010) 2 *Journal of Legal Analysis* 1; M. Kumm, 'Institutionalising Socratic Contestation: The Rationalist Human Rights Paradigm, Legitimate Authority and the Point of Judicial Review' (2007) 1 *European Journal of Legal Studies*, No. 2; M. Kumm, 'Democracy is not Enough: Rights, Proportionality and the Point of Judicial Review' in M. Klatt (ed.), *The Legal Philosophy of Robert Alexy* (Oxford University Press, 2009); W. Sadurski, 'Judicial Review and the Protection of Constitutional Rights' (2002) 22 *Oxford Journal of Legal Studies* 275; M. Tushnet, 'How Different are Waldron's and Fallon's Core Cases for and against Judicial Review' (2010) 30 *Oxford Journal of Legal Studies* 49; J. Waldron, 'The Core of the Case Against Judicial Review' (2006) 115 *Yale Law Journal* 1348.

[16] See, for example, Sadurski, 'Judicial Review and the Protection of Constitutional Rights'.

unsystematic.[17] Political rights review is a direct and alternative response to the standard concerns about legislative/majoritarian rights sensibilities that underlie the traditional argument for judicial review of legislation. Political rights review is designed to take this concern seriously and to address it directly, at the horse's mouth as it were, by ensuring that the general rights consciousness of both the executive that proposes bills and the legislature that considers and enacts them is raised, and that specific rights concerns are identified and aired during the legislative process.[18] In other words, political rights review provides an internal solution to this potential problem that transfers some of the responsibility for rights protection from the external and more indirect mechanism of judicial review to the legislature itself. As such, it also supplements a purely ex post technique of rights protection with an ex ante one, with many of the associated general advantages of this type of regulation. In this context, ex ante regulation provides the only protection against those outputs of the legislative process that are never litigated for one reason or another,[19] and a second layer in addition to ex post review for those that are.

The second technique of rights protection that is constitutive of the new model is weak-form judicial review. It is this technique that decouples judicial review from judicial supremacy, meaning that although courts have powers of constitutional review, they do not necessarily or

---

[17] Under their pre-new model parliamentary sovereignty systems, there were few such mechanisms or institutions so that, for the most part, new bodies and practices have been established at both executive and legislative levels. Australia has just adopted mandatory political rights review at the federal level for first time, but this is clearly based on the new model paradigm, see Chapter 8. Within systems of judicial supremacy, where it is undertaken at all, political rights review tends to occur in a less formal and more partisan way. Where there is abstract judicial review, for strategic reasons legislators sometimes express their policy differences in the language of constitutional law with an eye towards the final, judicial stage of the legislative process. See A. Stone Sweet, *Governing with Judges: Constitutional Politics in Europe* (Oxford University Press, 2000), ch. 3; J. Hiebert, 'Constitutional Experimentation: Rethinking How a Bill of Rights Functions' in T. Ginsburg and R. Dixon (eds.), *Comparative Constitutional Law* (Cheltenham: Edward Elgar, 2011), p. 307.

[18] See J. Hiebert, 'New Constitutional Ideas: Can New Parliamentary Models Resist Judicial Dominance when Interpreting Rights?' (2004) 82 *Texas Law Review* 1963; J. Hiebert, 'Parliamentary Bills of Rights: An Alternative Model?' (2006) 69 *Modern Law Review* 7; J. B. Kelly, 'The Commonwealth Model and Bills of Rights: Comparing Legislative Activism in Canada and New Zealand' Paper presented at the conference on Parliamentary Protection of Human Rights, University of Melbourne, 20–22 July 2006.

[19] B. Slattery, 'A Theory of the Charter' (1987) 25 *Osgoode Hall Law Journal* 714; J. Hiebert, *Charter Conflicts: What is Parliament's Role?* (Montreal: McGill-Queen's University Press, 2002), p. 14.

automatically have final authority on what the law of the land is. Unlike the
case under judicial supremacy, their decisions are not unreviewable by
ordinary legislative majority. This is because one of the defining features
of the technique (and so of the new model) is that it grants the legal power –
but not the duty – of the final word to the legislature. That is, in giving
political discretion to the legislature whether or not to use it in any
particular case, the new model creates a gap between this legal power and
its exercise that distinguishes it from both legal and political constitutionalism. Whereas under strong-form judicial review and legislative supremacy, the institution with the power of the final word is essentially bound to
exercise it and does so routinely, almost automatically – courts in the
context of deciding a case or abstract review and legislatures because the
act of passing a law *is* the final word – this is not so under the new model. In
deciding whether (rather than how) to use their power, legislatures may be
heavily influenced by the prior exercise of weak-form judicial review.

Here it is necessary to clarify both the relevant sense of judicial supremacy that the new model rejects and what is novel about the technique. The
term judicial supremacy has become a little clouded as a result of the rise of
dialogue theory alluded to in the introductory chapter. As we shall see in
detail in Chapter 5 on Canada, where the theory originated and has its
strongest hold, its proponents argue that, quite apart from the formal
section 33 override power, the frequency of 'legislative sequels' following
the judicial invalidation of a statute means there is judicial-legislative
dialogue and often de facto legislative supremacy, especially where such
sequels are upheld by the courts.[20] Even in the United States, it has been
noted that a similar practice of legislative sequels and inter-institutional
dialogue sometimes occurs, as exemplified by Congress's continuing to
create hundreds of legislative vetoes of executive action after the practice
was declared unconstitutional by the Supreme Court in *INS* v. *Chadha*.[21]
This, it has been argued, means that in reality the meaning of the
Constitution depends on interpretations put forward by legislators in
opposition to those proposed by the judiciary and that no single institution,
judiciary included, has the final word on constitutional questions.[22] Putting
aside the fact that the *Chadha* episode is unrepresentative of US constitutional law as a whole because on separation of powers (as distinct from
rights) issues it is well-known that legal resolutions generally play a lesser

---

[20] Hogg and Bushell, 'The Charter Dialogue between Courts and Legislatures'.
[21] 462 US 919 (1983). See Devins and Fisher, *The Democratic Constitution*, p. 94.
[22] Devins and Fisher, ibid. pp. 238–9.

role than political ones,[23] this train of thought misses the specific and relevant finality issue. This is who has the final legal word on the validity and continuing operation of the particular existing law at issue in the litigation, not whether the judicial decision binds *future* legislative or executive acts – an issue about which there has long been divided opinion in the United States.[24] But on this relevant issue for our purposes, there is no doubt or controversy: the judiciary has the final word on whether the specific law (or part of it) challenged in *Chadha* is the law of the land – and indeed, on the validity of any of the subsequently enacted legislative vetoes that may come before them. This is what, in context, strong-form judicial review refers to.[25] By contrast, weak-form judicial review under the new model means that the legislature and not the judiciary has de jure finality, the legal power of the final word with respect to the specific law at issue – unlike in the United States or other regimes of judicial supremacy.

On the novelty of the technique, as suggested in the introductory chapter, the concept of weak-form judicial review per se may not be original to the new model. This is because there are arguably other pre-existing constitutional theories that have a similar basic structure of

---

[23] See, for example, J. Barron and C. Thomas Dienes, *Constitutional Law* (St. Paul: West, Fourth Edition, 1999), p. 132 ('the courts have tended to avoid judicial review of executive actions, especially in the area of foreign affairs and national security'). Indeed, Dean Choper influentially argued that separation of powers questions should generally be treated as political questions inappropriate for judicial resolution. J. Choper, *Judicial Review and the National Political Process* (University of Chicago Press, 1980).

[24] Compare the US Supreme Court's statement in *Cooper* v. *Aaron* 358 US 1 (1958), that its interpretations of the Constitution are the supreme law of the land and bind all legislative and executive officials, with the statements to the contrary by Presidents Jefferson, Jackson, Lincoln, and Franklin Roosevelt; see K. Sullivan and G. Gunther, *Constitutional Law*, 17th edition (New York: Foundation Press, 2010), pp. 22–5, as well as then-incumbent Attorney General Edwin Meese. E. Meese, 'The Law of the Constitution' (1987) 61 *Tulane Law Journal* 979. It is uncontroversial that, under the doctrine of precedent, decisions of the Supreme Court bind all other courts in subsequent cases.

[25] See *Dickerson* v. *United States* 530 US 428 (2000): 'Congress may not legislatively supersede our decisions interpreting and applying the Constitution', per Rehnquist, C. J. There is, however, some controversy over the existence and scope of Congress's ability under its Article III, section 2 power to make 'Exceptions' to the Supreme Court's appellate jurisdiction to respond to judicial decisions by stripping the Supreme Court (and other federal courts) of jurisdiction over specific subject matters. Compare L. Tribe 'Jurisdictional Gerrymandering: Zoning Disfavored Rights Out of the Federal Courts' (1981) 16 *Harvard Civil Rights-Civil Liberties Law Review* 129 with G. Gunther, 'Congressional Power to Curtail Federal Court Jurisdiction: An Opinionated Guide to the Ongoing Debate' (1984) 36 *Stanford Law Review* 895.

judicial review without judicial finality and so can perhaps properly be called such. These include certain versions of departmentalism (each branch of government is the final interpreter of its own powers)[26] and popular constitutionalism (the people are the final interpreters of constitutional meaning).[27] Nonetheless, weak-form judicial review as institutionalized within the new model is innovative in at least three ways. First, it is the general mode of judicial review under the new model, whereas it is only a partial or supplementary mode under these other theories, employed in certain areas but not others (e.g., separation of powers type issues under departmentalism) or triggered exceptionally or only periodically (e.g., popular constitutionalism). Secondly, the new model's general mechanism of 'penultimate judicial review'[28] followed by possible exercise of the legislative override power is not one that seems to be present in the other theories, because either courts defer to the relevant other branch in the first place or it is the people themselves who have the final say. Indeed, the new model's distinctive allocation of powers provides a far more tangible and concrete institutional mechanism of judicial non-finality than is present in most versions of popular constitutionalism and departmentalism.[29] Thirdly, two of the new model's specific mechanisms of weak-form review were entirely novel when introduced: namely, the 'notwithstanding mechanism' contained in section 33 of the Charter and also section 2 of its predecessor, the CBOR,[30]

[26] See works cited in Chapter 1, n. 54 above.

[27] Kramer, *The People Themselves*. By contrast, where it exists, the judicial practice of deferring to the elective branches in particular areas or generally is not an instance of weak-form review because the judiciary still has the legal power of the final word, it simply chooses to exercise it in a way that tends to uphold the challenged governmental measure.

[28] This helpful term was coined by Michael Perry. M. Perry, 'Protecting Human Rights in a Democracy: What Role for Courts?' (2003) 38 *Wake Forest Law Review* 635.

[29] See Harel and Shinar, 'Between Judicial and Legislative Supremacy', p. 8.

[30] The notwithstanding mechanism is a Canadian invention that first appeared in the prototype new model bill of rights, the statutory CBOR, which under section 2 permits the federal Parliament to exempt a statute from its operation. 'Every law of Canada shall, unless it is expressly declared by an Act of Parliament of Canada that it shall operate notwithstanding the Canadian Bill of Rights, be so construed and applied as not to abrogate, abridge or infringe . . . any of the rights and freedoms herein recognized and declared.' Versions of this mechanism were also included in the pre-Charter provincial human rights codes of Quebec (1975, section 52), Saskatchewan (1979, section 44) and Alberta (1980, section 2). The version of the mechanism contained in section 33 of the Charter permits legislative override of a judicial decision as well as such pre-emptive use.

and the power of the higher UK courts to issue declarations of incompatibility under section 4 of the HRA.[31]

These two techniques of political rights review and weak-form judicial review, which in combination define and distinguish the new model, can be further broken down into the following four essential institutional features, or jointly necessary and sufficient conditions. The first is a legalized and codified charter or bill of rights – as distinct from purely moral and political rights, residual common law liberties or a piecemeal collection of specific, stand-alone statutory rights. This bill of rights forms the subject matter or focus of both political and weak-form judicial review and may have either constitutional or statutory status. In principle, it could even be judicially created, like pre-Charter EU human rights law,[32] which would satisfy the criterion of legal enforceability, although the codification requirement is likely to be inconsistent with the case-by-case, accretive methodology of the common law.

The second feature is mandatory rights review of legislation by the political branches before enactment. As we shall see, this is typically institutionalized by a requirement that a government minister provide a formal statement where he or she is of the opinion that a bill is incompatible with protected rights on its introduction in the legislature, which triggers both prior executive vetting and subsequent legislative scrutiny.

The third is some form of constitutional review of legislation by the courts. That is, a form of judicial power to protect and enforce these rights going beyond an interpretative presumption that the legislature does not intend to violate them or ordinary modes of statutory interpretation. From the perspective of traditional parliamentary sovereignty, these are *enhanced* or greater judicial powers to protect rights than previously existed. As we shall see below, the required form of constitutional review may range from a duty to interpret legislation consistently with protected rights where reasonably possible to a judicial power of invalidation.

---

[31] For details of this power, see Chapter 7. At the time of the HRA's enactment, no other system of constitutional review of legislation in the world – domestic or international, past or present, contained the same or a similar judicial power. It was subsequently adopted in New Zealand (by judicial implication), in Ireland as part of the European Convention on Human Rights Act (2003), and as part of both the ACT HRA and the VCHRR. The Supreme Court of Canada's suspended declaration of invalidity is quite different in that the legislature acts in the shadow of a legally authoritative reversion to a judicial order invalidating the relevant statute.

[32] See J. H. H. Weiler and N. Lockhart, '"Taking Rights Seriously" Seriously: The European Court and its Fundamental Rights Jurisprudence' Parts I & II (1995) 32 *Common Market Law Review* 51 and 579.

The fourth feature, notwithstanding this judicial role, is a formal legislative power to have the final word on what the law of the land is by ordinary majority vote. The specific form of this legislative power will vary according to the version of the constitutional review power granted to the courts – ranging from the power to amend legislation as interpreted by the courts under their rights-respecting duty to the power to override the judicial invalidation of legislation, with others in between. Practically speaking, a legislative power to amend the constitution by ordinary majority vote without any special procedures (such as a referendum or successive majorities) is a fully equivalent power to override a judicial decision and have the final word, which is why it is such a rarity among codified constitutions where courts have the invalidation power.[33] Although there is a conceptual difference between applying a constitution which empowers the legislature to trump the judicial view and amending a constitution which does not (even if by ordinary majority vote), this seems too fine and formal a distinction for denying that such a flexible amendment procedure would satisfy this necessary fourth feature.[34]

In combination, the first and third features distinguish the new model from traditional parliamentary sovereignty, and the fourth from judicial or constitutional supremacy. These essential features of the new model are quite general and permit a range of different specific instantiations, particularly with respect to the second and third features, some of which have in fact been adopted in various countries. So, on a spectrum in which traditional judicial and legislative supremacy mark the two poles, the new model has at least five different possible variations, thereby occupying five slightly different intermediate positions.

Starting from the judicial supremacy pole, the first of these is exemplified by the Canadian Charter: (1) a constitutional bill of rights (2) granting the judiciary power to invalidate conflicting statutes but (3) with a formal legislative final word in the form of the section 33 power

---

[33] Indeed, I am not aware of any written constitutions that have such flexible general amendment procedures. The Indian Constitution contains three specific exceptions to its general requirement under Article 368 of a two-thirds parliamentary majority for constitutional amendments. These exceptions, permitting amendment by simple majority, are citizenship matters (Article 11), abolition or creation of Legislative Councils of a State (Article 169) and the creation of local legislatures or councils of ministers for certain union territories (Article 239A).

[34] I am grateful to Vicki Jackson for persuading me of the need to include discussion of amendment procedures.

exercisable by ordinary majority vote.[35] The second is a statutory bill of rights granting the judiciary the same power to invalidate conflicting statutes, with a similar legislative override power. This position is most closely, although not exactly, illustrated by the still operative CBOR.[36] The third version is exemplified by the HRA, the ACTHRA and the VCHRR: a statutory bill of rights without the power of judicial invalidation of legislation but instead one new judicial power to declare statutes incompatible with protected rights that does not affect their continuing validity, and a second new judicial power (and obligation) to give statutes a rights-consistent interpretation wherever possible. Both types of judicial decision – declaratory and interpretative – are subject to the ordinary legal power of the legislature to have the final word: a default power in the case of the former and requiring affirmative action in the case of the latter. The fourth variation is a similar statutory bill of rights containing the second judicial power, the interpretive power/duty, but lacking the first or declaratory power. This was exemplified by the NZBORA, at least until 2000 when the latter power was seemingly implied by the courts.[37] A fifth variation would be granting the courts the declaratory power, but only ordinary and traditional powers of statutory interpretation.[38]

A statutory bill of rights alone without either the interpretive duty or the declaratory power would not satisfy the third necessary feature of the new model and thus, whatever its independent merits, does not depart from traditional parliamentary sovereignty. Similarly, pre-enactment political rights review alone, with or without a bill of rights.[39] Weak-form judicial review by itself is also insufficient, which is why certain stand-alone legislative override mechanisms in non-Commonwealth

---

[35] Under sections 33(3) and (4), a declaration made under section 33 ceases to have effect after five years but may be renewed any number of times.

[36] Under the CBOR, the judicial power to invalidate is not expressly granted but was implied by the SCC in the case of *R. v. Drybones* [1970] 3 SCC 355, analogously to *Marbury v. Madison* in the United States. It is not an exact example because the legislative override power granted was pre-emptive only, insulating legislation against subsequent judicial review. But there is no reason why a section 33-style power, or even a reactive only power, could not be included in a statutory bill of rights.

[37] Although the current status of the unused implied power is questionable. See Chapter 6.

[38] Arguably, this reflects the current position in both the ACT and Victoria, see Chapter 8.

[39] This is the current situation at the federal level in Australia, but without a bill of rights, following recent enactment of the Human Rights (Parliamentary Scrutiny) Act 2011. See Chapter 8.

jurisdictions noted above amount to no more than a 'partial' adoption of the new model.[40] Analytically, once again, a common law version of the new model is perhaps possible but would (among other things) require a judicially created bill of rights, along the lines of the one developed by the European Court of Justice, to satisfy the first criterion. Most problematic of all would seem to be the second, mandatory political rights review. If this could somehow be overcome, perhaps by development of a constitutional convention, there could in theory be common law versions of all three models of constitutionalism.

We have already seen that what is new about the new model is the following: (1) it transcends the standard dichotomy in institutional forms of constitutionalism, providing a third choice; (2) it does so by combining two novel techniques of rights protection; and (3) it provides a clear institutional mechanism for decoupling judicial review from judicial supremacy. Also as part and parcel of these characteristics, the new model establishes a distinctive and more balanced allocation of powers between courts and legislatures than under the two lopsided existing models. Thus, with their authority to engage in constitutional review, courts have greater powers than under political constitutionalism, but their lack of de jure finality means less power than under any form of legal constitutionalism. And conversely, legislatures are faced with greater legal and judicial constraints on their actions than under political constitutionalism, but fewer than under legal constitutionalism.

This allocation of powers demonstrates that the new third option is specifically an intermediate one in between the two standard and traditional choices. Its intermediate nature can be further elaborated and explained in the following ways. First, it takes certain key ideas from each of the other two models and combines them into a distinct third option. By borrowing from *both*, the new model creates something in between. From the 'big-C' version of legal constitutionalism, the new model first takes the importance of a comprehensive set of affirmative legal rights,[41] as distinct from the (a) mostly moral and political, (b) ad hoc statutory, and/or (c) default, or negative, conception of rights and liberties as whatever is left unregulated by government that characterizes the traditional model of parliamentary sovereignty. From both forms of legal constitutionalism – 'big-C' and common law – it also takes the

---

[40] See the examples in Chapter 1, n. 38 above.

[41] Affirmative in the sense of contrasting with a residual conception of rights, not in the sense of positive versus negative constitutional rights (i.e., constitutional entitlements).

importance of judicial protection and enforcement of rights, as compared with exclusively political. And from legislative supremacy, the new model takes the importance of the notion that there is no form of law set above and wholly immunized from legislative action.

Secondly, the new model can be said to create a distinct blending of legal and political constitutionalism across the board. Although the discourse of political versus legal constitutionalism tends to suggest that the choice is either–or, in reality, most legal systems have elements of both even where one or the other is predominant.[42] Thus, a paradigmatically legal constitutionalist regime such as the United States still has swathes of putatively constitutional law that are typically politically rather than judicially enforced, such as separation of powers between Congress and the President.[43] Australia is perhaps the best example of a formally 'mixed regime' at the national level, with a legal constitutionalist treatment of structural issues – federalism and separation of powers – and a mostly political constitutionalist treatment of rights.[44]

By contrast with such formally or informally mixed regimes that apply one or other model to different substantive areas, the new model blends political and legal constitutionalism across the board. It provides a sequenced role for both legal and political mechanisms of accountability as its general mode of operation. As we have previewed above and shall see in more detail in Chapter 4, in its various forms the new model begins with political rights review at the legislative stage, whereby the government is required to consider whether proposed legislation is compatible with protected rights and make its conclusion known to Parliament.[45] The second stage involves judicial rights review, whereby in the context of a litigated case, courts may exercise one or more of their enhanced powers to protect and enforce the rights. The third and final stage involves post-legislative political rights review, whereby the legislature may exercise its power of the final word and enforce any disagreement

---

[42] See Bellamy, *Political Constitutionalism*; T. Hickman, 'In Defence of the Legal Constitution', (2005) 55 *University of Toronto Law Journal* 981, 1016; G. Gee and G. Webber, 'What is a Political Constitution?' (2010) 30 *Oxford Journal of Legal Studies* 273.

[43] Again, this is why the example of the post-Chadha episode as calling into question judicial supremacy in the US is hardly characteristic of the system as a whole. On the role of law in limiting presidential power, see R. Pildes, 'Law and the President' (2012) 125 *Harvard Law Review* 1381.

[44] The one major exception is the judicially implied federal right of political speech.

[45] As we shall see in Part II, in some jurisdictions the government is required to make a formal statement only when it is of the opinion that a statute is inconsistent with rights; in others, either way.

with the courts. Indeed, the new model not only combines legal and political modes of accountability, but also (1) legal and moral/political conceptions of rights, and (2) judicial and legislative rights reasoning,[46] rather than a general systemic choice of one rather than the other.

Thirdly, and most formally, the new model offers a set of intermediate legal positions to the essential and conflicting postulates of constitutional and legislative supremacy. As we saw in the previous chapter, despite interesting differences in the institutionalization of the first form of legal constitutionalism – or 'big-C' constitutional law – since the end of World War II, most notably between centralized and decentralized judicial review, contemporary systems of constitutional supremacy around the world uniformly adhere to the basic principles first established by the United States in its legal revolution against Great Britain which closely followed the political one. These, of course, are that the written – or, rather codified – constitution, including its rights provisions, is (1) the supreme law of the land, (2) entrenched against ordinary majoritarian amendment or repeal, and (3) enforced by the judicial power to invalidate or disapply conflicting statutes and other government actions, against whose decisions the legislature is powerless to act by ordinary majority vote. The contrary principles of traditional parliamentary sovereignty, which the US Constitution was deliberately designed to reject, are that statutes are (1) the supreme law of the land, (2) not entrenched against ordinary majoritarian amendment or repeal, and (3) not subject to a judicial power of review and invalidation on substantive grounds.[47]

The new model provides intermediate positions on each of these three basic issues. In a legally significant sense, the protected rights have some form of higher law status compared to ordinary statutes, but not one that wholly immunizes them from legislative action. This may, for example, be conventional constitutional status but subject to a legislative override, as in Canada, or 'constitutional statute' status, as has been argued for under the HRA[48] and occasionally applied in practice in New Zealand,

---

[46] On the difference between the two, see J. Waldron, 'Judges as Moral Reasoners' (2009) 7 *International Journal of Constitutional Law* 2.

[47] Obviously, these general principles of parliamentary sovereignty do not require the absence of an uncodified constitution as traditionally in the Commonwealth. The first four French republics, for example, all had written constitutions, but adhered to the model of parliamentary sovereignty.

[48] *Thoburn v. Sunderland City Council* [2003] QB 151 at [60], per Laws L. J.

whereby the earlier statutory right prevails over a conflicting later ordinary statute unless expressly amended or repealed.[49] Such non-application of the normal doctrine of implied repeal also provides a mode of partial entrenchment that straddles the full entrenchment and no entrenchment of the other two models.[50] And, as discussed, the new model grants courts greater powers to protect rights than under traditional parliamentary sovereignty, powers that amount to forms of constitutional review, but not powers against which legislatures are wholly powerless to act by ordinary majority, as under constitutional supremacy. These include the power of Canadian courts to disapply conflicting statutes subject to the legislative power in section 33, the power of higher UK courts to issue declarations of incompatibility under section 4 of the HRA, and the power/duty of UK and New Zealand courts to interpret statutes consistently with rights provisions whenever possible.[51] These new, 'weak-form' powers occupy the space between strong-form judicial review against which there is no legislative recourse by ordinary majority vote vis-à-vis the particular statute at issue, and no constitutional review at all.

The Commonwealth model does not only, however, provide a new form of judicial review; it also provides a new justification of judicial review. For once shorn of judicial supremacy, the task of defending a judicial role in rights protection is a different – and easier – one. A model of constitutionalism that provides for judicial rights review of legislation but gives the legal power of the final word to ordinary majority vote in the legislature is normatively, and not only practically, different from one that does not. Indeed, even if it turns out (as certain critiques maintain) that there is little or no practical difference between the power of courts under certain instantiations of the new model and judicial supremacy, there is still a normative difference between them. Despite the current fairly strong political presumption against use of the legislative override in Canada,[52] there is still a straightforward sense in which exercises of judicial review are more democratically legitimate than in the United States because of the existence of the override power. I shall elaborate the content of this new and distinctive justification of judicial review in presenting the case for the new model in the following chapter.

---

[49] *R. v. Pora* [2001] 2 NZLR 37 (CA). See Chapter 6.
[50] As discussed in Chapter 7, there is some controversy as to whether this suspension of the normal rule of implied repeal applies under the HRA.
[51] Section 3 HRA and section 6 NZBORA.   [52] See Chapter 5.

III The fuller spectrum

From a systemic perspective, the new Commonwealth model suggests the novel possibility that the universe of constitutionalism, rather than a bifurcated one clustered around one or other of two mutually incompatible poles, is more of a continuum based on the scope and role of legal/judicial versus political/legislative decision-making in resolving rights issues and enforcing other limits on political power. The continuum stretches from pure political constitutionalism, or strong legislative supremacy, at one end, to pure legal constitutionalism, or what has been termed 'the total constitution',[53] at the other. On this continuum, unlike the bipolar model, many constitutionalist systems will occupy positions somewhere between the two ends.

For pure political constitutionalism, the answer to the general question of what type or number of rights-relevant issues and conflicts in a society should be resolved by judicially enforceable higher law is zero. All such issues/conflicts should be resolved politically, through ordinary, non-constitutional laws made and executed by political actors who remain fully accountable for them to the electorate. The judicial role is limited to fairly interpreting and applying this law. The opposite answer is given by pure legal constitutionalism. Its instrument is the 'total constitution', a constitution that decides or strongly influences virtually all rights-relevant issues and conflicts in a society. It does this by broadly defining the rights it contains, imposing affirmative duties on government and/or by creating greater horizontal effect on private law and private individuals.[54] In this way, the total constitution effectively constitutionalizes all law by requiring it to be not merely consistent with, but effectively superseded by, the comprehensive higher law of the constitution. Here there is relatively little room for discretionary, autonomous political decision-making or law making as the total constitution provides mandatory answers to almost all issues, leaving ordinary law in effect as a form of administrative law. What defines this polar position, then, is the scope or reach of legal constitutionalism.

Moving along the continuum from total constitutionalism, we come to more standard or limited versions of legal constitutionalism, in which the written or unwritten higher law as construed and applied by the

---

[53] M. Kumm, 'Who is Afraid of the Total Constitution? Constitutional Rights as Principles and the Constitutionalization of Private Law' (2006) 7 *German Law Journal* 341.
[54] *Ibid.*

constitutional judiciary resolves some but not all of the rights-relevant issues and conflicts in a society. Again, as compared with the polar version, this will typically be because of its fewer and more narrowly defined rights, lesser reach into the private sphere and/or fewer affirmative duties on government. Here, legal constitutionalism (in either its 'big-C' or common law form) still leaves significant space for discretionary and autonomous political decision-making in that it removes some but not all topics from the political sphere and, within those remaining, some but not all approaches to those topics. In other words, within conventional legal constitutionalism, higher law (as interpreted and applied by the courts) provides answers to certain issues and narrows the range of permissible political options on others, but its lesser scope compared to the pure or polar version maintains greater space for politically accountable decision-making. Just as important as its better-known function of taking some issues off the political agenda[55] is that ordinary legal constitutionalism *leaves others on it* – and this has been central to its appeal in an era that has seen the rise of world constitutionalism alongside, and as part and parcel of, the rise of world democracy.[56]

The new Commonwealth model occupies that part of the continuum in between this more limited and common form of legal constitutionalism on the one side and pure political constitutionalism on the other. With its blending and sequencing of legal and political accountability and modes of reasoning, its form of judicially enforced higher law influences but does not automatically or necessarily resolve any rights-related issues, distinguishing it from the neighbouring positions on either side. Within the space occupied by the new model and on the basis of the introductory discussion of the range of different specific instantiations above, it might be suggested that Canada is slightly closer to the limited legal constitutionalism part of the continuum than the other new model jurisdictions, with the original version of the NZBORA slightly closer to the political constitutionalism pole than the HRA, ACTHRA and VCHRR.

To give a concrete example of how these various positions on the continuum affect how and by whom rights issues are decided, let us consider the case of abortion. On this issue at least, Germany approximates

---

[55] S. Holmes, 'Gag Rules, or the Politics of Omission' in J. Elster and R. Slagstad (eds.), *Constitutionalism and Democracy* (Cambridge University Press, 1988), pp. 19–58.

[56] See S. Gardbaum, 'The Place of Constitutional Law in the Legal System' in M. Rosenfeld and A. Sajo (eds.), *The Oxford Handbook of Comparative Constitutional Law* (Oxford University Press, 2012).

pure legal or total constitutionalism.[57] As interpreted by the Federal Constitutional Court, the Basic Law largely determines how this most controversial issue is resolved, leaving relatively little space for discretionary political decision-making. As is well-known, because the right to life of a foetus is protected by Article 2(2),[58] and the state has a constitutional duty to protect this life even against its mother, the state must treat all abortions as unlawful, with the exception of the few judicially defined 'unexactable' situations, such as cases of rape, incest or severe birth defects.[59] Discretionary political decision-making is limited to the narrow window of selecting constitutionally permissible means, apart from the criminal law, for effectively fulfilling the state's duty whilst still maintaining the required general unlawfulness of abortion. Even here, however, the Federal Constitutional Court has prescribed much of the content of mandatory counselling as a permissible alternative.[60]

The United States exemplifies the second position on the continuum, the more conventional or limited version of legal constitutionalism, in its written or enacted form. Here, judicially enforced higher law determines what legislatures *cannot* do – namely, as currently interpreted by the Supreme Court, prohibit or place 'undue burdens' on pre-viability abortions or post-viability ones necessary to protect the life or health of the mother – but leaves a greater amount of space for discretionary political decision-making within the parameters of the constitutionally permissible.[61] Thus, the scope of legislative choice runs from no regulation of abortion at all, to twenty-four-hour waiting periods, prohibiting so-called partial birth abortions, and perhaps mandatory viewing of foetal ultrasounds.[62]

In the UK, the HRA as interpreted and applied by the judiciary may influence the abortion issue, but does not definitively decide any aspect of it – either what legislatures must or cannot do. So, even if a higher court were to interpret Convention rights as bestowing a right to life on the foetus and declare the current UK abortion statute inconsistent with it – or, conversely, declare a future statute criminalizing abortion

---

[57] Kumm argues it does more generally, see Kumm, 'Who is Afraid of the Total Constitution?'.

[58] 'Everyone has the right to life and physical integrity'.

[59] First Abortion Case, 39 BVerfGE 1 (1975).

[60] As affirmed and applied in the Second Abortion Case, 88 BVerfGE 203 (1993).

[61] Roe v. Wade 410 US 113 (1973); Planned Parenthood of Southeastern Pennsylvania v. Casey 505 US 833 (1992).

[62] See Casey, ibid.; Gonzalez v. Carhart 550 US 124 (2007).

inconsistent with a woman's right to privacy – Parliament would be free to exercise its power to disregard the declaration.[63] Indeed, this first was the specific scenario cited by the Home Secretary during legislative debate on the HRA as the type of situation where Parliament might reject a declaration.[64] Similarly, if a court were to interpret the current abortion statute narrowly to render it consistent with its finding of a right to life, Parliament would be free to amend the statute to make clear its intention and disagreement with the judicial decision.

At the federal level in Australia, one of the last surviving bastions of a fairly pure form of political constitutionalism in the rights context, the abortion issue is fully and exclusively decided by politically accountable lawmaking, with no substantive role for the judiciary – apart, of course, from interpreting it according to traditional principles of statutory interpretation and applying it in litigated cases.

To be sure, other factors than the four defining the new model and differentiating it from both conventional legal and pure political constitutionalism may also help to locate the relative position of any particular system on this continuum. These are factors that might be said to affect the depth or strength of legal/judicial decision-making, as distinct from its breadth or scope, such as the ease or difficulty of constitutional amendment,[65] the independence and tenure of the judiciary, and access to (individual standing) and systemic consequences of judicial review. Thus, on these issues, the US system, with its very high bar for constitutional amendment, life tenure for federal judges with no mandatory retirement age, relatively easy access to judicial review due to individual standing and decentralization, and system-wide effects of judicial decisions is closer to the polar position than most other systems of conventional legal constitutionalism or constitutional supremacy. At the margin, this may even result in some blurring of the boundary between

---

[63] Especially if the ECtHR continues its longstanding practice of staying out of the abortion issue.

[64] *Hansard*, 21 October 1998: 'Although I hope that it does not happen, it is possible to conceive that some time in the future, a particularly composed Judicial Committee of the House of Lords reaches the view that provision for abortion in ... the United Kingdom ... is incompatible with one or other article of the convention ... My guess – it can be no more than that – is that whichever party was in power would have to say that it was sorry, that it did not and would not accept that, and that it was going to continue with the existing abortion legislation.'

[65] Although, as noted above, at the extreme of ease, constitutional amendment by ordinary majority vote of the legislature satisfies the final element of the new model as a form of legislative override of judicial decisions.

pure and ordinary legal constitutionalism, especially if or where a total constitution bestows lesser depth to legal/judicial decision-making through its position on these issues. Ultimately, however, depth issues of this sort are subordinated to the prime criterion of the scope of such decision-making within the political system.

IV   Questioning the distinctness of the new model

Two different types of commentary have directly or indirectly called into question the claim that the new Commonwealth model is a new and distinct intermediate form of constitutionalism. The first is conceptual, and focuses on the issue of whether the new model is consistent with parliamentary sovereignty or political constitutionalism rather than an alternative to it.[66] To the extent the answer is yes, it might be thought to follow that it ushers in nothing new as far as forms of constitutionalism are concerned.[67] The second is practical and maintains that, in operation, the new model's claim of distinctness has in fact been, or is likely to be, refuted. This practical critique has come in three versions: (1) a general prediction that the new model is likely to be unstable and revert to one or other of the two traditional models;[68] (2) a verdict on the overall record of the HRA, in particular, as one of 'futility' in that there has not been any significant change from the pre-existing system in the

---

[66] R. Bellamy, 'Political Constitutionalism and the Human Rights Act' (2011) 9 *International Journal of Constitutional Law* 86, 89 (denying that 'the HRA, as well as parallel developments in other commonwealth countries, [gives] rise to a new model of constitutionalism that balances legal and political constitutionalism in a novel way while offering an alternative to both'). Jeffrey Goldsworthy and Alison Young have argued that the HRA is consistent with parliamentary sovereignty, whereas Aileen Kavanagh, Philip Joseph and Mark Elliott have claimed either that it is not, or that the latter has become redundant. Goldsworthy, *Parliamentary Sovereignty*, pp. 299–304; Young, *Parliamentary Sovereignty and the Human Rights Act*; Kavanagh, *Constitutional Review under the UK Human Rights Act*, ch. 11; P. Joseph, 'Parliament, the Courts, and the Collaborative Enterprise' (2005) 15 *King's College Law Journal* 321; M. Elliott, 'Parliamentary Sovereignty and the New Constitutional Order: Legislative Freedom, Political Reality, and Convention' (2002) *Legal Studies* 22.

[67] This is the view of Richard Bellamy, *ibid.*, although both Goldsworthy ('hybrid' model) and Young ('democratic dialogue model') treat the HRA as embodying an innovative form of constitutionalism despite its being (in their views) consistent with parliamentary sovereignty.

[68] M. Tushnet, 'Weak-Form Judicial Review: Its Implications for Legislatures' (2004) 23 *Supreme Court Law Review* (second series) 213, 234–1; Tushnet, *Weak Courts, Strong Rights*, ch. 3.

courts' traditional deference to the political branches;[69] and (3) the opposite assessment that the formal limits on judicial power have largely been illusory and that in substance the new model has proven to be little different from American-style judicial supremacy.[70]

Of the two, this second, practical critique of the distinctness claim has been the more major and direct. It would obviously be premature to address its two opposite and at least in part mutually incompatible strands before the practice under the various versions of the new model has been discussed and assessed, so this task will be postponed until Chapters 7 (on the HRA) and 9. So for now, let me focus only on the more conceptual issue about the new model's reconcilability with parliamentary sovereignty and/or political constitutionalism and its possible implications for my claim in this chapter.

It should be noted at the outset that this issue has mostly revolved around the HRA in particular. The Canadian Charter seems more obviously inconsistent with parliamentary sovereignty, notwithstanding the notwithstanding clause. This is because it has big-C constitutional status as supreme, formally entrenched higher law enforced by a judicial invalidation power, and because there are rights in the Charter that are expressly exempted from the scope of section 33.[71] These features impose substantive legal limits on legislative power. And yet, where section 33 does apply, there is equally clearly not de jure judicial supremacy. Accordingly, in this particular way, the Canadian example shows how the new model's mixed system spans the dichotomy between the two traditional forms.

The HRA debate on this issue (unlike the practical critique) has mostly[72] not been framed as a direct challenge to the new model's claim of distinctness or as having the goal of identifying its proper status;

---

[69] K. Ewing, 'The Futility of the Human Rights Act' (2004) *Public Law* 829; K. Ewing and J. Tham, 'The Continuing Futility of the Human Rights Act' (2008) *Public Law* 668; K. Ewing, *The Bonfire of the Liberties* (Oxford University Press, 2011).

[70] This assessment has in essence been made by proponents of both legal constitutionalism (i.e., positively) and political constitutionalism (negatively). For the former, see Kavanagh, *Constitutional Review under the UK Human Rights Act*, pp. 416–20; for the latter, see J. Allan, 'Statutory Bills of Rights: You Read Words In, You Read Words Out, You Take Parliament's Clear Intention and You Shake It All About – Doin' the Sanky Hanky Panky' in T. Campbell, K. Ewing and A. Tomkins (eds.), *Legal Protection of Human Rights: Sceptical Essays* (New York: Oxford University Press, 2011), p. 126.

[71] These are sections 3–6 and 16–23.

[72] The recent contribution by Richard Bellamy is one exception, see Bellamy, 'Political Constitutionalism and the Human Rights Act'.

indeed, it is not really a debate about the new model at all. Rather it has largely been conducted from the specific perspective of the opposition between legal and political constitutionalism, and is part of the ongoing skirmishes between their respective proponents. Thus, supporters of common law constitutionalism and judicial supremacy tend to view the HRA through the lens of their general opposition to parliamentary sovereignty and what they see is its wished-for demise.[73] Similarly, supporters of political constitutionalism tend to view the HRA through their own lens and see the preservation of parliamentary sovereignty.[74] Notwithstanding this opposite orientation and background set of commitments, there is more consensus on the conceptual issue than first meets the eye. I think both sides actually agree on the 'facts', that the HRA is formally consistent with the doctrine of parliamentary sovereignty in that it imposes no substantive legal limits on legislative power, but the practical significance of the doctrine is further reduced as the HRA increases the various constraints (moral, political, and particularly judicial-institutional) on its exercise.[75] Their disagreement is mostly about the next battle: resisting or 'inciting' further shifts towards greater judicial power in how the HRA comes to be applied and understood, in how much of a reduction in practical significance actually occurs, for in its subtle interplay of legal and political factors there is significant room in the joints for different outcomes and balances between the two.

More generally, and from the perspective of my claim in this chapter, it is true that for systemic coherence and rule of law-type reasons, (1) if both courts and legislatures are empowered to make judgments about whether legislation violates rights, one or the other must have the final or authoritative word where these judgments conflict,[76] and (2) the new

---

[73] Kavanagh, *Constitutional Review under the UK Human Rights Act*. As Goldsworthy I think accurately notes, there is some tension in her account of how much the HRA adds to pre-existing common law constitutionalism. See Goldsworthy, *Parliamentary Sovereignty*, p. 304.

[74] Bellamy, 'Political Constitutionalism and the Human Rights Act.'

[75] This view of consistency is expressed by Goldsworthy, *Parliamentary Sovereignty*, pp. 299–304.

[76] Although not focused on rights or legislatures, the imperative of final authority was expressed at least as long ago as Justice Story's opinion in *Martin* v. *Hunter's Lessee* 14 US 304 (1816) ('From the very nature of things, the absolute right of decision, in the last resort, must rest somewhere.'). As Mark Elliott observes, it is one of the features of British-style unwritten constitutionalism that it tends to obscure the answer to this question. Eliot, 'Interpretative Bills of Rights and the Mystery of the Unwritten Constitution'.

model gives the legislature the legal power of the final word, which it may or may not choose to exercise. In this important sense, I agree with Jeffrey Goldsworthy and what I take to be the actual consensus in the above debate that the HRA (like the other statutory versions of the new model) is formally *consistent with* the essential postulate of parliamentary sovereignty in that it does not contain substantive legal limits on what Parliament can do. Parliament can repeal the HRA and under its terms is not powerless to act in the face of either interpretive or declaratory judgments of the courts.[77] If political constitutionalism boils down to this single issue of the legal power of the final word, then the new model is indeed a version of it, rather than an outright alternative. At the same time, however, it is a different version, an alternative to the traditional form of political constitutionalism, just as it is consistent with, but not the *same as*, parliamentary sovereignty as traditionally practiced and institutionalized.

The new model creates an institutional alternative to the traditional form of political constitutionalism and parliamentary sovereignty because it creates a different division between legislative and judicial power – granting greater power and responsibility to the courts for the protection of rights and a greater role for legal argument as a practical constraint on political decision-making. This is why it can be thought of as creating not only weak-form judicial review but also weak-form legislative supremacy, as compared with the traditional strong one. Here, although there are still no formal substantive legal limits on legislative power, courts may review the content of legislation for conformity with protected rights and thereby add an institutionally focused and legal dimension to the pre-existing moral and political constraints on exercise of that power. Moreover, whereas under both judicial and traditional legislative supremacy, the institution with the power of the final word is essentially bound to exercise it and does so routinely, almost automatically – courts in the context of deciding a case (or abstract review), and legislatures because the act of passing a law *is* the final word – this is not so under the new model. Rather, what is 'weaker' about legislative supremacy is the gap between the formal power of the final word and its exercise, the existence of political discretion as to whether (rather than how) to use it that may be heavily influenced by the judicial view.

What makes the new model distinct is that, as discussed above, it takes something (though not everything) from both legal and political

---

[77] Goldsworthy, *Parliamentary Sovereignty*, p. 299.

constitutionalism and creates something new in between. If it is a version of political constitutionalism, then it is also a version of legal constitutionalism – as indeed some of its proponents have claimed[78] – in that it involves a legalized bill of rights and constitutional review by the courts. This is why it is properly thought of as a hybrid model.[79] After all, a hybrid petrol-electric car is distinct from both an all-petrol and an all-electric car. This, too, is why the new model suggests, or creates, a constitutionalism continuum. Accordingly, the distinctness of the new model cannot be seen by looking at either its judicial or legislative powers in isolation. Rather, the entire package – including the relationship between the two and the role of pre-enactment political rights review – must be considered in combination at the same time, for this is what creates its newness. The critical, and distinctive, hybrid feature of the new model is the legislative power to override the exercise of constitutional review of legislation by the courts.[80] Within a system of constitutional supremacy – that is, either general form of legal constitutionalism – there is, of course, no such legislative power; legislatures are disabled from overriding judicial decisions by ordinary majority vote. Within a system of legislative supremacy, as traditionally conceived and institutionalized, there is no judicial power of constitutional review in the first place. Accordingly, even though the new model can be understood as a version of political constitutionalism because of its allocation of the final word to the legislature, the difference between this 'impure' or limited version of political constitutionalism and conventional legal constitutionalism is smaller, finer than the traditional one. And for this reason, I take it that most political constitutionalists do or would not view the new model as their preferred standard-bearer but at most as an acceptable second-best to fall back on.

As we have seen, the various models of constitutionalism are importantly (although not exclusively) about the relative scope of legislative and judicial power, about different divisions of labour between legislatures and courts. Although both the polar model of pure political constitutionalism and (at least) the statutory versions of the new model are consistent with the essential postulate of the doctrine of parliamentary sovereignty, they are characterized and defined by a different allocation of authority between the two institutions. In this sense again, the new

---

[78] As we shall see in the following chapter.

[79] Goldsworthy uses this term and characterizes the new model in this way, even though he also argues that it is consistent with parliamentary sovereignty. See Goldsworthy, *Parliamentary Sovereignty*, pp. 79–80.

[80] That is, the essential feature of the new model with a hybrid source as distinct from those – a bill of rights and pre-enactment political rights review – that do not.

model can properly be viewed as a variation within parliamentary sovereignty or political constitutionalism – a weaker variation – rather than an outright alternative to it, just as it can also be viewed as an even weaker version of legal constitutionalism than either the polar total constitutionalism or ordinary legal constitutionalism. The major question is whether it is meaningful, helpful and accurate to draw the conceptual map on this larger scale and alternative basis so that these differences and potential options, as well as the overarching continuum, can be seen. Or, is it better to confine it to the bipolar universe, perhaps supplemented with some very general conception, and acknowledgement, of 'balance' between the two poles? On this larger-scale map, the new model occupies distinct, intermediate space in between ordinary legal constitutionalism and traditional or pure political constitutionalism.

To my mind, even though (or where) the new model is formally consistent with the essential postulate of parliamentary sovereignty because there are no substantive legal limits on what legislatures can do, it seems an unnecessarily high bar to deny that, as an institutional form of constitutionalism, it is distinct from traditional parliamentary sovereignty or political constitutionalism in some significant, non-trivial sense. Certainly citizens, lawyers and politicians in Australia believed they were assessing two meaningfully different options during the recent vigorous debate about whether to maintain the status quo or to enact a national human rights act along the lines of the HRA and the ones already operating in the ACT and state of Victoria. Similarly, it seems unnecessarily rigid and limiting to deny that the commonalities in techniques, essential features and allocations of powers between the Canadian Charter and the four statutory bills of rights are insufficient to view them all as instances of a single new model because the former is at least partially inconsistent with the core principle of parliamentary sovereignty.

3

The case for the new Commonwealth model

I Introduction

If the new Commonwealth model is a distinct institutional form of constitutionalism, as I have argued in the previous chapter, then the next issue – to be taken up in this one – is how attractive or compelling an alternative is it. In what ways might it be thought preferable or advantageous? As with any normatively grounded institutional practice, whether communism or federalism, the full case for (or against) the new model cannot consist of relatively abstract arguments alone but must also include an assessment of whether practice is bearing out the theory. The latter is particularly important because, as already mentioned, the most powerful critiques of the new model thus far have been practice-oriented: claims that it is not in fact functioning as a distinct model, and predictions that it will be unstable in operation. This empirical part of the case, however, must wait until after the practice has been reviewed in the second part of this book. In this chapter, I focus on the normative case for the new model, which will also help to provide the criteria for the subsequent assessment of its success or failure in practice.

Presenting this case has become an urgent task not only because it remains unfamiliar by contrast with the very well-known and developed arguments for and against the other two traditional options, but also because, in the increasingly sophisticated debate between their respective proponents, both sides have begun to move from ignoring the new model, to co-opting it for their own camp.

As previously mentioned, in the last few years there has been a spirited, high-quality and original set of contributions to the old debate about the merits of constitutional or judicial review by both its proponents and opponents. Some of these contributions have been made in the specific context of the opposition between legal and political constitutionalism in the UK.[1] Others have been more general and usefully taken the form of a colloquy between the two sides.[2] Although this 'latest round of contributions'[3] has undoubtedly enriched the overall debate and helpfully focused attention on the critical issues, it has not, however, altered the fact that it is conducted within the traditional bipolar conceptual framework. There are still two, and only two, sides. Despite paying certain lip-service to the new model, as discussed below, the debate continues to presuppose that these are the only options: to be a proponent of judicial review is to be a proponent of judicial rather than legislative supremacy; to be an opponent of judicial review is to be – and is the only way to be – an opponent of judicial rather than legislative supremacy. What is exciting about the new model is that it recasts this fundamental debate by providing a third, fully-fledged alternative option at the outset.

Indeed, both sides in the debate have at least implicitly conceded that the new model is relevant, can no longer simply be ignored and must be taken into account, although both sides have significantly understated how and to what extent, in attempting to co-opt it for their own camp and deny its independent status. Among recent proponents of judicial review, Mattias Kumm has acknowledged the new model, but relegates it to an institutional design option within his insightful and sophisticated defence of judicial review as a form of Socratic contestation that, in fulfilling the requirement of reasonable justification of all public acts, is a precondition of the legitimacy of law.[4] Kumm states that 'what deserves a great deal of thought is how to design the procedures and institutions that institutionalize Socratic contestation ... Should judges just have the power to declare a law incompatible with human rights, leaving it to the legislature to abolish or maintain the law?'[5] Similarly, Richard Fallon suggests that the choice between strong and weak forms of judicial review is a 'design question' within the overall institution of judicial review he is defending, and that the desirability of one or the other may depend contextually on the 'pathological proclivities' of particular societies.[6] Among opponents of judicial review, Jeremy Waldron has also acknowledged the existence of the new model by distinguishing what he terms 'weak' from 'strong judicial review', and stating that only the latter is

---

[1] See Tomkins, *Our Republican Constitution*; Bellamy, *Political Constitutionalism*; Kavanagh, *Constitutional Review under the UK Human Rights Act*, pp. 338–403.
[2] See works cited in Chapter 2, n. 15.
[3] Kumm, 'Institutionalising Socratic Contestation', p. 1.   [4] *Ibid.*
[5] Kumm, 'Democracy is not Enough', p. 38.
[6] Fallon, 'The Core of an Uneasy Case', pp. 1733–4.

the 'target of his critique'.[7] More positively, although somewhat cryptically and equivocally, he 'suspect[s] . . . there is a place for some sort of [judicial] alert mechanism along these lines, say, in the context of a system of weak judicial review – with declarations of incompatibility – along the lines of those provided for under the United Kingdom's Human Rights Act.'[8] Otherwise, he has not engaged it.

Interestingly, from this it appears that the new model may be acceptable, if grudgingly, to both those who defend and oppose judicial review, which perhaps further suggests its intermediate normative status and appeal. But this appeal needs to be fleshed out and the case for the new model explicitly and systematically presented[9] as a full, independent and distinct option in its own right at the outset – to counter this common attempt to smother it at birth and relegate the new model to the status of institutional or contextual detail within one or other pole of the traditional framework and as not worthy of serious normative consideration. For on the one hand, whether courts or legislatures should have the power of the final word does not seem like a mere institutional detail, but a question at the same level of discourse as whether to have judicial review itself, part of the same important normative issue. On the other hand, *all* of these issues are in a sense matters of institutional detail, for the point of all three models is to answer the question of how the normative commitment to constitutionalism should be institutionalized within a democratic political system. Moreover, as refined and sharpened by these and other recent contributions, the cases for the two traditional options are well-known and developed; the case for the new model is not. In what follows, I aim to present this case.

Two final preliminary points before I begin. First, the case to be presented depends on certain assumptions about the institutions and rights commitments of a political society that entail it is most centrally and generally applicable to mature democracies. These assumptions are the same as those listed by Jeremy Waldron in presenting his case against judicial review: namely, a reasonably well-functioning legislature and

---

[7] Waldron, 'The Core of the Case', p. 1354.
[8] Waldron, 'Judges as Moral Reasoners', p. 24.
[9] For previous, briefer arguments for the new model generally, see Gardbaum, 'The New Commonwealth Model', pp. 744–8; S. Gardbaum, 'Reassessing the New Commonwealth Model of Constitutionalism' (2010) 8 *International Journal of Constitutional Law*, 167, 171–5; J. Goldsworthy, 'Homogenizing Constitutions' (2003) 23 *Oxford Journal of Legal Studies* 483; Perry, 'Protecting Human Rights in a Democracy: What Role for Courts?'.

judiciary, broad commitment to individual and minority rights in society, and persistent, good faith disagreement about what specific rights there are and what they amount to.[10] Where these conditions obtain, as in many mature democracies, my normative argument, like his, is a general one: that is, the new model is a better institutional form of constitutionalism than the other two. Where they do not, as in many transitional, newer or fragile democracies, the normative case for one of the other models may be stronger – or, indeed, this entire design issue less important than certain others. If either legislatures or courts are not reasonably well-functioning, this should affect their relative allocation of power, so that contextual factors of this sort will be relevant to the issue of which legal regime will likely better protect rights.[11] Other contextual factors, such as the desire for radical regime change and a 'new beginning',[12] may also be highly relevant. So, for example, in the new constitutions of post-Nazi Germany and post-apartheid South Africa, judicial supremacy and strong-form review may have represented the sharper break with the past that was deemed necessary for expressive and practical reasons. And at the empirical level, even in mature democracies where the assumptions hold, there may be circumstances and contexts that undermine the general normative case for the new model, so that one of the other two models might be better in practice. For example, if or where the new model actually operates (or would operate) no differently than judicial supremacy, as some claim, and reforms to push it into a more intermediate position are unlikely to be enacted or to work, then there may be good reason to prefer political constitutionalism. Conversely, if and where it operates in practice no differently than traditional legislative supremacy, and the result is that individual or minority rights are insufficiently protected, there may be good reason to think that conventional legal constitutionalism is the better choice in the context. In short, my claim is that the normative case to be presented is generally compelling for mature democracies; for others, this case affords the new model its rightful place as a third form of constitutionalism to be considered on its contextual merits alongside judicial and legislative supremacy.

---

[10] Waldron, 'The Core of the Case Against Judicial Review', pp. 1359–69.

[11] As Wojciech Sadurski persuasively argues in the context of central and eastern Europe, although his argument is premised on the two traditional choices only. See Sadursky, 'Judicial Review'.

[12] Ackerman, 'The Rise of World Constitutionalism'.

The second point is that I am also presenting a general case for the new model in a different sense: as a general, or regime-level, alternative to the other two existing options. In particular, I shall not be addressing the issue of whether there are specific rights for which the new model is the better option; or indeed whether there are specific rights for which, even assuming the general superiority of the new model, either judicial or legislative supremacy may be the optimal choice. So, for example, the Canadian Charter exempts voting and language rights from the operation of section 33.[13] Similarly, it has been argued that social welfare rights may be particularly suited to the new model,[14] although a more conventional argument finds them to be properly subject to political constitutionalism and some, inspired by the *Grootboom* and *Treatment Action Campaign* decisions of the South African Constitutional Court,[15] claim they can and should be enforced, at least in part, by means of judicial supremacy, like other rights. It will be noted in Chapters 5–8 that one of the common features of all five of the bills of rights considered in this book is that they are limited to civil and political rights, and contain no social welfare rights. In any event, my argument for the new model is a general, or regime-level, one and is not rights-specific: it does not focus on or distinguish between particular rights or types of rights in this way. That said, it would be surprising (and disappointing) if the discussion that follows was not highly relevant to this related but separate issue.[16]

II   The strengths and weaknesses of legal and political constitutionalism

The essential case for the new Commonwealth model is that it is to forms of constitutionalism what the mixed economy is to forms of economic organization: a distinct and appealing third way in between two purer but flawed extremes. Just as the mixed economy is a hybrid economic form combining the core benefits of capitalism and socialism whilst

---

[13] Section 33(1) is stated to apply to section 2 and sections 7 to 15 of the Charter.

[14] See, for example, M. Tushnet, 'Social Welfare Rights and the Forms of Judicial Review' (2004) 82 *Texas Law Review* 1895; R. Dixon, 'Creating Dialogue About Socio-Economic Rights: Strong v. Weak-Form Judicial Review Revisited' (2007) 5 *International Journal of Constitutional Law* 391.

[15] *Government of the Republic of South Africa* v. *Grootboom* 2001 (1) SA 46 (CC); *Minister of Health* v. *Treatment Action Campaign* 2002 (5) SA 721 (CC).

[16] I am grateful to Michael Perry and Susan Williams for independently raising this issue with me.

minimizing their well-known costs, so too the new model offers an alternative to the old choice of judicial supremacy or traditional parliamentary sovereignty by combining the strengths of each whilst avoiding their major weaknesses. Like the mixed economy's countering of the lopsided allocation of power under capitalism to markets, and under socialism to planning, the new model counters legal and political constitutionalism's lopsided allocations of power to courts and legislatures, respectively. It recalibrates these two existing choice options by effectively protecting rights through a reallocation[17] of power between the judiciary and the political branches (adding to judicial power if starting from parliamentary sovereignty, and reducing it if starting from judicial supremacy) that brings them into greater balance and denies too much power to either. As such, it is largely an argument about greater subtlety in constitutional engineering. The result is a more optimal institutional form of constitutionalism within a democratic polity than provided by either traditional model alone, one that provides a better working coexistence of democratic self-governance and the constraints of constitutionalism, the twin concepts underlying constitutional democracy.

After the latest round of the debate about judicial review conducted within the conventional bipolar framework, it seems clearer than ever that there are powerful arguments both for and against legal constitutionalism and that no unanswerable, knock-down case – for one side or the other – that persuades all reasonable people is likely anytime soon. Although political constitutionalists have generally been more comfortable in critical mode, focusing rather more on presenting arguments against legal constitutionalism than on the positive case for their own position,[18] these are simply two sides of the same coin within a bipolar debate so that which one to pick mostly reflects choice of rhetorical strategy. Indeed, one of the benefits of the new three-way debate ushered in by the new model is that it becomes necessary to specify what position is being argued for, and not only against, as there is no single, dichotomous default option but rather two separate alternatives. So, for example, a successful critique of judicial supremacy is no longer sufficient

---

[17] A 'reallocation' does not necessarily mean a 'transfer' of power from one institution to the other. Thus, in being given the two new powers of declaring an incompatibility and interpreting statutes in a rights-consistent way wherever possible, UK courts are not exercising powers previously held by Parliament. See Kavanagh, *Constitutional Review*, pp. 277–8.

[18] This point is perhaps best represented by the title of Waldron's celebrated article, 'The Core of the Case Against Judicial Review'. See also, Tomkins, *Our Republican Constitution* and Bellamy, *Political Constitutionalism*.

to justify traditional parliamentary sovereignty, for whilst the new model is also opposed to judicial supremacy, it supports a judicial role in rights issues. The net effect is that this high-quality bipolar debate has helpfully isolated the two key issues as (1) which model better protects rights, and (2) whether judicial review is politically legitimate within a democracy,[19] and has also provided an enhanced assessment of the strengths and weaknesses of both traditional models with respect to them.

This enhanced assessment is particularly helpful because in order to explain how the new model combines the core strengths of both traditional ones whilst avoiding their major weaknesses, it is of course first necessary to specify what these are. As an institutional form of constitutionalism in a democratic political system, political constitutionalism (or legislative supremacy) has two major strengths or benefits. First, on the issue of legitimacy, by institutionalizing limits on governmental power as political in nature and enforcing them through the twin mechanisms of electoral accountability and structural checks and balances – such as parliamentary oversight of the executive – political constitutionalism coheres easily and unproblematically with democracy as the basic principle for the organization of the governmental power that it limits. Whether these limits that protect individual rights and liberties remain exclusively in the political sphere as moral or political rights, or are given legal effect as common law or statutory rights, they are ultimately within the scope of the democratic principles of equal participation and electorally accountable decision-making as determined or changeable by ordinary legislative act. Secondly, on the issue of outcomes, given the nature of many, if not most, rights issues that arise in contemporary mature democracies – including the existence of reasonable disagreement about how they should be resolved – legislative reasoning about rights may often be superior to legal/judicial reasoning. As powerfully argued by Adam Tomkins and Jeremy Waldron, high-quality rights reasoning often calls for direct focus on the moral and policy issues involved free of the legalistic and distorting concerns with text, precedent, fact-particularity and the legitimacy of the enterprise that constrain judicial reasoning about rights.[20] Moreover, electorally accountable representatives are able to bring

---

[19] Waldron, 'The Core of the Case'; Fallon, 'The Core of an Uneasy Case'; Kumm, 'Institutionalising Socratic Contestation'; Sadursky, 'Judicial Review.'

[20] See Tomkins, *Our Republican Constitution*, pp. 27–9; Waldron, 'Judges as Moral Reasoners'. Mattias Kumm argues that the sort of legalistic distortions they describe are not a feature of contemporary rights adjudication in Europe under proportionality analysis, see 'Institutionalising Socratic Contestation', pp. 5–13. However, the second-order task of assessing the reasonableness of the government's justification for a law,

a greater diversity of views and perspectives to bear on rights deliberations compared to the numerically smaller, cloistered and elite world of the higher judiciary.

At the same time, proponents of judicial review have identified two major weaknesses of political constitutionalism on the key issues. The first is the risk of either understating or under-enforcing constitutionalism's limits on governmental power, especially individual rights, as the result of various 'pathologies' or 'blind spots' to which electorally accountable legislatures (and executives) may be prone. These include sensitivity to the rights and rights claims of various electoral minorities – whether criminal defendants, asylum-seekers, or minority racial, ethnic or religious groups – given the exigencies and logic of re-election, legislative inertia deriving from tradition or the blocking power of parties or interest groups, and government hyperbole or ideology.[21] Under-enforcement of rights may also result from the circumstance that however high the quality of legislative rights reasoning, it inevitably competes in this forum with other deliberative and decisional frameworks. Undoubtedly, these standard, well-known concerns were primarily responsible for the massive switch away from political constitutionalism towards judicial supremacy around the world during the post-war 'rights revolution', as the resources of representative democracy alone were perceived to provide insufficient protection.

Secondly, just as political constitutionalists have attempted to turn the tables on the conventional argument that rights are better protected with judicial review in the way we have just seen, legal constitutionalists have tried to do the same with the standard argument that judicial review is democratically illegitimate. Thus, Richard Fallon has argued that important though democratic legitimacy undoubtedly is, it is not the exclusive source or type of legitimacy in constitutional democracies, and that the substantive justice of a society also contributes to its overall political legitimacy. Accordingly, to the extent that political constitutionalism may undermine substantive justice by under-enforcing rights for the above-stated reasons, it

which Kumm argues is the point of judicial review, arguably replaces one set of distorting filters with another so that courts still do not directly address the merits of the rights issues. Moreover, the absence of such law-like reasoning may heighten the internal concerns about the legitimacy of the enterprise.

[21] See, for example, A. Bickel, *The Least Dangerous Branch* (New Haven: Yale University Press, 1962); R. Dixon, 'The Supreme Court of Canada, Charter Dialogue, and Deference' (2009) 47 *Osgoode Hall Law Journal* 235; Kumm, 'Institutionalising Socratic Contestation'; Perry, 'Protecting Human Rights in a Democracy' (in making the case for the new model); Fallon, 'The Core of an Uneasy Case'.

also detracts from the overall political legitimacy of a democratic regime.[22] More generally, Mattias Kumm has argued that in addition to electorally accountable decision-making, a second precondition for the legitimacy of law in constitutional democracies is the requirement of substantively reasonable public justification for all governmental acts, including legislation, burdening individuals' rights. As part of our commitment to constitutionalism, legislation unsupported by a reasonable public justification for the burdens it imposes on individuals is illegitimate regardless of majority support. Political constitutionalism, however, provides no adequate forum for critically scrutinizing the justification for a piece of legislation to determine if it meets the minimum standard of plausibility in terms of public reasons. Given the various potential pathologies noted above, legislative deliberation and political accountability are insufficient to ensure that burdened individuals are provided with the reasonable justification to which they are entitled, as evidenced by many decisions of domestic and international constitutional courts.[23]

If these are the most important strengths and weaknesses of political constitutionalism that emerge from the recent academic debate, what are the equivalents for legal constitutionalism? One of its strengths is fostering public recognition and consciousness of rights. A reasonably comprehensive statement of rights and liberties, as found in the typical constitutional bill of rights, renders rights less scattered and more visible or transparent, more part of general public consciousness than either an 'unwritten' set of moral and political rights or a regime of residual common law liberties supplemented by certain specific statutory rights.

A second strength of legal constitutionalism – in either its 'big-C' or common law variations – is that it may help to protect against the above-mentioned tendency towards the under-enforcement of rights resulting from the potential pathologies and blind spots affecting politically accountable legislatures and executives. Where they are politically independent in the sense of not needing to seek re-election or renewal in office after initial appointment, judges exercising the power of judicial review are in a better institutional position to counter or resist such electorally induced risk of under-enforcement.[24] This is not so much an argument about expertise as

---

[22] Fallon, 'The Core of an Uneasy Case', pp. 1718–22.
[23] Kumm, 'Democracy is not Enough', pp. 21–8.
[24] Kyritsis, 'Constitutional Review in a Representative Democracy'; Perry, 'Protecting Human Rights in a Democracy'.

about incentives and institutional structure. Courts also decide cases upon concrete facts, some of which may have been unforeseen by legislators,[25] and indeed bring a more context-specific or 'applied' dimension to rights deliberation that complements the necessarily greater generality of that undertaken by legislatures.

Thirdly, in the positive version of the argument noted above, legal constitutionalists have made the case that judicial review is essential to the overall legitimacy of a constitutional democracy. Thus, Richard Fallon argues that to the extent judicial review promotes substantive justice by helping to protect against under-enforcement of rights, it might 'actually enhance the overall political legitimacy of an otherwise reasonably democratic constitutional regime'.[26] In this sense, judicial review may result in a trade-off among different sources of legitimacy, but not between rights protection and overall political legitimacy. Mattias Kumm has argued that judicial review provides the forum, required for the legitimacy of legislation, in which individual rights claimants can put the government to its burden of providing a reasonable public justification for its acts. As he puts it:

> Human and constitutional rights adjudication, as it has developed in much of Europe ... is a form of legally institutionalized Socratic contestation. When individuals bring claims grounded in human or constitutional rights, they enlist courts to critically engage public authorities in order to assess whether their acts and the burdens they impose on the rights-claimants are susceptible to plausible justification ... Legally institutionalized Socratic contestation is desirable, both because it tends to improve outcomes and because it expresses a central liberal commitment about the conditions that must be met, in order for law to be legitimate.[27]

Thus, for example, judicial review aims to ensure that an individual burdened by a statutory ban on gays in the military is able to put the government to the task of providing a reasonable public justification for the enacted law, one not relying on prejudice, tradition, disproportionate means, etc., failing which it is illegitimate.[28]

---

[25] Fallon, 'The Core of an Uneasy Case', p. 1709.   [26] *Ibid.*, p. 1728.

[27] Kumm, 'Institutionalising Socratic Contestation', p. 4. In 'The Easy Core Case', Harel and Kahana present a broadly similar justification of judicial review, which they argue is designed to provide individuals with a necessary and intrinsic right to a hearing to challenge decisions that impinge on their rights, although they do not embed their justification in terms of the general legitimacy of law.

[28] Kumm gives this example, based on the 1981 ECHR case of *Dudgeon* v. *United Kingdom*, *ibid.* pp. 22–4.

And what are the weaknesses or costs of legal constitutionalism as an institutional form in a democracy? Starting with the issue of rights protection, one is that just as there may be under-enforcement of rights due to electorally induced or other legislative pathologies, there may also be under-enforcement resulting from certain judicial pathologies.[29] These include: (1) the risk of rights-relevant timidity that comes with responsibility for the final decision and its real world consequences; (2) concerns about lack of policy expertise or legitimacy in the context of assessing justifications for limiting rights – the universal second stage of modern rights analysis; (3) the artificially and legalistically constrained nature of judicial reasoning about rights; and (4) the relative lack of diversity of perspectives among the elite members of the higher judiciary. Now, it might be thought that, even if it exists, the risk of judicial under-enforcement of rights is not much of a concern because it is premised on, and simply mirrors, a prior under-enforcement by the legislature. Where it occurs, it is true that the countering force of judicial review does not take place, but we are no worse off in terms of rights-enforcement than before the judicial decision.

This response strikes me as at least partially misguided, for two reasons. First, assuming a court has under-enforced the right, it is not true that we are no worse off. The judicial decision formally legitimates the statute and the legislative under-enforcement in a way that would not be the case without; there would simply be a controversial statute on the books which many people reasonably believe violates rights and should be repealed. Moreover, there is now a judicial precedent in place, which may affect the political and/or legal treatment of other or future statutes. It is for these reasons that Justice Jackson famously chided the US Supreme Court for taking the case of *Korematsu v. United States*.[30] It is one thing for the elective branches to under-enforce rights during a perceived national emergency; it is another for the highest court to give its seal of legitimacy to that under-enforcement. Secondly, the response assumes that the existence of judicial review has no effect on the rights deliberations otherwise undertaken by the legislature itself in the course of enacting the statute, that judicial review provides an additional and supplementary layer of rights scrutiny – a safety net – over

---

[29] On judicial under-enforcement of rights generally, see L. Sager, 'Fair Measure: The Legal Status of Underenforced Constitutional Norms' (1978) 91 *Harvard Law Review* 1212. On the argument that rights have been under-enforced by the judiciary under the HRA, see the works cited in Chapter 2, n. 63.

[30] 323 US 214 (1944).

and above the legislative one. There are plausible reasons to believe, however, that judicial review within a legal constitutionalist framework results in the processes of political rights review being reduced or even bypassed altogether in favour of relying on the courts, which after all have the final word.[31] Why spend precious time on matters you do not decide? That is, judicial and political review may well be more substitutes for each other than supplements within legal constitutionalism, so that before opting for the latter one would need to be persuaded that on balance the rights under-enforcement stemming from judicial pathologies is likely to be less than from legislative ones.

A second weakness of legal constitutionalism is that it may also lead to the overstatement or over-enforcement of constitutionalist limits on governmental power. There is a term for this weakness, and it is 'Lochner'.[32] So even if, very generally speaking, potential under-enforcement of rights is worse than potential over-enforcement,[33] over-enforcement of the *Lochner* variety is far from harmless error. That is, where courts use their supreme interpretative power to read into a constitutional text certain controversial rights that are the subject of reasonable disagreement, they may be artificially limiting the scope of governmental power in the service of substantive injustice. This type of over-enforcement undermines the overall political legitimacy of an otherwise democratic constitutional regime.

A third weakness of legal constitutionalism is the general weakness and relative ineffectiveness of relying on ex post regulatory mechanisms to the exclusion of ex ante ones.[34] If constitutionalism imposes limits on governmental power, some of which take the form of individual rights, then relying primarily or exclusively on courts to enforce them will often

---

[31] The classic statement of this argument was made by James Bradley Thayer in his book, *John Marshall*. Thayer considered that the tendency of legislatures within a system of judicial supremacy to leave consideration of constitutional limits to the courts and to assume that whatever they can constitutionally do they may do, meant that 'honor and fair dealing and common honesty were not relevant to their inquiries'. Even more famously, he argued that as judicial review involved the correction of legislative mistakes from the outside, it results in the people losing the 'political experience, and the moral education and stimulus that come from . . . correcting their own errors. [The] tendency of a common and easy resort to this great function [is] to dwarf the political capacity of the people, and to deaden its sense of moral responsibility'. *Ibid.*, pp. 103–7.

[32] *Lochner* v. *New York*, 198 US 45 (1905).

[33] This argument is made by Fallon, 'The Uneasy Case', p. 1709.

[34] For general works on this issue, see S. Shavell, *Economic Analysis of Accident Law* (Cambridge, MA: Harvard University Press, 1987); C. Kolstad, T. Ulen and G. Johnson, 'Ex Post Liability for Harm vs. Ex Ante Safety Regulations: Substitutes or Complements?' (1990) 80 *American Economic Review* 888.

be tantamount to closing the barn door after the horse has bolted. Some laws that raise serious rights issues may never be challenged in court, others may be challenged but under-enforced, and in most cases laws will not be challenged until at least some of the damage they are judicially assessed to impose has already been caused. Abstract judicial review acknowledges, and is designed to deal with, this problem but several systems do not permit this type of review and those that do usually limit standing to elected representatives of a certain number or office, whose political interest in challenging a law may or may not coincide with those likely to be adversely affected by it.[35]

Fourthly, there is a strong tendency within legal constitutionalism for courts to become the primary expositors of rights in society, and yet there are serious weaknesses in judicial modes of rights deliberation from the perspective of this important function. Judicial review may be conceptualized and defended (in common law jurisdictions at least) as incidental to the ordinary judicial function of deciding a case,[36] but deciding a specific case is far from all that a highest court typically does when exercising this power in the context of a controversial rights issue. Rather, depending on the scope of its judgment, it resolves not only the case but the rights issue raised in it as far as lower courts in future cases are concerned, and, depending on its accepted or perceived interpretive supremacy within the entire political system, its resolution becomes the authoritative one for all purposes. In this way, the highest court tends to speak for, and in the name of, society as a whole. Here again, the 'limitations inherent within judicial forms of decision-making'[37] discussed by Tomkins and Waldron come to the fore, as does the concern with over-legalization or judicialization of principled public discourse generally, whereby the legal component or conception of rights is over-emphasized at the expense of the moral and political.[38]

---

[35] For the few exceptions to this standing limitation and for general discussion of the merits and critiques of abstract review, see V. Ferreres Comella, *Constitutional Courts and Democratic Values* (New Haven, CT: Yale University Press, 2009), pp. 66–70.

[36] This conceptualization and defence were first presented in *Marbury v. Madison*. Harel and Kahana's argument in 'The Easy Core Case' seeks to justify 'case-specific judicial review' only and not the broader precedential force of these decisions underlying claims of judicial supremacy, although they believe their argument has 'implications' for the latter.

[37] Tomkins, *Our Republican Constitution*, p. 29.

[38] See, for example, M. Glendon, *Rights Talk: The Impoverishment of Political Discourse* (Cambridge, MA: Harvard University Press, 1991); Waldron, 'The Core of the Case'; Stone Sweet, *Governing with Judges*.

These first four weaknesses mostly address the issue of whether or not rights are better protected with judicial review. Last, but by no means least, is the familiar and standard concern with legal constitutionalism from the perspective of legitimacy in a democratically organized polity, the concern that Fallon and Kumm have attempted to outflank. As this concern is so familiar, I shall be brief. It may perhaps be expressed or captured this way: in the name of attempting to ensure against under-protection of rights, legal constitutionalism gives to an electorally unaccountable committee of experts unreviewable power to decide many of the most important and weighty normative issues that virtually all contemporary democratic political systems face, even though it turns out that these issues are not ones for which the committee's expertise is especially or uniquely relevant.

The easy, conventional and mostly rhetorical response to this concern is premised on a legal fiction: namely, that a supermajority of citizens has self-consciously, deliberately and clearly pre-committed to a set of higher law solutions to rights issues, and the function of the courts is simply to apply these – in essentially the same way as any other type of law.[39] The legal reality is that many of the most important rights issues as and where they present themselves are inevitably the subject of reasonable disagreement among and between judges, legislators and citizens – as routinely evidenced by closely divided courts, legislatures and referenda on some of the most controversial and difficult topics. Such disagreement – about which rights exist, their meaning, scope and application, as well as permissible limits on them – persists whether or not rights and rights claims are left in the realm of moral and political discourse only, are deemed part of the common law or have been incorporated into the particular textual formulas of a statutory or constitutional bill of rights. As Jeremy Waldron puts it, 'the Bill of Rights does not settle the disagreements that exist in the society about individual and minority rights. It bears on them but it does not settle them. At most, the abstract terms of the Bill of Rights are popularly selected sites for disputes about these issues.'[40]

In this context, the case for some of the most fundamental, important and divisive moral and political issues confronting a self-governing society of equal citizens being subject to the rule that the decision of a judicial majority is final and effectively unreviewable, on the legal fiction that they are wholly questions of law akin to the interpretation of a statute or a contract, appears

---

[39] This argument originates with Alexander Hamilton in *Federalist Paper* 78.
[40] Waldron, 'The Core of the Case', 1393.

weak – if not duplicitous. So too on the frequently proffered alternative basis that they concern matters of principle (as distinct from policy) best left to, and answered by, courts alone.[41] Even were the distinction between principle and policy to be successfully explained and justified, if 'constitutional democracy' is taken to require excluding the participation and reasonable judgments of equal citizens and their electorally accountable legislative representatives on all rights-relevant issues of principle in favour of the reasonable judgments of judicial majorities, then the qualifying adjective has largely swallowed what it qualifies.

III   The new model as a normatively appealing third way

The persistence of these weaknesses with both traditional models alongside each of their strengths is a major problem because of the structure of the choice between them. In the either-or universe of the bipolar model, we are stuck with one or the other in a 'winner-takes-all' institutional system that requires the weaknesses of the chosen model to be endured alongside its strengths, whilst the complementary merits of the other model are lost entirely. It is legal constitutionalism *versus* political constitutionalism, judicial supremacy or no judicial review at all. But this 'warts-and-all' structure of institutional design choice is unnecessarily crude and disproportionate with respect to the normative costs and benefits of the two models. By contrast, a major advantage of the new model as an intermediate hybrid is that it makes possible a form of 'proportional representation' among the strengths of both legal and political constitutionalism, whilst also severing or minimizing the major weaknesses of each.

The core of the case for the new model is the argument for *both* weaker-form judicial review and weaker-form legislative supremacy versus *either* strong-form judicial review or strong-form legislative supremacy. The central problem with strong-form judicial review is not that rights-based judicial review has no value or cannot be justified at all, but that it is too strong. In the familiar language of proportionality, it is not the least restrictive way of achieving this value with respect to others that are also central and essential within a constitutional democracy. Moreover, as already previewed in the previous section, there are good reasons for believing that at least part of this value – protecting against under-enforcement of

---

[41]   R. Dworkin, *Taking Rights Seriously* (Cambridge, MA: Harvard University Press, 1977), ch. 4. In the UK, and drawing on Dworkin, see J. Jowell, 'Of Vires and Vacuums: The Constitutional Context of Judicial Review' (1999) *Public Law* 448.

rights – may not be optimally or best promoted by strong judicial review, even if it were the case that on balance it affords better protection than political constitutionalism.

Similarly, the central problem with traditional strong-form legislative supremacy is also that it is unnecessarily strong. Just as judicial supremacy effectively gives exclusive voice to the highest court, traditional strong-form legislative supremacy needlessly creates a monopoly for elected representatives in terms of whose voice counts or has legal authority on rights issues. If the core concept of parliamentary sovereignty is perfectly consistent with the existence of moral, political and procedural constraints on legislative decision-making, as Jeffery Goldsworthy reminds us,[42] the new model adds two concrete and specific types of such constraint: the procedural requirement of pre-enactment rights review and the very visible political constraint of a formal, but not necessarily legally final, judicial opinion on rights issues raised by enacted laws. By challenging the legislature's institutional monopoly of authoritative voice on rights issues, this second constraint in particular can be said to weaken legislative supremacy compared to the traditional version that remains part and parcel of political constitutionalism.

I have claimed that the general case for the new model, like the arguments for the mixed economy, is that it combines the strengths of the two purer but flawed extremes whilst avoiding their weaknesses. It is now time to make good on this claim by explaining how this is achieved. As we have seen, to the extent that proponents of legal and political constitutionalism have engaged each others' arguments, it has mostly been in a debate about judicial review, in which the common ground is that the two main issues are whether there is reason to suppose that rights are better protected with or without judicial review and whether judicial review is democratically legitimate. Although, at times, political constitutionalists almost seem to rue the focus on rights – which they acknowledge has been the trigger for the growth of legal constitutionalism[43] – as misplaced, it is too late in the rights revolution (at least in the context of mature liberal democracies) to cede this territory to the opposition.

How exactly does the new model accommodate and combine the strengths of both polar positions, whilst severing their weaknesses as inessential and dispensable? And what is the argument that the resulting intermediate position better protects rights whilst also maintaining political legitimacy in a democracy? To begin with the issue of rights

---

[42] Goldsworthy, *Parliamentary Sovereignty*, pp. 302–3.
[43] Bellamy, *Political Constitutionalism*, p. 15.

protection, the case for the new model accepts almost everything that critics of legal constitutionalism say as to why legislative reasoning about the sorts of rights issues confronting all modern societies is or may be better/more appropriate than judicial reasoning, with its inherently artificial and constrained nature and relative inability to focus directly on the moral issues involved. This acceptance is institutionalized in pre- and post-enactment political rights review. At the same time, it also accepts and accommodates the legal constitutionalist argument that judicial review may sometimes help to reduce the risk of certain types of under-enforcement of rights, hence the role of courts in between the two stages of political review. Given what has just been said, this is obviously not because courts are better or more expert than legislatures at rights deliberation, but because each institution comes to the task from a different perspective, with different strengths and weaknesses that may usefully be brought to bear on rights issues to help improve outcomes and protect against under-enforcement. Again, the relative strengths of legislatures are those expressed by Tomkins and Waldron, as well as the greater diversity of views mentioned above. The relative weaknesses of legislatures are the potential rights-relevant pathologies to which they may be subject. The relative advantage of courts here is independence from these potential electorally induced pathologies and the dimension of fact-specific, applied rights deliberation versus the more general and abstract approach of legislatures, but the weaknesses are the parallel tendencies towards pathologies of their own and the general problem of relying exclusively on ex post regulation discussed above.

What the argument for the new model rejects as uncompelling, disproportionate and dispensable in the two polar models on this issue is the following. First, in the case for political constitutionalism, it does not accept the consequence of concluding that, on balance, legislative reasoning about rights is superior to (or no worse than) judicial; namely, that rights issues should be left exclusively to the former. This consequence is a function of the either-or universe of the bipolar framework, in which it is necessary to choose between legislative and judicial modes of reasoning about rights. The appeal of the new model here is that it revises the standard implication of this argument by recognizing the respective strengths and weakness of courts and legislatures and providing a significant and appropriate role for both. Accepting the net superiority of legislative over judicial reasoning about rights may determine which has the formal power of the final word but it does not entail that no role is served by, or afforded to, the latter.

Secondly, with respect to the legal constitutionalist case for judicial review, the argument for the new model rejects the implication that under-enforcement concerns justify not only *a* judicial role in the protection of rights but also a judicial veto over legislation – what Fallon refers to as one of the 'multiple veto points' in the system[44] – or at least one that is not defeasible by ordinary majority vote of the legislature. Rather, for the new model, under-enforcement concerns mean that courts should be a 'checking point' in the system, having an interpretative, alerting and informing function with respect to rights issues, somewhat akin to the delaying power of the UK House of Lords as the second legislative chamber versus the veto power of the US Senate.[45] This revision, of course, reflects and expresses the difference between weak-form and strong-form judicial review. To the significant extent that the case for legal constitutionalism turns on the incentives and potential rights-relevant pathologies of elected officials, the case for the new model here is that the combined impact of mandatory political rights review and non-final judicial review will sufficiently alter those incentives and counter the pathologies to render the solution of judicial finality unnecessary and disproportionate. This distinct mode of judicial input into rights discourse can be helpful as the legally penultimate word in both informing/spurring rights review by the political branches and raising the costs of legislative disagreement through an alerted citizenry. As with the criminal jury trial to which Fallon analogizes the argument for judicial review as protection against under-enforcement of rights, we may give citizen-members of the jury a veto power in order to minimize erroneous conviction of the innocent, but (and this is the limit of the analogy) we do not give such a power to second-guess their decisions to judges. Accordingly, unlike the two traditional models, the new model recognizes and reaps the respective benefits of *both* legislative and judicial reasoning in terms of their contributions to rights deliberation and protection against under-enforcement, but within an institutional structure that affords the power of the final word to the former.

Let us now turn to the issue of legitimacy. Once again, the case for the new model is that it is able to combine and accommodate the core insights of both opponents and proponents of judicial review into a package that is more compelling and proportionate than either alone. The democratic legitimacy of collective decision-making procedures (and especially higher

---

[44] Fallon, 'The Uneasy Case', p. 1707.

[45] The current delaying power of the House of Lords is one year, under the 1949 Parliament Act.

lawmaking procedures) is obviously a centrally important value within constitutional democracies. By granting the legal power of the final word to the legislature, the new model preserves and promotes this value. At the same time, the new model acknowledges and accommodates the broader legitimacy concerns raised by Fallon and Kumm in their defences of judicial review. To the extent that weak-form judicial review helps to protect against under-enforcement of rights by giving courts checking, alerting, informing and decision-making functions that supplement legislative rights deliberations and counter characteristic potential pathologies, it promotes justice and so enhances overall political legitimacy. But it does so, too, when also countering *judicial* under- and over-enforcement of rights, against which legal constitutionalism is generally powerless.

With respect to Kumm's argument, it is first necessary to distinguish reasonable public justification for general legislative acts that burden individuals from administrative and judicial decisions, which are typically subject to forms of judicial review for reasonableness even in systems that do not provide for constitutional review of legislation.[46] These are not at issue, and clearly perform the legitimating, rule of law function that Kumm prescribes. As for legislative acts, the new model obviously provides the judicial forum for the required critical assessment of reasons. The question, therefore, is whether strong-form judicial review rather than weak is necessary or essential to fulfil this condition of legitimacy and so is justified as a proportionate departure from the norm of democratically accountable decision-making.[47] I believe the answer is no. To explain why, let me begin by making explicit what has been left implicit in the argument so far and will be discussed at greater length in the next chapter: the case for the new model's override power is premised on reasonable disagreement with the courts on a rights issue. The basic principle at work here is that democracy requires a reasonable legislative judgment to trump a reasonable judicial one.[48] In one sense, therefore, if courts and legislatures both adhere to their normatively

---

[46] Most famously, 'the Wednesbury unreasonableness' test in the UK. *Associated Provincial Picture Houses* v. *Wednesbury Corporation* [1947] 1 KB 223.

[47] Alon Harel and Adam Shinar ask the different, if not unrelated, question of whether strong-form judicial review ('a strong right to a hearing') rather than 'constrained judicial review' is necessary to satisfy the right to a hearing that they claim grounds the justification of judicial review. Harel and Shiner, 'Between Legislative and Judicial Supremacy'.

[48] See Perry, 'Protecting Human Rights in a Democracy', p. 661. Mattias Kumm also appears to accept this principle, which is why for him judicial review is limited to policing the boundaries of the reasonable.

assigned roles and (as in Kumm's theory) courts only invalidate legislation for which there is no reasonable public justification, then legislatures would never exercise their override power – which perhaps
becomes redundant. But by the same token, under this scenario it cannot
be said that strong-form judicial review is necessary, as weak-form
review would achieve exactly the same result.

More realistically, however, the risk that both will depart from their
normatively circumscribed powers must be taken into account: that courts
will invalidate reasonable legislative decisions in favour of the court's view
of the correct one, and legislatures will exercise their override power in
support of unreasonable legislative decisions. In these circumstances, is
strong-form judicial review, rather than weak, justified? In current practice,
Kumm's normative standard is not in fact the one that is generally understood to govern judicial review, and courts regularly overturn legislative
decisions which cannot be said to be unreasonable.[49] But what if it were?
Under strong-form review, there is little to counter the risk of judicial
overreaching on this issue – as by reason of their very independence, courts
face no direct political constraint – and the legislative override power
would be a useful institutional check in the absence of others as a form
of separation of powers. Moreover, we are by hypothesis here – a court has
invalidated a reasonable legislative act – in the situation where the principle
of a reasonable legislative judgment trumping a reasonable judicial one
applies, so that use of the override would be justified. By contrast, unlike
the strong-form judicial power, this legislative power would be subject to a
significant institutional or political constraint against the risk of misuse;
namely, the fact that a court has issued a formal judgment finding there to
be no reasonable public justification for the legislation violating individual
rights. Finally, so far we have been discussing the situation in which there
have been clear departures from the standard of reasonableness, but as
Kumm notes, the limits of reasonable disagreement may themselves also be
subject to reasonable disagreement.[50] That is, courts and legislatures may

---

[49] That is, in applying the second and third prongs of the proportionality principle courts
tend to ask whether the legislature's justification for limiting a right is in fact necessary
(or the least restrictive means) and proportionate in the strict sense, rather than
reasonably necessary and proportionate. I, too, have argued that under ordinary (i.e.,
strong-form) judicial review courts should limit themselves to asking whether the
government's justification for limiting a right is reasonable, contrary to the general
practice – although for a somewhat different reason than Kumm. See Gardbaum,
'Limiting Constitutional Rights'.

[50] Kumm, 'Institutionalising Socratic Contestation', p. 28, fn. 43.

reasonably disagree about whether a legislative act is within the bounds of the reasonable. For the same two reasons just noted – the checking function of the override and the default or tie-breaking nature of legislative power that democracy requires – weak-form review also seems the more justified solution here.

In sum, the conventional democratic legitimacy concerns with judicial review are genuine and powerful in the context of pervasive rights indeterminacy. Again, given this context, the argument that democratic legitimacy requires the reasonable view of a legislative majority to trump the reasonable view of a judicial majority seems compelling. Fallon and Kumm are correct that democratic legitimacy is not the only source or type of political legitimacy in constitutional democracies, but it is a critically important and presumptive one. Departures from it carry a strong burden of justification. If protecting against under-enforcement of rights, and/or the requirement of reasonable public justification for legislative burdens on individuals, are the potential bases for such a justified departure, the means of furthering these components of political legitimacy must be proportionate; in particular, they must promote their objectives in ways that least restrictively depart from the democratic legitimacy of electorally accountable decision-making. Weak-form judicial review is that least restrictive means; strong-form judicial review is not.

Institutionally, then, the strengths of legal and political constitutionalism that the new model combines in its hybrid status are as follows. From the latter, it employs the benefits of the more unconstrained and all-things-considered legislative style of moral reasoning about rights both before and after the exercise of weak-form judicial review. As part of the 'after', of course, the new model also retains the possibility of ultimate reliance on the principles of electorally accountable decision-making and political equality. From legal constitutionalism, the new model first takes the enhancement of general rights-consciousness that usually comes with a specific and fairly comprehensive statement of legal rights. It then attempts to counter potential legislative under-enforcement of rights in part by empowering politically independent and unaccountable judges to give their considered opinions on the merits of rights claims filed by individuals, thereby providing a forum to critically assess the public justification of laws and bolstering the broader legitimacy of the political system.

At the same time, the new model also avoids or seeks to minimize the major weaknesses of both traditional models. From political constitutionalism, it counters the rights-relevant pathologies or blind spots to which electorally accountable institutions may be prone by, first, mandating rights consciousness and review in the legislative process itself and, secondly, establishing judicial review. Of the weaknesses of legal constitutionalism, the new model counters certain judicial pathologies that may result in both the under- and over-enforcement of rights by not relying solely on courts for protection of rights but also on rights review and deliberation by the political institutions. This enables the benefits of legislative reasoning about rights to supplement the limitations of judicial rights reasoning. At the pre-enactment stage, this political rights review also introduces the advantages of ex ante regulation in addition to the ex post regulation of judicial review, which may help to prevent rights violations from occurring in the first place. And at the post-enactment stage, it permits the new model to neutralize legal constitutionalism's democratic legitimacy problem.

As part of its hybrid nature, and like the analogous mixed economy, the new model not only selectively incorporates and combines certain existing features (i.e., the strengths) from each of the two polar ones whilst discarding others (the weaknesses), but also *revises* them and in the process creates at least two wholly novel features that are not part of either traditional model. The normative appeal of these two exclusive features contributes substantially to the overall case for the new model. The first of these is the checking and alerting rights-protective roles of the courts compared to the full veto power of judicial supremacy just discussed in the context of Richard Fallon's arguments. More akin to the delaying power of the UK's second legislative chamber, the House of Lords, than the outright veto of the US Senate – and for similar reasons of democratic legitimacy – one version of these more limited powers is institutionalized in the judicial declaration of incompatibility, a novel judicial power when enacted as part of the HRA.[51] The second exclusive feature is the new model's dispersal of responsibility for rights among all three branches of government rather than its centralization in either the courts (judicial supremacy) or the legislature (legislative supremacy). It is achieved in the three sequenced stages of mandatory pre-enactment political rights review by the executive and legislature, post-enactment judicial rights review, and post-litigation political rights review by the legislature. In this way, the new model not only produces a better, more proportionate *general* balance of power between courts and legislatures than the two more lopsided models

---

[51] See Chapter 2, n. 30.

of legislative and judicial supremacy, but also specifically with respect to the recognition and protection of rights.

This dispersal of rights responsibilities has the goal of fostering a stronger and deeper rights consciousness in all institutions exercising public power and is an essential part of the aggregate rights protective features of the new model. Overall, in the three following ways, it creates a different, and arguably more attractive, rights culture than the one produced under judicial supremacy. First, in the context of reasonable disagreement about rights, the dispersal rather than the concentration of responsibility is likely to affect the content of the recognized rights. This is due to both types of 'judicial pathologies' about rights discussed above: (1) the artificially and legalistically constrained nature of judicial reasoning about rights that largely excludes direct engagement with the moral issues involved; and (2) the greater diversity of views and perspectives that electorally account- able representatives can openly bring to rights deliberations compared to the numerically smaller, cloistered and elite world of the higher judiciary. Secondly, in terms of procedure, rights discussions will be far more inclusive and participatory, leading to greater rights consciousness among both elected representatives and electorate. In affirming rather than denying Waldron's 'right of rights',[52] the new model here institutionalizes a demo- cratically legitimate rights regime. Thirdly, for standard checks and balan- ces reasons the dispersal rather than the concentration of rights responsibilities reduces the risk of under-enforcement that comes with relying exclusively on any one institution – whether courts or legislatures. As noted above, although better known, under-enforcement concerns are hardly limited to the legislature. The key innovation here is the distinctive new model feature of supplementing ex post judicial rights review with ex ante political rights review by the executive and legislature. For its goal is to internalize rights consciousness within the processes of policy-making and thereby reduce or minimize rights violations in legislative outputs at the outset.

A final argument for the new model, at least as against legal constitu- tionalism, relates to judicial appointments. Under judicial supremacy, because of the power that they wield, the claim that constitutional court judges should have whatever partial or indirect democratic accountability they can be given is an irresistible one. As a result, judicial appointments to these courts become political appointments, with several variations in the precise mode of legislative and/or executive selection but in almost all of

---

[52] J. Waldron, 'Participation: The Rights of Rights', p. 307.

which political affiliation is taken into account.[53] Yet, for some, observing constitutional court judges deciding important and close cases politically, along predictable ideological lines, is unedifying and problematic, and at least partly in tension with the very independence that the argument for judicial review centrally relies upon. To be clear, this practice does not necessarily affect one aspect or sense of judicial independence – that once in office, judges are no longer beholden or answerable to politicians (although it may do so where judges sit for renewable terms) – but it does in the sense of having impartial, relatively disinterested, non-party political, or at least non-partisan, individuals appointed to judicial office in the first place. For others, the desirability or acceptability of political appointments to the constitutional judiciary is not intrinsic, something that is independently valuable or justified, but rather is instrumentally and essentially tied to the nature of judicial supremacy within a democracy.

Understandably, there have been calls for the new model jurisdictions to follow the same path. As judges now exercise powers of constitutional review, they too should be given whatever indirect democratic accountability is available through the practices of political nomination and public hearings.[54] At the same time, this is anathema to many others within the Commonwealth common law culture in which the new model currently operates, given the long-standing official norms of merit, seniority and peer review for high judicial office and the irrelevance – indeed invisibility – of partisan political views and affiliations. The United Kingdom has recently moved even further in the direction of greater insulation from political factors, and also greater transparency, by instituting the fully independent Judicial Appointments Committee to replace the opaque method of selection by the Lord Chancellor.

Depending on one's point of view on this issue, one advantage of the new model is that, unlike judicial supremacy, it has the resources to resist this call for indirect democratic accountability and political appointments to the highest courts. This, of course, is the *direct* mode of democratic accountability for rights outcomes resulting from the existence of the legislative power of the final word. Accordingly, there is no necessary requirement for the politically tinged constitutional decision-making everywhere characteristic of judicial supremacy in

---

[53] See Stone Sweet, *Governing with Judges*, pp. 45–9; Tushnet and Jackson, *Comparative Constitutional Law*, pp. 498–500.

[54] Canada held its first-ever public hearing for a nominee to the SCC in 2006, albeit brief and non-partisan, but so far this has not been repeated for subsequent appointments.

practice. This can be left to the elected and accountable politicians under the new model. Here, by contrast, the designated task of the courts is to be as independent of political decision-making as possible and in all senses, to provide a complement rather than a supplement to such reasoning by bringing the best of the distinctive judicial technique, including its technical, impartial, disinterested and non-partisan nature, to bear on rights issues. To be sure, these norms are never fully realised in practice, and the limitations of this technique speak against its automatically having the final word on contestable rights issues, but it is what justifies a judicial role in the process, if anything does. In short, the new model arguably provides the best of both worlds, and judicial supremacy the worst: more politically independent judicial reasoning *and* more direct democratic accountability for the ultimate resolution of rights issues versus politically tinged and, at this point, wholly unaccountable judicial decisions that are final.

IV The comparative plausibility of existing counter-majoritarian conscious justifications of judicial review

Whilst some legal constitutionalists acknowledge that democracy and judicial review coexist in some inherent and ongoing tension with each other as twin pillars of constitutional democracy,[55] others have sought to solve the 'counter-majoritarian difficulty'[56] by denying, or at least minimizing, the tension. Indeed, for some, judicial review affirmatively promotes democracy.[57] Part of the case for the new model is that it provides a better, more direct solution – indeed, a radical dissolution – of the problem than these previously offered ones, premised as they are upon strong judicial review and the binary opposition with legislative supremacy: either judicial supremacy or no judicial review at all. That is, these existing 'counter-majoritarian conscious' justifications of strong judicial review tend to lose whatever plausibility they might otherwise have when faced with the new alternative of an intermediate, less powerful judicial role. In explaining why this is so in briefly considering the three most influential justifications of this sort, I will also be underscoring that the new model provides not only a new form of judicial review but also a new and distinctive justification of judicial review.

---

[55] For example, Kumm, 'Democracy is Not Enough'.
[56] Bickel, *The Least Dangerous Branch*, p. 16.   [57] See the first and second theories below.

The first of these existing justifications is the 'representation rein-forcement theory' associated with John Hart Ely[58] and footnote 4 of *Carolene Products*,[59] the origins of which may be traced at least as far back as Chief Justice Marshall's opinion in *McCulloch* v. *Maryland*.[60] The argument is that judicial review is not only compatible with, but actually enhances, representative democracy and popular sovereignty if and when its exercise is limited to perfecting the democratic process by enforcing those rights that bear on full and equal partic-ipation in it. These include voting, free speech and anti-discrimina-tion rights.

Although admittedly offered as a theory of US constitutionalism, when considered in the general or comparative context of the new model, there appear to be two serious problems with it. First, whatever the extent to which the United States Constitution may best be inter-preted as containing predominantly procedural rights of democratic participation, this is not a plausible account of the fundamental or human rights contained in the constitutions framed in the aftermath and knowledge of World War II – the post-war rights revolution – and so cannot provide a justification for strong-form judicial review of the many substantive provisions they incontrovertibly contain.[61] Secondly, the gap between popular sovereignty and legislative supremacy on which the theory relies runs counter to the political traditions of most countries apart from the United States, in which for historical reasons the legis-lature is conceived of as the distinctive political organ of the people.[62] In this context, the goal of perfecting democracy by disabling the demo-cratic institutions seems paradoxical. By contrast, the new model pro-tects both procedural and substantive rights, but in ways that do not completely disable the representative institutions in the name of their own perfection. It limits the general power of judicial review rather than its scope of operation.

---

[58] J. H. Ely, *Democracy and Distrust* (Cambridge MA: Harvard University Press, 1971).

[59] *United States* v. *Carolene Products Co.* 304 US 144 (1938).   [60] 17 US 316 (1819).

[61] For example, Germany's Basic Law places the substantive value of human dignity first, and at the centre of its scheme of constitutional values. In the (representative) view of one commentator, the German Constitutional Court has made it clear that Article 1(1) (which states that the 'dignity of man is inviolable. To respect and protect it is the duty of all state authority') 'expresses the highest value of the Basic Law, informing the spirit and substance of the entire document'. D. Kommers, *The Constitutional Jurisprudence of the Federal Republic of Germany*, 2nd edn (South Bend, IN: Notre Dame University Press, 1997), p. 298.

[62] See Gardbaum, 'The New Commonwealth Model', pp. 740–1.

The second theory makes an even more direct democratic appeal to the people over the heads of the institution that claims to represent and express its sovereignty. This theory minimizes not the exercise of judicial review, as with Thayer's argument for deference under the 'clear error rule',[63] but the conception of what judges who exercise it are doing. Finding its source in the defences of judicial review provided by Chief Justice Marshall and Alexander Hamilton,[64] the argument relies on the democratic source and authorship of the constitution by we the people, and sees the task of the courts as simply protecting and enforcing their work product against the legislature, with little independent input. This is the argument I referred to above as the 'easy, conventional and mostly rhetorical case' for judicial supremacy.[65] Bruce Ackerman has given far greater sophistication and dynamic form to this venerable argument by positing a more complex and creative judicial function of interpretive synthesis of successive interventions by we the people over time during 'constitutional moments' inside and outside the formal amendment process.[66]

The general problems associated with the original version of this solution are well-known. First, it is driven by justification rather than observation, and does not plausibly describe the actual process of constitutional adjudication, especially, but not only, in a context of reasonable rights disagreements. Even with the most tightly drawn text conceivable, this is necessarily less mechanical and gives more discretion to courts than the structure of the solution would seem to permit, as *Marbury* v. *Madison* itself amply and ironically illustrates.[67] Secondly, given the entrenchment of rights and the consequent difficulty of amendment, it gives primacy not to current popular sovereignty but to that of the past, without adequate justification. But even with Ackerman's heroic revision to address these problems, the theory itself, like the others considered, was framed in the context of the bipolar choice. The challenge that the new model poses is whether its constitutive limits on judicial power might better comport with the underlying

---

[63] Thayer, 'The Origin and Scope of the American Doctrine of Constitutional Law', p. 144.

[64] See Chapter 2, nn. 6 and 7.   [65] See p. 59 above.

[66] B. Ackerman, *We the People: Foundations* (Cambridge, MA: Harvard University Press, 1991).

[67] Marshall's interpretations of both the relevant statutory and constitutional provisions in the case are widely regarded as questionable and, at the very least, leave room for reasonable disagreement.

structure of the theory's appeal to popular sovereignty. In other words, might the judicial role in protecting rights be more appropriately a checking function on the legislature, rather than a trumping one, requiring the legislature to think in serious and principled terms before it exercises its weaker-form version of supremacy? The courts' role becomes that of alerting the people to potential rights-violating acts, so that the legislature can be made fully, directly and self-consciously answerable to them.

Finally, there is the justification of judicial review associated with Ronald Dworkin[68] and Alexander Bickel, the latter of whom, of course, coined the term 'the counter-majoritarian difficulty' and so was acutely aware of the need to try and solve it.[69] This justification stresses the division of function and relative abilities of courts and legislatures so that the necessary discussion of general or moral principle (versus policy) is best undertaken by the former because only it has the requisite independence, expertise, time and motivation. As we have seen above, the expertise part of the argument has tended to drop out of the most recent defences of judicial review but, from the broadly Thayerian perspective that informs the argument for the new model, even if it were true,[70] this unique judicial capacity for high principle is not a purely independent variable but is at least part of the product of judicial review itself. In other words, there is a bootstrapping element to this third justification of strong-form judicial review: legislatures might be 'unprincipled' if and where their rights deliberations do not count. It takes the consequence of judicial review as a justification of it. As we have seen, one of the most important potential advantages of the new model is that it attempts to transcend any strict division of function by creating strong incentives for legislatures to enter into constitutional modes of discourse. If there is constitutional review by courts, there is also constitutional deliberation by legislatures.

V   Conclusion

The essential argument for the new model as against judicial supremacy is that, whilst affording varied modes and a high standard of rights protection, it produces a better, more democratically defensible balance of power

---

[68] Dworkin, *Taking Rights Seriously*.   [69] Bickel, *The Least Dangerous Branch*.
[70] Of course, as we have seen, those identifying the limitations of judicial (versus legislative) moral and rights reasoning deny the truth of this claim.

between courts and legislatures. Judicial supremacy, with its associated tendency towards exclusivity and monologue in rights reasoning, is especially problematic in the inevitable real world context of reasonable disagreement about the meaning, scope, application, and permissible limits on the relatively abstract text of a bill of rights among judges, between courts and legislatures, and among citizens. Moreover, the second-stage of modern rights adjudication, the stage involving means-end analysis to determine whether limits on rights are justified, is largely devoid of specifically legal analysis. The new model permits the rights contained in a legalized charter to be protected in a less court-centric way that provides a greater role in rights deliberation for both the political branches and the citizenry. In so doing, it may also address and help to resolve the well-known problems of (1) the over-legalization or judicialization of principled public discourse[71] and (2) legislative and popular debilitation that have long been identified as major institutional costs of constitutionalization.[72] More broadly, the new model radically and directly dissolves the countermajoritarian difficulty.

The essential argument for the new model as against traditional legislative supremacy is that whilst maintaining democratic legitimacy through the legal power of the final word, it provides a more secure, comprehensive and pluralistic scheme of rights protection. The argument consists of the following steps: (1) basic or fundamental or human rights are an important and valuable way of thinking about collective life; (2) they both can and should be more effectively recognized and protected than under either a purely moral/political conception of rights or a system of residual common law liberties supplemented by certain specific statutory rights; (3) this more effective protection requires a concise, legalized statement of rights; and (4) courts have an important, indeed essential, role to play in this more effective protection; not an exclusive or necessarily final one but rather a role that exists alongside, and is ultimately legally subordinate to, that of the legislative branch of government.

Part of the reason that rights might be more effectively protected under a charter is that the legalized dimension of rights discourse that inevitably comes with a bill of rights (whether statutory or constitutional) is a valuable way of rendering rights and their limits more concrete and specific, of mooring potentially abstract or hypothetical issues in reality. Moreover, however vague and indeterminate a bill

---

[71] See works cited in n. 32 above.
[72] For an early identification, see Thayer, *John Marshall*.

of rights may be – which is part of the reason for not granting judicial supremacy – as a form of legalization it is generally far *less* vague and indeterminate than the primarily common law liberties of the Westminster-based parliamentary sovereignty model. Some form of judicial enforcement power is important to help deal with the standard concern of certain rights-relevant pathologies or blind spots that legislatures and executives may be subject to. If granting the judiciary the legal final word is problematic, this does not necessarily apply to all judicial input into rights discourse. To the contrary, such input can be helpful as the legally penultimate word in both informing/spurring rights review by the political branches both before and after judicial consideration and raising the political costs of legislative disagreement by alerting the citizenry. In these ways, a judicial role promises to enhance the quality of legislative rights debate compared to the status quo.[73]

As a new intermediate option that breaks open the old bipolar, either-or choice, the new model provides an institutional arrangement that treats legal and political protection of rights as supplementary rather than as alternatives, and in so doing combines the strengths of each without also importing their characteristic weaknesses. Whilst acknowledging the merits of the core case for judicial review, the new model also acknowledges the merits of the core case against it by providing a more democratically legitimate, and overall no less effective, legal rights regime than the model of constitutional supremacy.

---

[73] See Gardbaum, 'The New Commonwealth Model', pp. 744–8; Perry, 'Protecting Human Rights in a Democracy', p. 667.

4

An internal theory of the new model

I Introduction

In Chapter 2, we saw that the new model is defined in large part by its novel allocation of powers (and duties) among legislatures, executives and courts resulting in a blending and sequencing of political and legal deliberations about rights. It is this overall package of powers, and not any one viewed in isolation, that renders the model distinct. The previous chapter presented the 'external' normative case for the new model as against the other two standard forms of constitutionalism. By contrast, this chapter will develop the 'internal' normative case for it, in the sense of articulating a theory of how – in light of its distinctive institutional features, objectives and comparative justification – the new model ought best to operate. In other words, I shall be developing a sort of ideal type, a general normative account of how a well-functioning version of the new model operates to ensure that its distinctness is maintained and its objectives and benefits realized. This, I believe, is currently the most pressing and least developed theoretical issue surrounding the new model. In developing a general account, or ideal type, this chapter helps to establish the basic criteria and lays the groundwork for the assessments of specific instantiations of the new model in the second part of this book. It also provides a platform from which to consider reforms of, or alternatives to, these versions.

As an intermediate institutional form of constitutionalism occupying what was previously understood to be inherently bipolar conceptual space, it is unsurprising that there should be concerns about the new model's stability and distinctness. As we have seen, some of these concerns are more formal or conceptual, and I have attempted to address them in Chapter 2. Others are more practically orientated, focusing on how the new model is likely to, does or must actually work, and I shall be discussing these generally in Chapter 9. For current purposes, however, it is timely and relevant to state my view that the new model does not in practice collapse into traditional parliamentary sovereignty in all but name simply because (or where) final authority with respect to legislation is given to the legislature across the board. This, after all, is one of the general and defining features of the model. Rather, it collapses in practice either where courts do not use their (also model-defining) powers of constitutional review but routinely defer to the political branches, or where legislatures too routinely use theirs. Similarly, the new model does not in practice collapse into judicial supremacy simply because (or where) courts have new powers of constitutional review that are not so different in effect from the power to invalidate legislation.[1] For one thing, as we shall see, how these powers operate varies considerably from jurisdiction to jurisdiction; they have no fixed or inherent strength. For another, Canada gives its courts a formal invalidation power but is still a new model jurisdiction. Rather, it collapses in practice either where legislatures do not use their power of the final word to the extent that it becomes irrelevant and so act like legislatures under judicial supremacy, or where courts misuse theirs – similarly acting as if operating in a system of judicial supremacy.[2] In short, it is non-use or misuse of powers that threatens the practical stability and/or distinctness of the new model and not where these powers are placed at the outset.

Accordingly, a theory of when and how respective legislative and judicial powers should be used under the new model is essential but is mostly lacking. Not only would this help to clarify and maintain the distinctness of the new model but might also bolster legislative use as there is currently no general normative account of the proper, legitimate exercise of the power of the final word.[3] In this context, arguably legislatures are likely to be risk averse in political cultures long governed more generally by the rule of law and its constitutive norm that governments obey their own courts. It is this theory that I hope to develop in this chapter.

---

[1] Cf. Kavanagh, *Constitutional Review*, p. 419.

[2] These criteria of collapse are very broadly similar to the conditions under which Mark Tushnet predicts weak-form judicial review will be unstable. Tushnet, 'Weak-Form Judicial Review'.

[3] There are a few country-specific theories. Tsvi Kahana has presented a normative account of the legitimate use of section 33 in Canada and Alison Young of the judicial and legislative uses of respective powers under sections 3 and 4 of the UK's HRA. T. Kahana, 'Understanding the Notwithstanding Mechanism' (2002) 52 *University of Toronto Law Journal* 221; T. Kahana, 'What Makes for a Good Use of the Notwithstanding Mechanism?' (2004) 23 *Supreme Court Law Review* (second series) 191; A. Young, 'Is Dialogue Working Under the Human Rights Act 1998?' (2011) *Public Law* 773, 774–8.

One final preliminary word concerning the general nature of the internal normative account is in order. In practice, even (de jure) judicial supremacy can effectively collapse into legislative supremacy, where there is a strong norm that the formal power of judicial invalidation is rarely, if ever, used or triggered by only the clearest, most blatant violation of a higher law provision, as in several Scandinavian countries and Japan.[4] No one believes, however, that such examples undermine the general stability or distinctness of the model of judicial supremacy. So, too, with the new model qua model. Although it is obviously true that the number of sample jurisdictions is far smaller – more akin to that for traditional legislative supremacy – the general critique of the new model cannot be that in practice a particular instance of it may collapse, or has collapsed, into one or other of the two traditional forms of constitutionalism, but rather that this is a general, and perhaps even inherent and unavoidable, practical consequence of its combination of defining features. Accordingly, part of the point of developing an internal normative theory is to help build a bulwark against such collapse.

II   Pre-enactment political rights review

The new model contains a general blending and sequencing of political and legal deliberation about rights that constitutes both its distinct character and part of the normative case for it, as compared with the other two traditional models of constitutionalism. Consequently, in order to develop an account of the proper employment of respective powers, it is important that the role and contribution of each sequenced stage be understood.

As discussed in Chapter 2, the deliberate institutional engineering of the new model combines mandatory political rights review and weak-form judicial review. This combination of novel mechanisms breaks down into three distinct stages during which the protected rights may come into play, three stages of rights review rather than the single one associated with judicial supremacy. The first stage is pre-enactment

---

[4] In Scandinavia, Sweden and Finland expressly limit the power of judicial review in this way. See Husa, 'Guarding the Constitutionality of Laws'; K. Tuori, 'Judicial Constitutional Review as a Last Resort' in T. Campbell, K. Ewing and A. Tomkins (eds.), *The Legal Protection of Human Rights: Sceptical Essays* (Oxford University Press, 2011). On Japan, see D. Law, 'Why Has Judicial Review Failed in Japan?' (2011) 88 *Washington University Law Review* 1425.

political rights review; the second is judicial rights review; and the third and final is post-enactment, post-litigation political rights review.

As its name suggests, pre-enactment political rights review is defined by three features which it may be helpful to unpack. First, by *who* engages in it, namely, political actors including executive officials, legislators and administrators, subject to the normal oversight of the media and citizenry. Secondly, by *when* it is undertaken, namely, at the outset of and during the legislative process and, in particular, prior to any form of judicial review. Thirdly, by *what* it consists in, namely, political and moral deliberation and not only or primarily legal reasoning. That is, political rights review refers to the content of the review as well as to the identity of the reviewers. Accordingly, it should not be excessively legal in nature; that is, focused on reasonable interpretive pluralism within the law or (worse still) predicting what the courts will ultimately do. Rather it should bring a broader, freer perspective of principle to the issue than is typical of judicial reasoning. This is because part of the point of political rights review is to distinguish rights deliberation under the new model from that under judicial supremacy, to provide space for legislative-style rights reasoning – for both the outcome-related and democratic legitimacy reasons discussed in the previous chapter.

Having explored the empirical dimensions of pre-enactment political rights review, Janet Hiebert concluded (in 2004) that 'for now, the political interpretation of rights before rather than after judicial review is what most differentiates parliamentary institutional practice with respect to rights [under the new model] from that in the United States'.[5] Whether or not one agrees with this specific judgment ('most differentiates'), there is no doubt that this first stage is an important and distinctive feature of the new model. It is distinctive both normatively, as part of the bottom-up or dispersal of responsibility for rights approach, and practically, in that a form of it is legally mandated in each of the new model jurisdictions but not generally elsewhere.

In Canada, the federal Minister of Justice is required by statute to certify that bills have been assessed in light of the Charter and, when inconsistent with its provisions, to report such inconsistencies to Parliament.[6] Section 7 of the NZBORA requires New Zealand's Attorney-General to 'bring to the attention of the House of Representatives any provision in the Bill that

---

[5] Hiebert, 'New Constitutional Ideas', p. 1985. Given her more recent work, to be discussed in Chapters 5 to 7 below, it is not obvious whether she still believes this to be the case.

[6] For the statutory source of this duty, see Chapter 5 below.

appears to be inconsistent with any of the [protected] rights'. Section 19 of the UK's HRA requires the minister in charge of a bill in either House of Parliament 'to make a statement in writing to the effect [either] that in his view the provisions of the Bill are compatible with the Convention rights . . . or . . . if unable to make a statement of compatibility the government nevertheless wishes the House to proceed with the Bill'. In Australia, the ACTHRA and the VCHRR similarly require the Attorney-General and a Member of Parliament introducing a bill respectively to make a 'compatibility statement' as to whether or not the bill is consistent with human rights.[7] By contrast, in both judicial and legislative supremacy jurisdictions, any such pre-enactment review that occurs tends to be a voluntary and ad hoc, rather than a mandatory and formal, part of the legislative process.

Pre-enactment political rights review performs at least six functions within the overall matrix of the new model. First, it aims to ensure that the executive thinks and acts in a rights-conscious way when considering and preparing legislative proposals (and so perhaps also more generally), thereby helping to disperse responsibilities for rights review among all three branches of government. It is not something that should just be left to the courts. Mandating formal ministerial consideration of the rights implications of bills is likely to have ripple-effects at all departmental levels and also, of course, implications for the legislative text. Secondly, full and free legislative deliberation about potential rights issues raised by proposed statutes is a central component of the new model and may helpfully be triggered, informed and alerted by the required ministerial statements. Thirdly, as part of a broader, more ground-up rights culture, executive and legislative rights deliberations at this pre-enactment stage may, in turn, spur popular engagement with rights-issues in a more direct, open and relevant way than is typically possible under judicial supremacy where such issues are raised and considered primarily in the context of an ongoing lawsuit. Fourthly, pre-enactment review is intended to provide a forum for the type of freer, unrestricted political and moral deliberations about relevant rights issues that (as Hiebert implies) may only be practically possible *before* a specific and potentially constraining or framing legal decision is handed down by the judiciary.[8]

---

[7] ACTHRA, section 37; VCHHR, section 28. Under the former, if not, the Attorney-General must state how it is incompatible; under the latter, the MP must state whether and how the bill is consistent.

[8] Hiebert, 'New Constitutional Ideas', p. 1985.

Fifthly (and subject to rules of admissibility), this first stage also makes it more likely that there is some record of political deliberation and judgment on the relevant rights-issues for the courts to take into account if and when legislation is the subject of litigation, rather than only the subsequently prepared legal arguments of the government's lawyers. Finally, and perhaps most obviously, it helps to protect rights by potentially identifying and resolving rights concerns that might never be litigated (i.e., for which this will be the *only* stage of rights review), that the judiciary might not otherwise find or address (here, countering possible judicial under-enforcement), or simply at an earlier stage than under judicial supremacy. As compared with this latter, by transferring some of the responsibility for rights protection from the courts to the electorally accountable institutions, the new model seeks to reap the benefits of ex ante review compared to the judicial ex post.

These general functions or objectives of pre-enactment review within the new model directly suggest the ideal way in which such review would operate in practice. From the very beginning, as soon as the substance of a proposed bill starts to take form, its rights impact and implications would be taken seriously at all political and administrative levels within the sponsoring government department – and not only by its lawyers – and ultimately by the Cabinet in deciding whether and where to place it on the legislative agenda. This would culminate in a detailed written report presented by the relevant minister (rather than the attorney general or other senior specifically legal official) to the legislature, setting out whether and why the minister is of the opinion that the bill is or is not compatible with protected rights. This report would be submitted to a specialized and non-partisan legislative committee with the exclusive task of bringing to the attention of the full legislature any rights concerns in pending bills, whether or not deemed compatible by the minister and aiding it in its future debates of them. After holding hearings in which independent witnesses would provide opinions on the rights issues, the committee would present a clear, non-technical statement of any rights concerns it has to the legislature, which in turn would have sufficient time to debate them in full. Like the minister's report, this statement should be fully available to the public, triggering discussion in the media and elsewhere ahead of the legislative debate. This debate would be understood to be informed by, but not limited to, the types of legal reasoning found in relevant previous judicial decisions, with the aim of achieving a broader, freer discussion of the moral and political aspects of the rights issues involved. Although framed within the context of a parliamentary system, these norms are readily convertible for use within a presidential one.[9]

III Judicial rights review

If and when it arises, the second stage of rights review is undertaken by the judiciary under its new model powers of constitutional review. As we have seen, these range from giving statutes rights-consistent interpretations where possible to invalidation. Adhering to the 'who, when, what' formula above, in the case of legislation this second stage takes place post-enactment in the course of concrete litigation[10] and consists in the attempt by the relevant members of the judiciary to reach the best legal view on the merits of the relevant rights issue. That is, a good faith, independent and professionally skilful employment of the tools, techniques and reasoning styles of the courts.

As with pre-enactment political rights review, this second stage has several distinct functions within the overall matrix of the new model. First, although the new model departs from judicial supremacy in directly and deliberately seeking to foster greater rights consciousness and to distribute rights responsibilities among all three branches of government (as well as the citizenry) and not only the courts, it also of course departs from the traditional model of legislative supremacy that sees no rights reviewing role for courts in the context of enacted statutes. So this second stage is the designated one in which judicial rights-consciousness and responsibility is developed and exhibited. It provides the form and the space that rights review of state legislative action takes in the courts.

Secondly, this stage institutionalizes and executes the specific, affirmative reasons for granting the courts powers of constitutional review

---

[9] Thus, for example, in the US, either the sponsoring government department or responsible member of Congress could be required to make a compatibility statement, which is then scrutinized by the relevant congressional committee and is the subject of subsequent floor debate.

[10] Although not entirely ruling out the possibility of abstract judicial review within the new model, I am of course here attempting to describe the ideal type. From this perspective, the advantage of concrete judicial review is that it is more likely to separate political and legal rights review as the model requires – understanding that the latter is more tied to specific facts etc. For the dangers of abstract review pre-empting political rights review and causing legislatures to focus on predicting what courts will ultimately say, see A. Stone, 'Abstract Constitutional Review and Policy Making in Western Europe' in D. Jackson and C. N. Tate (eds.), *Comparative Judicial Review and Public Policy* (New York: Greenwood Press, 1992).

presented in the previous chapter. Most notably, it provides for a relatively fact-specific, applied dimension to rights deliberation that contrasts with the legislative approach of generality, and addresses the risk of under-enforcement of rights resulting from certain potential tendencies or path-ologies of electoral majoritarianism that are not filtered out during the first stage. Moreover, to the extent that the risk of under-enforcement is also or additionally a general function of institutional responsibility for the final practical consequences of decision-making, the withdrawal of this responsibility from the courts under the new model, as compared with judicial supremacy (i.e., the existence of the third stage of review), provides another basis for their role in countering this phenomenon.

Thirdly, and connectedly, the courts exercise their rights responsibilities during the second stage under the shadow of the third. That is, one important function that the courts perform – in addition, of course, to their adjudicatory one – is to inform the legislature and alert the citizenry of their rights concerns from a legal perspective posed by a piece of legislation. Here, the virtues of skilled professionalism and judicial independence from electoral accountability within a majoritarian political system, especially a parliamentary one, play their role – not by conclusively or automatically rendering the ultimate decision, but by bringing a perspective to bear on it that may otherwise not be brought. If the legislature has the power (but not the duty) to have the final word, the decision whether to exercise that power should be as fully informed as possible, with the addition of an authoritative legal perspective and its dissemination among the voters marking an important new piece of information as compared to when it reached its previous decision at the end of the first stage.

In light of these functions, how should the constitutional review powers of the courts be exercised? What norms ought to govern their use? What standard of review should the courts employ? Because of the new model's conception of rights responsibility and deliberation as a joint institutional enterprise,[11] courts should take seriously the political rights review at stage one, and not ignore or treat contemptuously as a usurpation of the judicial function any rights deliberations undertaken by the political branches, as sometimes occurs in US-style systems.[12]

---

[11] Tsvi Kahana refers to the proper relationship between courts and legislatures under the Charter, given the existence of section 33, as one of 'partnership'. Kahana, 'Understanding the Notwithstanding Mechanism', pp. 255–72.

[12] For an example of such alleged usurpation, see *City of Boerne* v. *Flores* 521 US 526 (1997). This critique of judicial supremacy, among others, is made in Waldron, 'Some

This judicial posture also properly acknowledges the reality and inevitability of reasonable, good faith disagreement about the resolution of many rights issues, which is one of the major justifications for the new model in the first place. Obviously, to the extent that the political rights review at the first stage approaches the ideal version sketched above, the basis for this judicial posture toward it is further strengthened. At the same time, however, their informing and alerting function – which, under the model, exists alongside their adjudicatory one – requires that the courts provide an independent judgment that seeks to present the best legal view on the merits. That is, they should take into account but not be foreclosed by, or formally deferential to, the views of the political branches expressed at the previous stage. Judicial rights review should be respectful but unapologetic. Not only is it unconstrained by full practical responsibility for the final decision and its consequences that can lead to under-enforcement of rights within judicial supremacy, but cultivating the 'passive virtues'[13] would be structurally misplaced and counterproductive in a system of penultimate judicial review. For here it is the non-use or under-use of deliberately granted powers that threatens to undermine the distinctness and stability of this system.

Accordingly, as an exercise in reasoned persuasion rather than 'raw judicial power',[14] judicial rights review should be characterized by transparency and candour, permitting a full airing of the issues from a legal perspective. It should attempt to be as clear and accessible as possible, for its most important intended audience is not fellow lawyers, but members of the legislature and the public. Because the judicial decision is not necessarily the final one, there is no need to assume an air of 'infallibility'[15] or false objectivity; its authority will be as much a function of its quality as its pedigree. Here, colloquies and differences among judges will be particularly important, and their absence, except in very clear cases, will likely detract from rather than add to its influence.

To be specific about the standard of judicial review, the better practice is for the courts to engage in merits rather than reasonableness review. That is, courts should ask whether the legislation in question is consistent with protected rights as they see it, and not whether the prior

---

Models of Dialogue Between Judges and Legislators' (2004) 23 *Supreme Court Law Review* (second series) 7, 39–46.

[13] Bickel, *The Least Dangerous Branch.*

[14] White J., dissenting in *Roe* v. *Wade* 410 US 113 (1973).

[15] 'We are not final because we are infallible, but we are infallible only because we are final', *Brown* v. *Allen*, 344 US 443 (1953), per Jackson, J.

political judgment is a reasonable one.[16] Not only does this standard of review enable the courts to best perform – most usefully and clearly – their informing and alerting function, but the seemingly 'weaker' reasonableness standard would threaten to undermine the legislative power of the final word. This is because, given the norm of substantive reasonableness that (I shall argue) constrains the legitimate use of this power, for courts to effectively declare in finding an incompatibility at the second stage that the legislature has not acted within the bounds of legal reasonableness would be to create an excessively narrow window for the legislature at the third. Its power could legitimately be used only where it (1) reasonably disagrees with the court that its position is unreasonable, or (2) finds that the legal perspective on the rights issue is too narrow and supplements it to arrive at a broader but substantively reasonable overall resolution of the rights issue. This first possibility is rather a subtle and complex one for the third-stage political debate, and its condition would only fairly rarely be satisfied. Moreover, the political costs of rejecting a judicial decision of legislative unreasonableness are likely to be very high, so that overall legitimate use of the power would be infrequent. There would also be the additional risk of judicial over-reaching whereby the courts in effect disguise merits review within the approved language of reasonableness, further stymieing the operation of the third stage.

It is at most only an apparent paradox that, as a result, the standard of judicial review is stronger under weak-form review than under strong-form. For the most part, merits review is either the acknowledged norm under contemporary strong-form judicial review, or reflects the actual practice even where it is not, especially given the vagaries of self-policing and the absence of any checks on judicial over-reaching noted above.[17] But even where reasonableness review is both norm and practice under strong-form judicial review, it reflects the fact that democratic concerns are built into the standard of review – in part because they have nowhere else to go.[18] By contrast, under weak-form review, these concerns are

---

[16] Usually, this prior political judgment will be of consistency with protected rights but where it is of inconsistency and the legislation is nonetheless enacted, courts will have the opportunity of giving an independent assessment that may agree or disagree with it.

[17] That is, under the near-ubiquitous test of proportionality, courts typically ask whether a law limiting a right is in fact necessary/the least restrictive means and proportionate, rather than whether the legislative judgment on these prongs of the test was reasonable, although there are both country-specific and subject-matter exceptions.

[18] See, for example, Kumm's theory of judicial review as policing the boundaries of the reasonable: Kumm, 'Institutionalising Socratic Contestation; Gardbaum, 'Limiting

institutionalized in the external check provided by the independent legislative power of the final word, which is why it is structurally important that the norms of its legitimate use are clarified. Moreover, given the broad scope of reasonable disagreement on rights issues, it will be relatively rare that the legislative resolution is objectively unreasonable, so that there will be relatively few exercises of the new judicial powers and even fewer exercises of the new legislative one. As a result, the new model would likely operate overall in a less distinct manner under a reasonableness standard of judicial review.

Although this 'better' judicial practice is thus based on the likelihood that a reasonableness standard of review would result in too few exercises of both judicial and post-enactment legislative powers under the new model, it is possible that the proposed merits review would lead to too many judicial findings of inconsistency, that in turn, would overwhelm the political ability of the legislature to reject them. If this is the general or widespread consequence, then the norm should be adjusted to incorporate the second-best.

IV   Legislative reconsideration

The third and final stage of rights review is the possible exercise of the final legislative word in light of the judicial review at the second stage. Again, it is the gap between this power and its exercise that is a distinguishing feature of the new model. Obviously, this review is conducted by the legislature – although it may be instigated by the executive – and takes place following an exercise of judicial rights review that is, in some significant sense, in tension with the legislative one undertaken at the first stage. The most obvious example is where a court finds that legislation is incompatible with a protected right, in exercise of its invalidation or declaratory power, but it can also be triggered by exercise of the judicial power/duty to give statutes a rights-consistent interpretation where possible, even where such a reading would not be the result of more traditional modes of interpretation.[19] Like the first stage, this is a form of political rights review not only in the sense of who engages in it but also what it consists in. It would make little structural sense to insist

Constitutional Rights'. This idea goes back at least as far as Thayer, 'The Origin and Scope of the American Doctrine of Constitutional Law'.

[19] As we shall see, in practice exercise of this interpretive power/duty is also premised on first finding an inconsistency between the legislation based on ordinary modes of statutory interpretation and the bill of rights.

that this third stage be exclusively restricted to duplicating and reviewing the reasoning style of the courts at the second stage.

Conceptually, this stage is the most distinctive one of the three, in that the pre-enactment political rights review of the first stage is not necessarily inconsistent with either judicial or legislative supremacy.[20] That is, it appears to be a contingent and not a necessary feature of both systems that this stage is not legally mandated. By contrast, the function performed by the third stage is the key one of decoupling constitutional review from judicial supremacy, of permitting the legislative view about rights to prevail over the expressed judicial one.

The critical normative question that has not yet been fully aired and addressed is when this ought to happen.[21] The routine use or non-use of this power of the final word, although obviously legally permitted, would undoubtedly reduce – although perhaps not eliminate altogether – the distinctness of the new model in practice. Accordingly, it is easy and obvious to say that its exercise should fall somewhere in between these two extremes, but what is more difficult and urgently required is a general normative theory of its legitimate use. This is because there is a widespread perception in practice, at least in Canada and the United Kingdom, that there is no such use, which may in turn help to explain its relative dormancy. As a result, development of this norm of legitimate use is a critical and urgent task for the new model.

To begin to address it, it may be helpful to return to the general normative goals of the new model and the specific reasons for granting the legal power of the final word to the legislature, as discussed in Chapter 3. The fundamental objective of the new model is to provide an institutional form of constitutionalism that effectively protects rights whilst maintaining greater balance or equality of power between legislatures and courts than under either of the two lopsided traditional ones. As an integral part of this greater balance, the new model disperses responsibility for rights among the three branches of government rather than allocating it more or less exclusively to either the courts or the legislature, thereby seeking to create a 'ground up' or more democratic rights culture. In a nutshell, the specific reasons it is both unnecessary and unjustified to always give courts the legal final word on rights issues are threefold. First, judicial reasoning is inherently too narrow and artificially

---

[20] To prove this latter point, the federal legislature in Australia has recently borrowed from the new model to enact a stand-alone requirement of pre-enactment political rights review – without a bill of rights or new judicial powers. See Chapter 8.

[21] Again, there have been a few country-specific discussions of this issue, see n. 3 above.

constrained for courts to definitively resolve most rights issues, issues that are not conclusively legal or interpretive in nature. Secondly, certain potential, rights-relevant legislative pathologies can be countered by less restrictive procedural and/or substantive constraints on outcomes than a full judicial veto. Thirdly, whilst enhancing the specifically democratic legitimacy of the rights regime, these same lesser constraints can also satisfy more general criteria of political legitimacy, such as reasonable public justification of government action or preventing the under-enforcement of rights.

The norms for the legitimate exercise of the legislative power of the final word are strongly suggested by these reasons for rejecting judicial supremacy. The first is procedural. To counter concerns about legislative pathologies and rights-relevant blind spots – indeed legislative deliberative capacities more generally – the legislature must engage in serious and principled reconsideration of the judicial decision on the rights issue.[22] The criteria for such reconsideration cannot be exhaustively fixed in advance, but at a minimum require sufficient time allotted for debate and genuine, good faith deliberation on the issues of principle involved versus mere lip service or purely partisan discussion. In a similar but inverse way from the second stage, the legislature should engage seriously and respectfully with the judicial view but not automatically defer to it. Indeed, overall, the process here at the third stage is the most important thing and not the outcome, so that principled and serious legislative reconsideration resulting in decisions to comply with the courts' view manifest what the new model seeks to achieve as much as do decisions not to comply, at least so long as the latter is generally taken to be a realistic political possibility. For it enhances both the democratic legitimacy of the rights regime and the content/quality of rights deliberation. In other words, compliance per se is not a problem, although a 'culture of compliance' is.[23]

The second norm is substantive. Where, as a result of the above process, the legislature concludes that the judicial reasoning on the relevant rights issue, though perhaps compelling in its own terms, is nonetheless too narrow, technical or path-dependent, and that broader, fresher, or more direct engagement with applicable moral and political principles leads it to a different resolution, this would be a legitimate basis for exercise of the

---

[22] On the need for, and criteria of, such procedural seriousness in the context of a 'good use' of section 33 in Canada, see Kahana, 'What Makes for a Good Use'.

[23] Danny Nicol uses this term to refer to one of two ways legislatures might respond to judicial rights decisions, the other being a 'culture of controversy'. See D. Nicol, 'The Human Rights Act and the Politicians' (2004) 24 *Legal Studies* 451.

final word as long as this resolution remains within the bounds of overall substantive reasonableness. So, too, where the legislature concludes that the judicial reasoning on any of the relevant sub-issues – interpretation, scope, application of the right or the justification of limits on it – is not compelling in its own terms and reasonably disagrees with it, typically because after due consideration it is unpersuaded by the merits of the majority opinion and agrees with a dissenting one. For within the normative framework of the new model, there is no good reason for not permitting a procedurally sound and substantively reasonable legislative view to prevail. By the same token, however, it is not a legitimate exercise of the legislative power to sustain either a non-deliberative or an unreasonable decision on rights.

In practice, the legitimacy of a potential use of the legislative power as just enunciated would be a necessary but not a sufficient condition for its exercise; for the legislature will, in addition, most likely take an assessment of the political costs into account. In a sense, as discussed, an important practical goal of developing norms of legitimate use is to reduce the general political costs widely thought to be currently associated with exercise of the power – to explain that, and how, its use may reflect 'rights disagreements' and not only 'rights misgivings'.[24] But even once this general case is successfully made, it does not of course mean that on a specific rights issue there will not be (prohibitively) high political costs of a legitimate exercise, because, for example, a particular judicial outcome is widely supported by the public. On the other hand, as legitimate use is a necessary condition, political benefits (rather than costs) alone would not justify an exercise of the legislative power.

Two objections to my position might be anticipated at this point. First, mere norms – as distinct from legal limits – will likely inadequately constrain exercise of the legislative power so that the attempt to maintain a gap between the power of the final word and its exercise collapses. Of course, the greater practical problem at the moment, at least according to many, is the non-use of the power rather than its misuse. Putting this to one side, however, as a general matter the entire 'norms literature' of recent years testifies to the powerful and independent conduct-shaping role of norms in social life.[25] Closer to home and more specifically, the consensus

---

[24] These terms appear in Waldron, 'Some Models of Dialogue Between Judges and Legislators', pp. 37–8.

[25] Perhaps the seminal work in the legal literature on norms is R. Ellickson, *Order Without Law: How Neighbors Settle Disputes* (Cambridge, MA: Harvard University Press, 1991).

view is that a norm of non-use with respect to the section 33 power is governing the conduct of federal and provincial legislatures in Canada. Relying on a legal limit, certainly a judicially enforceable one, may not only be unnecessary but would risk undermining the new model's careful balance between judicial and legislative power by giving at least *a* final word to the courts. Conceivably, in the case of a section 33-type power, the two requirements of legitimate use could be expressed in the relevant text as legally binding but not judicially enforceable, although this would not work for declaration of incompatibility mechanisms because they have no legal effect; legislatures are not required to do anything in order to 'override' the judicial decision.

Secondly, the particular norms I have suggested are too vague to be useful and/or too easy to abuse. Whilst certainly not wedded to these precise formulations, given the goal of placing political/moral conditions on the exercise of the power of the final word rather than legal ones for the reasons just stated, I believe that anything significantly more specific or determinate would (1) likely make use of the power too rare or difficult, (2) be too formalistic, as, for example, with a procedural norm of at least *x* hours of legislative debate, and (3) not be possible with respect to outcomes as reasonable legislative judgment is the only normative standard that coheres with the reasons for granting the power in the first place.

My general theory of the legitimate use of the legislative power employs criteria that overlap to some extent with the work of at least two other scholars, and it may help to further elaborate this theory by explaining how its focus and content differ from theirs.[26] As discussed in the previous chapter, Jeremy Waldron has in recent years explored the distinction between the models of judicial and legislative moral reasoning about rights as part of his longstanding but evolving case against judicial review.[27] The former focuses more narrowly and legalistically on reconciling decisions with existing texts and precedents, whilst the latter takes a freer, more direct approach to the moral issues on the merits. Because, for him, the questions about rights which are the subject matter of the controversy regarding judicial review are 'mostly watershed'[28] ones involving major issues of political philosophy with significant practical implications that confront

---

[26] As indicated above, the procedural component of my general theory of legitimate use also overlaps in part with Tsvi Kahana's normative account of the proper use of section 33 in Canada, see Kahana, 'What Makes for a Good Use', although mine also has a substantive component. For one point of disagreement with respect to the use of section 33, see Chapter 5 below.

[27] Waldon, 'Judges as Moral Reasoners'.   [28] *Ibid.*

all societies, and not essentially issues of interpretation even where there is a bill of rights, they are better – and should mostly be – resolved by the ideal of legislative reasoning without a subsequent judicial veto.[29] In this way, he challenges the claim that rights are better protected by the practice of judicial review.

Although, as previously mentioned, Waldron has briefly acknowledged and recently reaffirmed that his arguments are not inconsistent with, or hostile to, weak-form judicial review,[30] they are still directed at (what he terms) strong judicial review and made as part of that lively, ongoing bipolar debate. Once again, in the three-way debate ushered in by the new model, it becomes critical to make clear what you are arguing *for*, and not only against. Both my argument for the new model as a whole and my specification of the criteria for the legitimate use of the legislative power incorporate a similar point – that the legislature should have the final word where it reasonably concludes that the prior judicial decision is too narrow and legalistic to resolve the issue. But I am employing it in the context of making the case for the new model as against both of the other two; indeed, as part of that case, I believe this sort of argument provides a stronger case for the new model than it does for legislative supremacy. In other words, for me the point is not only *consistent* with, but helps to make the affirmative case for, weak-form judicial review and the new model as against both judicial and legislative supremacy. This is because the argument does not assume or rely on the either/or choice between the two but combines them in presenting a sequenced model of judicial and legislative deliberation about rights. And as part of the normative ideal of the new model developed in this chapter it is, moreover, not an ex ante theory of who should decide the issue at the outset – courts or legislature – but an ex post theory of the circumstances under which the legislature should exercise its normatively conditioned power to override a prior judicial decision.

As part of her theory of democratic dialogue, Alison Young draws on Waldron's concept of 'watershed' issues but argues that, at least when properly limited to legal reasoning, not all human rights issues that arise under a given bill of rights are of this sort.[31] Thus, for her, some decisions about rights raise watershed issues and should presumptively be resolved

---

[29] Although Waldron states that, conceptually, the ideal of legislative reasoning is not limited to the legislature, in practice he seems to suggest that it is the legislature that should resolve the relevant rights issues. *Ibid*, pp. 22–4.

[30] See Chapter 3 above.   [31] Young, 'Is Dialogue Working', pp. 774–8.

by legislatures; whereas others do not and should presumptively be resolved by courts. Young refers to the former as raising 'contestable' rights issues and the latter as 'non-contestable' ones.[32] In her view, such a division of relative authority is essential if a theory of democratic dialogue is to be both stable and distinct from either judicial or legislative supremacy. A theory that places final authority in the hands of the courts or legislature across the board is in danger of collapsing into a purely judicial or legislative protection of rights in all but name.[33]

It should immediately be underscored that Young's theory of democratic dialogue employing the distinction between contestable and non-contestable rights issues is geared towards the HRA specifically and, in particular, to providing an account of the proper use by the courts of their new powers under section 3 (the interpretive power/duty, to be used primarily for non-contestable issues) and section 4 (the declaration of incompatibility power, primarily for contestable issues). At least as a general theory of the new model, however, Young's exclusion of non-legal sources of contestability is perhaps questionable, given the difficulty or artificiality of separating the legal and moral/political dimensions of rights issues under relatively abstractly framed rights and where proportionality plays a central role in the analysis. Even within her own terms of legal contestability, Young is perhaps unduly optimistic about how many non-contestable rights issues there are likely to be, especially given these two features, in which case by her account the risk of instability towards legislative supremacy would seem to remain.

The main point I wish to make, however, is a structural rather than a critical one. Like Waldron's, Young's theory is static or ex ante, focusing on the question of who should have the authority in advance to resolve a given type of rights issue. It allocates authority by type or nature of the issue, in her case by dividing authority between courts and legislatures based on the contestability criterion, and in Waldron's by having legislatures resolve most rights issues. For both, at the time the issue is raised it can be determined who has normative authority to – who should – resolve it, and at that point the choice is mostly an either/or one. My approach is more dynamic or ex post in nature, focusing less on who should be given authority or should resolve certain issues in the first place and more on when and under what circumstances that authority is

---

[32] Although some non-contestable issues should also be resolved by Parliament for practical reasons, *ibid.*, pp. 777–8.
[33] Young, *Parliamentary Sovereignty*, Chapter 5.

legitimately exercised; less on whether there is a contestable or watershed issue at the outset than whether there is in fact reasonable disagreement after due legislative process. It distinguishes between formal allocation of power to the legislature and normative constraints on when the legislature is entitled to use it. Such conditions on the exercise of the legislative power mean that in practice sometimes courts and sometimes legislatures will have the final word even where the legal power to do so is always given to the legislature. In this way, there is a de facto division of authority that maintains the distinctness and stability of the new model.

The theoretical exploration of the new model is now complete. Having discussed in this and the two previous chapters how and why it amounts to a new and distinct intermediate form of constitutionalism, what the general case for adopting it looks like, and how it should best operate, it is time to evaluate whether the practice of the new model is living up to this theory. If the proof of the pudding is in the eating, then the merits of the model are in the working. The next four chapters explore how the new model is working in each of its existing variations. The final chapter, Chapter 9, pulls this evidence together to present a general evaluation of its success and distinctness.

PART II

Practice

5

Canada

Canada has been the pioneer in institutionalizing the new Commonwealth model of constitutionalism – not once, but twice. Perhaps this is due to a sense of being pulled in two opposite directions by its combination of geographical location adjoining the United States and historical-cultural tradition as the oldest Westminster-based parliamentary system outside the United Kingdom.[1] The first time was in 1960, near the mid-point of the Warren Court era in the United States, with the enactment of the ordinary statute CBOR; the second time in 1982 with the coming into force of the Charter as an integral part of the Constitution of Canada newly 'repatriated' from the United Kingdom. Both introduced the two central innovatory features of the new model – mandatory political rights review and new judicial powers of rights protection without judicial supremacy – and pre-dated developments elsewhere. New Zealand, the United Kingdom and eventually the ACT and state of Victoria, jurisdictions that share legal, political and cultural traditions with Canada, observed, learned from and ultimately adapted the Canadian example which they used as a common starting point for discussion when they came to adopt their own versions of the new model.

I   Structural features of the CBOR and Charter regimes

For most of their history, Canada's federal and provincial legislatures collectively exercised the same parliamentary sovereignty traditionally enjoyed by the mother Parliament at Westminster. Although under the British North America Act of 1867, effectively Canada's pre-existing constitution, the allocation of legislative power was constitutionally divided among federal and provincial legislatures, no power was legally withheld

---

[1] The parliamentary system in Canada dates to 1791, when the Province of Quebec was divided into Lower and Upper Canada, each with its own elected legislative assembly and an appointed legislative council.

from the division. None was 'reserved to the people' as beyond the authority of all legislatures, so that total, combined legislative power was
unlimited and no court had power to set aside any legislative act except
on allocative, or federalism, grounds. As Peter Hogg described the situation, the only constitutional question was 'which jurisdiction [federal or
provincial] should have the power to work the injustice not whether the
injustice should be prohibited completely'.[2]

In 1960, the Parliament of Canada enacted the CBOR, a statutory bill
of rights binding the federal government only and not the provinces,
which was the first version of the new model and forms the backdrop
against which all the later variations were considered and compared.[3]
Section 2 of the CBOR requires that 'every law of Canada shall, unless it
is expressly declared by an Act of Parliament of Canada that it shall
operate notwithstanding the Canadian Bill of Rights, be so construed
and applied as not to abrogate, abridge or infringe . . . any of the rights
and freedoms herein recognized and declared'.[4] These rights, set out in
section 1, which declares them to 'exist without discrimination by reason
of race, national origin, colour, religion, or sex', include 'the right . . . to
life, liberty, security of the person and enjoyment of property, and the
right not to be deprived thereof except by due process of law; the right . . .
to equality before the law and the protection of the law; freedom of
religion; freedom of speech; freedom of assembly and association; and
freedom of the press'.[5] The CBOR does not specify what the courts are
empowered or required to do if, in the absence of an express parliamentary declaration, a statute cannot be construed consistently with any of
the protected rights. Are they to apply or disapply the statute? Although
eventually, ten years after its enactment, a bare majority of the Supreme
Court of Canada (SCC) agreed on the latter, the case in which they did so
was the only occasion on which the CBOR was ever employed to declare
an inconsistent statute 'inoperative' prior to the Charter.[6] The legislature
could reinstate such a statute by re-enacting it together with a

---

[2] P. Hogg, *Constitutional Law of Canada* (Toronto: Thomson, 1977), p. 429.
[3] The CBOR has not been repealed and is still in effect, although it is relatively rarely
employed because of its effective supercession by the Charter, apart from those few rights
only it contains, such as 'enjoyment of property'.
[4] Canadian Bill of Rights, S.C. 1960, c. 44, section 2.   [5] *Ibid.*, section 1.
[6] *R v. Drybones* [1970] S.C.R. 282. By a majority of five to four, the SCC held that it had
power to declare 'inoperative' a statute that, in the absence of an express parliamentary
override, could not be read consistently with a protected right. Section 94 of the Indian
Act 1952, which made it an offence for an Indian to be intoxicated off a reserve, was held
inoperative as in conflict with the provision of the CBOR containing the right to equality

declaration under section 2 by ordinary majority vote. Section 3 of the CBOR contains its provisions for pre-enactment political rights review, requiring the justice minister to examine all bills introduced into the House of Commons and report any inconsistencies with the protected rights.[7] Accordingly, the CBOR contains both innovative features of the new model and satisfies its various criteria.

Overall, and notwithstanding the decision in *Drybones*, the CBOR is almost universally thought to have been ineffective because of the courts' tendency to interpret its impact and their power through the traditional lens of parliamentary sovereignty, thereby limiting the scope and effectiveness of the rights protected.[8] Thus, whether or not they agreed that courts were empowered to invalidate inconsistent statutes, many judges diluted the CBOR by adopting the so-called 'frozen concepts theory', which interpreted it as merely codifying the existing (largely common law) rights of citizens as they stood in 1960, and not creating any new ones.[9] This interpretation had the effect both of immunizing all pre-1960 statutes, since such statutes expressed and determined the content of these rights, and giving narrow scope to the meaning of the rights when assessing them against subsequent statutes. In addition, the textually unqualified and abstractly expressed rights were sometimes interpreted as too general to affect the interpretation of, or be held in conflict with, subsequent parliamentary measures.[10] In these ways, the ordinary statute, unentrenched bill of rights was adjudged to have less reconciled parliamentary sovereignty and judicial review of legislation than permitted the former to swallow the latter in precisely the way that the standard binary model would predict. Its perceived failure only seemed to confirm

---

before the law, since non-Indians were not subject to a similar prohibition. The four dissenting judges argued that they were required to apply the statute, notwithstanding the conflict on the basis that had Parliament intended to grant them this novel power, it would have done so expressly.

[7] CBOR, section 3, as subsequently amended by section 29 of the Statutory Instruments Act 1971.

[8] See, e.g., W. Tarnopolsky, 'The Historical and Constitutional Context of the Proposed Canadian Charter of Rights and Freedoms' (1981) 44 *Law & Contemporary Problems* 169 (describing weaknesses of the CBOR).

[9] The term was coined by Tarnopolsky, see *ibid*. The language of section 1 which gave rise to this 'frozen concepts' interpretation is the following: 'It is hereby declared that in Canada there have existed and shall continue to exist ... the following human rights and fundamental freedoms'. The 'have existed' language was interpreted by these judges to mean that the laws in existence at the time of the bill of rights expressed and determined the content of the rights, thus meaning they could not be in violation of any of the rights.

[10] See the dissenting opinion of Pigeon, J. in *Drybones*.

the stark choice: either legislative or judicial supremacy, no middle ground is available. But neither Canada nor other Commonwealth countries were finished with the experiment of reconciliation.

The next major development was enactment of the Charter as Part 1 of the Constitution Act of 1982. The Charter contains a reasonably comprehensive set of civil and political rights. Section 2 contains the 'fundamental freedoms' of conscience, religion, thought, expression, peaceful assembly and association; section 3 the right of every citizen to vote; section 6 the right to enter, remain in and leave the country; section 7 the right to life, liberty and security of the person; sections 8–14 various specific criminal procedure rights; section 15 the right to equal protection and benefit of the law without discrimination on various specified grounds; and sections 16–22 a miscellany of language rights. Noticeably absent are any express property or social welfare rights.[11] All rights in the Charter are subject to the general limitations clause of section 1, which states that the Charter 'guarantees the rights and freedoms set out in it subject only to such reasonable limits prescribed by law as can be demonstrably justified in a free and democratic society.'[12]

The Charter is, by virtue of section 52 of the Constitution Act, part of the supreme law of Canada, against which any inconsistent law is of no effect and, under section 32, it applies to the legislatures and governments of both Canada and the provinces (unlike the CBOR). The Charter is also entrenched in that the Constitution of which it is part can be amended only under the provisions contained in sections 38–49 of the Constitution Act, the general formula of which requires the consent of both Houses of Parliament and at least two-thirds of the provinces containing a minimum of 50 per cent of the population of all the provinces.[13]

Although there is no provision explicitly granting the courts the power to invalidate laws inconsistent with the Charter, this seems the clear

---

[11] On the former, see S. Choudhry, 'The Lochner Era and Comparative Constitutionalism' (2004) 2 *International Journal of Constitutional Law* 1.

[12] On the history of the inclusion of section 1, see J. Hiebert, *Limiting Rights: The Dilemmas of Judicial Review* (Montreal: McGill-Queen's University Press, 1996).

[13] Constitution Act 1982, section 38(1). There are additional specific requirements for certain types of amendments, which include provincial vetoes, contained in sections 39–47, and a federal statute that prevents a minister from proposing a constitutional amendment unless it has first been consented to by Quebec, Ontario and British Columbia as part of a majority of provinces. An Act Respecting Constitutional Amendments, S.C. 1996, c.1.

intent of section 52 (the supremacy clause) and section 24 (the enforce-ment clause) taken together,[14] and the SCC has acted accordingly since 1982. As stated above, with the exception of the one deeply divided occasion under the CBOR, this was a new departure for Canadian courts which had previously exercised such power only in relation to the task of policing the federal-provincial allocation of legislative powers. Sections 24 and 52 have also been interpreted to empower a broad range of judicial remedies in the case of infringement of rights which, in addition to striking down statutes in whole or part and granting both injunctions and damages, also include modifying them by reading in and reading down provisions, constitutional exemptions for particular individuals, and temporary suspensions of invalidity.[15]

Thus far, as Part I of the Constitution Act, the Charter has all the essential features of the model of constitutional supremacy: (1) a bill of rights with the status of supreme law (2) entrenched against amendment or repeal by ordinary legislative majority, and (3) enforced by courts with the power to strike down inconsistent statutes. The compromise extracted by those against complete abandonment of parliamentary sovereignty and which was designed to prevent full adoption of the model of judicial supremacy is the provision contained in section 33 of the Charter. For this provision rejects the very last feature of this model, which is that the judiciary always has the legal power of the final word on the validity of any statute challenged in the courts, against whose deci-sions the legislature is powerless to act by ordinary majority. Although judicial supremacy is the default position, section 33 empowers legisla-tures to exercise the final word by ordinary majority vote for renewable five-year periods. As such, this power is both a Canadian invention[16] and one of the two distinctive new model features of the Charter regime. Section 33(1) states that 'Parliament or the legislature of a province may expressly declare in an Act of Parliament or of the legislature, as the case

---

[14] 'The Constitution of Canada is the supreme law of Canada, and any law that is incon-sistent with the provisions of the Constitution is, to the extent of the inconsistency, of no force or effect'. Constitution Act, 1982, section 52(1). 'Anyone whose rights or freedoms, as guaranteed by this Charter, have been infringed or denied may apply to a court of competent jurisdiction to obtain such remedy as the court considers appropriate and just in the circumstances.' Ibid., section 24(1).

[15] R. Sharpe and K. Roach, The Charter of Rights and Freedoms, 4th edn (Toronto: Irwin Law, 2009).

[16] That is, the mechanism is not novel to the Charter per se, but to Canada, as earlier versions of it were used in the CBOR (section 2) and in some pre-Charter provincial bills of rights. See Chapter 2, section II above.

may be, that the Act or a provision thereof shall operate notwithstanding a provision included in section 2 or sections 7 to 15 of this Charter.' Under sections 33(3) and (4), such a declaration has effect for a maximum period of five years but may be re-enacted indefinitely.

Finally, the second distinctive new model feature of the Charter regime is its mandatory provisions for pre-enactment political rights review. Although the Charter itself does not contain an obligation to examine proposed bills and report on any inconsistencies, unlike section 3 of the CBOR, in 1985 Parliament amended the Department of Justice Act to create similar duties.[17] Thus, section 4(1) of this Act requires the Minister of Justice[18] to examine all government bills introduced in Parliament to determine whether any provisions are inconsistent with the Charter, certify that bills have been so examined, and report to the House of Commons any such inconsistency in the event that any provision in a government bill is inconsistent with the purposes and provisions of the Charter.

II   The Charter in operation

One thing even so-called Charter 'believers' and 'sceptics' agree on is that, unlike the CBOR, the Charter has brought fundamental change to the Canadian legal system and political culture. The idea of rights has become central to political discourse, the impact of the Charter on issues of public policy is broad, and the role and power of the courts has increased significantly. This section will provide a brief survey of how the Charter system has been operating in practice in relevant respects, in an attempt to lay the groundwork for an assessment of it as an instance of the new model in sections III and IV. It takes the new model's three stages in order beginning with pre-enactment political rights review. Recall that the basic objectives of this first stage are: (1) to help ensure effective rights protection long before a statute is ever litigated; (2) to disperse rights responsibilities and consciousness to all three branches of government and not only the judiciary; and (3) to provide space for

---

[17] P. Hogg, *Constitutional Law of Canada*, Fifth Edition, 2 vols. (Toronto: Thomson, 2007), Vol. 2, p. 26.

[18] The Minister of Justice is *ex officio* the Attorney General of Canada, Department of Justice Act 1985, section 2(2). For an argument that the offices should be split to enhance the working of political rights review, see J. B. Kelly and M. A. Hennigar, 'The Canadian Charter of Rights and the minister of justice: Weak-form review within a constitutional Charter of Rights' (2012) 10 *International Journal of Constitutional Law* 35.

political/legislative reasoning about rights independently of, and in addition to, legal/judicial reasoning.

The Attorney General's reporting duty has triggered systematic pre-legislative rights review by the executive.[19] Much of this is undertaken by the Human Rights Law Section of the Department of Justice, which was created in 1982 to review legislation for Charter consistency, although sponsoring departments are responsible for drafting the required memorandum to Cabinet for policy approval setting out the objectives and implications of a legislative proposal, including whether it is consistent with the Charter. The Department of Justice lawyers take a risk-assessment approach to the task of scrutiny on a scale from minimal to unacceptable in terms of the likelihood of justifying legislation under the Charter, and the ultimate political threshold for determining whether an Attorney General's report is required is whether or not a credible case for Charter consistency can be made. The number of reports of inconsistency by the Minister of Justice/Attorney General to Parliament on the introduction of a government bill since the Charter came into effect is precisely zero. This is so even though, as we shall see, on at least two occasions federal legislation was introduced with the objective of reversing or overruling prior SCC decisions.[20] Although no official explanation is given for not finding an inconsistency and the review process remains secretive and opaque, the practice suggests there is a strong political presumption against reports. If Ministers of Justice find that the threshold of a credible case is not satisfied, then either the bill is amended so that such a case becomes arguable, or the risk of judicial invalidation will cause the Cabinet to withdraw the bill before it is introduced. If the Cabinet were intent on pursuing a bill that is so clearly inconsistent with the Charter that it requires a report, the Minister of Justice would likely feel compelled to resign.[21] The absence of any such resignations alongside the absence of reports suggests that amendments are made.

---

[19] See Hiebert, *Charter Conflicts*, pp. 7–13; J. Kelly, 'Bureaucratic Activism and the Charter of Rights and Freedoms: The Department of Justice and its Entry into the Centre of Government' (1999) 42 *Canadian Public Administration* 476.

[20] These were Bills C-72 (1995) and C-46 (1996) (responding to the SCC decisions in *R. v. Daviault*, [1994] 3 SCR 63 and *R. v. O'Connor*, [1995] 4 SCR 1411.

[21] Hiebert, *Charter Conflicts*, p. 10; Hiebert, 'Parliamentary Bills of Rights', p. 12; G. Huscroft, 'Reconciling Duty and Discretion: The Attorney General in the Charter Era' (2009) 34 *Queens' Law Journal* 773.

Parliament has provided relatively little additional check on government bills, and usually 'remains on the periphery of political rights review'.[22] This fact has been explained by the dominance of the government in the House of Commons resulting from the strong party/whip system, the relatively weak parliamentary committee system generally and not only on rights issues, and the lack of warning and information, given the absence of any ministerial reports of inconsistency combined with the secrecy and confidentiality of the executive rights-vetting process. There are standing committees in each House of Parliament that consider the Charter-consistency of bills – the House of Commons Standing Committee on Justice and Legal Affairs and the Senate Standing Committee on Legal and Constitutional Affairs – but their general weakness is a function of lack of time, resources and specialization, not having their own legal advisors, and the routine denial by the government of requests for access to its documents prepared during executive review.[23] Although they hear witnesses and summon Department of Justice lawyers, the latter are responsible to the government and not Parliament. In rare cases, mostly where the government's legislation has the objective of reversing SCC decisions, the executive has consciously cooperated with Parliament and focused on it as a venue for the sort of full and principled deliberations that might impress the SCC in any subsequent litigation.[24]

In terms of judicial rights review, the SCC has exercised its power under the Charter to invalidate inconsistent federal and provincial laws on approximately sixty occasions since 1982.[25] Contrary to the dominant 'frozen concepts' approach under the CBOR, the SCC has consistently affirmed the 'living tree' methodology of constitutional interpretation and a broad, 'generous' approach to the content of Charter rights.[26] More

---

[22] Hiebert, 'Parliamentary Bills of Rights', p. 12.

[23] Hiebert, *Charter Conflicts*, pp. 14–18.

[24] *Ibid.*, pp. 17–18, especially with respect to legislation in response to the SCC decisions in *Daviault* and *O'Connor*.

[25] This approximation is based on Rosalind Dixon's calculation of fifty-four invalidating decisions between 1982 and the end of 2004. Dixon, 'The Supreme Court of Canada, *Charter* Dialogue, and Deference', p. 282. Dixon reports that her number is based on Manfredi and Kelly's study of cases between 1982 and 1995, a further study by Kelly between 1995 and 1997, and independent examination of cases decided between 1998 and 2004. Peter Hogg and co-authors state that there were sixty-six invalidations by the SCC and certain lower courts between 1982 and 1997, and a further twenty-three invalidations by the SCC alone between 1997 and 2006. Hogg, Bushell and Wright, '*Charter* Dialogue Revisited', p. 51.

[26] See, for example, *Manitoba (A.G.)* v. *Metropolitan Stores (MTS) Ltd* [1987] 1 SCR 110 at 124 (Charter rights not 'frozen' in content but had to 'remain susceptible to evolve in the

generally, although its constitutional status and clearer bestowal of the invalidation power were obvious enabling factors, the courts are significantly responsible for the fact that the Charter has had a profound impact on Canadian law, public culture and government conduct in a way that the CBOR did not. They have taken Charter rights seriously and been prepared to exercise their power of judicial review robustly, particularly in certain areas.

Under section 15's equality rights, the courts have adopted the general approach of 'substantive equality', 'indirect' or 'systemic discrimination' rather than 'formal equality' or 'direct discrimination', so that a law not expressly employing any of the categories listed in section 15 but having a disproportionately adverse effect on one of these prohibited bases still falls within the section.[27] They have also exhibited specific commitment to gay and lesbian equality in particular, as evidenced by decisions in a well-known series of sexual orientation discrimination and same-sex marriage cases.[28] These latter firmly put the issue on the legislative agenda, culminating in the passage of the federal Civil Marriage Act in 2005 legalizing same-sex marriage across the country. Under the section 7 right to life, liberty and security of the person,[29] the SCC established that the internal limit of 'the principles of fundamental justice' to which the right is subject have substantive and not only procedural content (i.e., limits must not violate substantive principles of justice). It was under this section that the SCC invalidated the criminal code provisions on abortion,

future'); *Reference Re Same-Sex Marriage*, [2004] 3 SCR 698 at [22]–[30] (rejecting view that Parliament's jurisdiction over marriage under the BNA 1867 was limited to marriages as understood at the time of Confederation); *R. v. Big M Drug Mart* [1985] 1 SCR 295 at 344 (describing the nature of the required purposive interpretation).

[27] Despite this general commitment, only two claims of indirect discrimination have been successful. See Hogg, *Constitutional Law of Canada*, p. 650.

[28] *Egan v. Canada* [1995] 2 SCR 513 (sexual orientation discrimination is analogous to the enumerated grounds of discrimination in section 15); *Vriend v. Alberta* [1998] 1 SCR 493 (omission of protection against sexual orientation discrimination in Alberta's human rights code constituted unjustified discrimination); *M. v. H.* [1999] 2 SCR 3 (limitation of support provisions in Ontario's family law legislation to opposite-sex partners was unjustified discrimination); *Reference Re Same-Sex Marriage* (proposed federal legislation stating that marriage for civil purposes is the lawful union of two persons to the exclusion of all others was within the jurisdiction of Parliament and consistent with the Charter, although the SCC refused to answer the separate question of whether the opposite-sex requirement established in the common law, that had been invalidated by the Court of Appeal for Ontario under section 15, was consistent with the Charter).

[29] 'Everyone has the right to life, liberty and security of the person and the right not to be deprived thereof except in accordance with the principles of fundamental justice.'

albeit primarily due to procedural arbitrariness in the application of the requirement for an exemption that could presumably be fixed.[30] Although the SCC has thus far refused to interpret section 7 as including social and economic rights, it has also refused to rule out this possibility.[31] A third area of relatively vigorous review has been certain criminal procedure rights – under both section 7 and specific provisions in sections 8 to 14 – especially rights to disclosure of prosecutorial evidence, to make full answer and defence, to bail, as well as the development of a presumption that most statements obtained in violation of the Charter should be excluded from evidence at trial.[32] In the field of freedom of conscience and religion under section 2(a), the SCC has been solicitous of the rights of religious minorities.[33] With respect to freedom of expression under section 2(b), the SCC has applied the 'generous' interpretive approach to give broad protection under the first stage of rights analysis, while permitting certain limits under section 1 on a case-by-case basis that resulted in upholding laws prohibiting hate speech, pornography, defamation and third party spending during elections.[34] At the same time, the SCC has invalidated a different hate speech law, given more protection to commercial speech than many initially anticipated, and modified the law of defamation to provide greater protection for free expression on issues of public interest (and less to reputation) by creating the defence of responsible communication on matters of public interest.[35]

The Charter's general limitations clause in section 1 has played a central role in the SCC's constitutional jurisprudence as the second stage in the analyses of rights claims. Where a court finds that a right is infringed under the first stage, it proceeds to the 'section 1 analysis' to determine whether the government can justify the infringement as a reasonable limit 'in a free and democratic society'. As is well-known, in

---

[30] *R. v. Morgantaler* [1988] 1 SCR 30.

[31] *Gosselin v. Quebec (Attorney General)* [2002] 4 SCR 429.

[32] See Sharpe and Roach, *The Charter of Rights*, ch. 14.

[33] See, for example, *Syndicat Northcrest v. Amselem* [2004] 2 SCR 551 (ban on ability of Orthodox Jews to build a temporary structure on their balconies in order to observe religious festival is unjustified violation of freedom of religion); *Multani v. Commission scolaire Marguerite-Bourgeoys* [2006] 1 SCR 256 (prohibition on Sikh student from bringing kirpan to school violated religious freedom).

[34] *R. v. Keegstra* [1990] 3 SCR 697 (hate speech); *R. v. Butler* [1992] 1 SCR 452 (pornography); *Hill v. Church of Scientology of Toronto* [1995] 2 SCR 1130 (defamation); *Harper v. Canada (Attorney General)* [2004] 1 SCR 827.

[35] *R. v. Zundel* [1992] 2 SCR 731; *RJR-MacDonald Inc. v. Canada (Attorney General)* [1995] 3 SCR 199; *Grant v. Torstar Corp.* 2009 SCC 61.

addition to the 'prescribed by law' requirement, the SCC employs the following four-pronged test first set out in *R* v. *Oakes*, 'the *Oakes* test', to operationalize the section 1 analysis, absent much guidance in its text:

1. The objective must be of sufficient importance ('pressing and substantial') to warrant limiting or overriding a constitutionally protected right.
2. The measures adopted must be rationally connected to the objective.
3. The measures 'should impair as little as possible' the right in question.
4. There must be proportionality between the deleterious effects of the measures and the sufficiently important objective.[36]

The SCC typically addresses the four prongs in order, although in practice the third, the minimum impairment test, has been the core of section 1 analysis.[37] Only infrequently have laws been held to fail the first or second prongs and, until relatively recently, the final prong was considered as virtually redundant, in that a law satisfying the first three was ipso facto proportionate. It has, however, in the past decade assumed greater importance as an independent test balancing the benefit of the limit against the extent and harm of the rights violation.[38] The minimum impairment prong remains the central test even though the SCC has, since *Oakes* itself, retreated from requiring that the 'least intrusive means' be employed to finding that a law will fail the test 'only if there are measures clearly superior to the measures currently in use'[39] or, as elsewhere stated, that the law 'must be *reasonably* tailored to its objectives; it must impair the right no more than *reasonably* necessary'.[40]

Given (1) that all Charter rights are subject to reasonable limits under section 1, and (2) that the SCC has been fairly deferential towards legislative judgments about the importance of the objective under the first prong of this analysis, it follows that legislatures have significant

---

[36] [1986] 1 SCR 103.

[37] According to Hogg and Bushell, of the fifty limitations that failed the Oakes test between 1986 and 1997, 86 per cent failed the minimum impairment test; Hogg and Bushell, 'Charter Dialogue', p. 100.

[38] See, for example, the SCC's decision in *JIT-Macdonald* at [46]–[47]. The SCC expressly elevated the importance of the final prong in *Alberta* v. *Hutterian Brethren of Wilson County* [2009] 2 SCR 567.

[39] *Libman* v. *Quebec (Attorney General)* [1997] 3 SCR 569.

[40] *R.* v. *Sharpe*. For a detailed critical analysis of the development of the Oakes test, see S. Choudhry, 'So What Is the Real Legacy of Oakes? Two Decades of Proportionality Analysis under the Canadian Charter's Section 1' (2006) 34 *Supreme Court Law Review* (second series) 501.

constitutional leeway to respond to judicial invalidations by enacting a new statute with a better means-end fit under the other three prongs. In particular, by responding with less restrictive and/or more proportionate means to achieve their authorized objective, legislatures may be able to both comply with the court's decision and justify the new law. This phenomenon of legislative responses to judicial decisions, known in the literature as 'legislative sequels', has become common practice under the Charter[41] and also the basis for 'dialogue theory', the dominant academic discourse concerning its distinctiveness, as we shall see in the next section. Not all such legislative sequels, however, have been of the dutiful implementation variety and, on a few occasions, Parliament has effectively attempted to overrule the prior judicial decision by reinstating the law held to be unconstitutional either essentially as-is, or along the lines of a dissenting opinion in the original case – and without using the section 33 power. Overall, there has been a range of legislative responses along the spectrum from clear acceptance to minor, but not necessarily incompatible differences/disagreements to clear challenging of judicial decisions. As such, different people may count the cases differently, but at least two are widely agreed to fall into this latter category.

In the 1994 case of R. v. Daviault,[42] the SCC held by six to three that the common law rule denying the defence of extreme intoxication to a general intent offence such as sexual assault violated the accused's rights to due process and a fair trial under sections 7 and 11(d) of the Charter, and must be changed. Parliament responded by essentially enacting the pre-existing common law rule into statute, but without using section 33. A lengthy preamble set out its views that the rights of the accused had to be balanced against the equality rights of women under section 15, and that the concept of responsibility for one's actions, emphasized by the dissenting opinion in Daviault, was implicit in the Charter.[43] The SCC has yet to rule on the law.[44] In the 1995 case of R. v. O'Connor,[45] a five-justice majority established the preferred and 'Charter-informed'[46] common law regime for ordering production of private records about the

---

[41] According to Peter Hogg and co-authors, there have been fifty-nine legislative sequels out of eighty-nine invalidated laws between 1982 and 2006. Hogg, Thornton and Wright, 'Charter Dialogue Revisited', pp. 51–2.

[42] [1994] 3 SCR 63.   [43] See preamble to Bill C-72 (1995).

[44] Although the British Columbia Supreme Court upheld the amendment to the Criminal Code and thus disagreed with the SCC's prior ruling. R. v. Vickberg (1998) 16 CR (5th) 164 (BCSC).

[45] [1995] 4 SCR 1411.   [46] Mills at [133].

complainant in the hands of third parties at the request of the accused in sexual assault cases.[47] This regime, which was expressed to accommodate the defendant's Charter right to a fair trial, created a relatively low threshold for the defendant to obtain access; four judges dissented and would have imposed a significantly higher one. Parliament responded by enacting legislation rejecting the majority approach as insufficiently taking the conflicting Charter value of equality into account, again without using section 33. Bill C-46 followed the dissenting opinion in *O'Connor* accepting that records must be produced where relevant but narrowing the criteria of relevancy. In *R. v. Mills*,[48] decided in 1999, the SCC upheld the new law.

Mills is an example of what have come to be known as 'second-look' cases, in which the SCC considers the consistency under the Charter of legislative responses to its initial decisions, although as noted, it is not a typical example because of the nature of that response.[49] As reported by Peter Hogg, as of 2006 there had been a total of nine second-look cases under the Charter; four of which resulted in holdings that the new legislation violated the Charter in whole or part.[50] To these must be added the important 2007 second-look case of *JTI-Macdonald*,[51] upholding in full the amended tobacco advertising statute.

As noted, the legislative sequels to neither *Daviault* nor *O'Connor* employed the section 33 power. But what has been the general practice with respect to this distinctive provision of the Charter? The power has been used on seventeen occasions since 1982, the last in 2000, and all by provincial or territorial legislatures rather than the federal Parliament.[52] Indeed, fourteen of these uses have been by Quebec, with one each by the Yukon Territory, Saskatchewan and Alberta, and three federal prime ministers, Brian Mulroney, Paul Martin and Jean Chrétien, publicly pledged never to use section 33. Moreover, only one of these seventeen uses was in

---

[47] Although both *Daviault* and *O'Connor* involved common law rules rather than statutes, and the SCC has held that the Charter does not apply (directly) to common law rules at issue in purely private litigation, the Charter applied to these rules because they were employed by the government in the context of criminal prosecutions.

[48] [1999] 3 SCR 668.

[49] Also, because the 'first-look' case involved a common law rule rather than a statute.

[50] Hogg, Thornton and Wright, '*Charter* Dialogue Revisited', pp. 63–5. Or, as Rosalind Dixon states, only one legislative sequel was struck down in its entirety, in *Sauvé II*. Dixon, 'The Supreme Court of Canada', 278.

[51] *Canada (Attorney General)* v. *JTI-MacDonald Corp.* [2007] 2 SCR 610.

[52] T. Kahana, 'The Notwithstanding Mechanism and Public Discussion: Lessons from the Ignored Practice of Section 33' (2001) 43 *Canadian Public Administration* 255.

direct response to a judicial invalidation of a law, all the others being pre-emptive exercises of the power, shielding legislation from judicial rights review under the Charter.[53] This latter type of use seems fairly clearly to be permitted by the language of section 33 and has never been litigated, although both textual and normative arguments against pre-emptive use have been made.[54] Only three of the seventeen uses – the reactive use by Quebec in 1988 after the SCC invalidated its French-only sign law, and the pre-emptive uses by Saskatchewan in 1986 to shield its back-to-work law and by Alberta in 2000 to protect its opposite-sex only marriage statute – received public attention and discussion.[55]

As a result, it is undisputed that, as a descriptive matter, section 33 has largely fallen into non-use. More contestable are, first, whether it can be said that it has become unusable or, more formally, that a constitutional convention has arisen against its use (i.e., whether there is now thought to be any legitimate use), at least among the other provinces and Parliament and, secondly, the best explanation of this fact of non-use. Among the candidates are (1) the particular history of perceived initial illegitimate use of section 33 by Quebec, (2) the relatively non-controversial and restrained nature of the SCC's exercise of its judicial review powers, (3) the specific wording of section 33 as seemingly involving 'rights misgivings' rather than 'rights disagreements'[56] on the part of legislatures, and (4) the combi-nation of normative qualms about pre-emptive use and the inherent political costs of reactive use, where a legislature is affirmatively required to override a court decision. The perceived return on political capital expended is perhaps further reduced by the need to renew the declaration after five years.

---

[53] The one reactive use followed *Ford* v. *Quebec (Attorney General)*, [1988] 2 SCR 712. The use by Saskatchewan was part responsive and part pre-emptive in that it occurred after a lower court decision holding that the Charter protected the right to collective bargain-ing. See Kahana, *Ibid.*

[54] The textual argument against pre-emptive use of section 33 is that otherwise the legislative provision does not operate 'notwithstanding' the Charter's other provisions. Absent a prior declaration of unconstitutionality, the legislature presumably assumes that its acts are consistent with the Charter. See D. Greschner and K. Norman, 'The Courts and Section 33' (1987) 12 *Queen's Law Journal* 155, 188. For normative argu-ments, see P. Weiler, 'Rights and Judges in a Democracy: A New Canadian Version' (1984) 18 *University of Michigan Journal of Law Reform* 51, 90; C. Manfredi, *Judicial Power and the Charter*, Second Edition (Toronto: Oxford University Press, 2001), p. 192; T. Kahana, 'Understanding the Notwithstanding Mechanism'.

[55] Kahana, 'The Notwithstanding Mechanism and Public Discussion'.

[56] See Waldron, 'Some Models of Dialogue', 34–9.

III Dialogue theory and the distinctness of the charter regime

Although important decisions of the SCC are now front-page news, debates about the merits of the transformed judicial role and powers under the Charter have largely been confined to the academy, as the general public seems mostly to have welcomed or at least accepted the change.[57] And within the academy, dialogue theory has become the leading approach to assessing the success and particularly the distinctness of the Charter regime, an approach that has in turn been taken up by the courts to characterize the nature of their relationships with legislatures.[58] Moreover, dialogue theory has spread from Canada to New Zealand, the UK and Australia, where the new model as a whole is now often referred to as 'the dialogue model' and/or justified on the basis that it promotes 'democratic dialogue'.[59]

General references to 'dialogue' between courts and legislatures as one of the features or advantages of the Charter regime had been made in the academic literature before,[60] but it was the seminal 1997 article by Peter Hogg and Alison Bushell[61] that propelled the metaphor into the spotlight by providing a concrete and specific account of the contribution it could make to understanding how the Charter operates in practice. In the article, 'dialogue' refers to 'cases in which a judicial decision striking down a law on Charter grounds is followed by some action by the competent legislative body'[62] or, as stated in a later piece, to the empirically documented fact that such judicial decisions 'usually leave room for a legislative response, and usually receive a legislative response'.[63] Accordingly, for the authors, due to the possibility and prevalence of such 'legislative sequels' – fifty-nine times out of eighty-nine invalidated laws between 1982 and 2007[64] – the normal situation is that courts do not have the last word; rather, legislatures can usually overcome a negative judicial decision and pursue their chosen objective.[65] In this way, dialogue theory is claimed to demonstrate that Canada has a weaker

---

[57] See the public opinion poll numbers in Chapter 1, p. 9, n. 29 above.
[58] The SCC has explicitly invoked the notion of dialogue in several cases, starting with *Vriend* v. *Alberta* (1998) and including the second-look case of *Mills*, see page 134 below.
[59] See Chapter 1, section III above.
[60] See, L. Weinrib, 'Learning to Live with the Override' (1990) 35 *McGill Law Journal* 542, 565; P. Weiler, 'Rights and Judges in a Democracy'.
[61] Hogg and Bushell, 'The *Charter* Dialogue'. [62] *Ibid.*, 82.
[63] Hogg, Thornton and Wade, '*Charter* Dialogue Revisited', 4. [64] *Ibid.*, 51.
[65] *Ibid.*, 4; Hogg and Bushell, 'The *Charter* Dialogue', 80.

system of judicial review than the United States, where the Supreme Court almost always has the final word de jure and de facto. Canadian dialogue theory has come to have a normative dimension in addition to the mostly empirical one established by Hogg and Bushell, with Kent Roach in particular presenting a systematic justification for what he refers to as 'dialogic judicial review'.[66]

Of course, as an academic theory within an academic debate (albeit one taken up in part by the judiciary), no part of dialogue theory has gone unchallenged. In essence, there are three general positions in the Canadian dialogue debate. The first is the one advanced by dialogue proponents just mentioned which, in a little more detail, holds that Canada has a weaker system of judicial review than the United States because of the distinctive dialogic features of the Charter that permit legislatures to respond to court decisions invalidating laws by enacting sequels and thereby often having the final word. There are three such dialogic features. First, section 33, which empowers the override (or pre-emption) of a judicial decision by ordinary majority vote of the legislature as compared with the cumbersome and multiple supermajority requirements of the US and Canadian constitutional amendment processes. Secondly, section 1 which, as interpreted and applied by the SCC, usually permits legislatures to further their authorized objective by re-enacting an invalidated law with less restrictive means, thereby replacing a judicially determined unreasonable limit on a right with a reasonable one, as exemplified in the 2007 second-look tobacco advertising case of *JTI-Macdonald*.[67] Thirdly, the courts have exercised their broad remedial discretion to create the suspended declaration of invalidity, a dialogic remedy which gives the legislature time to fashion an amended law or face the invalidity of the old one.[68] For Hogg and Roach, even though section 33 has been used only once as the basis for a legislative sequel, section 1 in particular remains a much-used and centrally important dialogic vehicle within the Charter regime.

The second position is deeply sceptical of dialogue theory and its claim to demonstrate that judicial review is weaker in Canada than the United States. Indeed, proponents of this second position believe the claim is false because Canada has strong-form judicial review that is little

---

[66] Roach, 'Dialogic Judicial Review'.

[67] *Canada (Attorney General)* v. *JTI-Macdonald Corp.* [2007] 2 SCR 610. In *RJR*, the SCC invalidated a blanket ban on tobacco advertising as an unreasonable limit on free expression, suggesting that a more targeted less restrictive ban would satisfy section 1 analysis. Parliament responded as suggested, and the new law was upheld.

[68] Roach, 'Dialogic Judicial Review', 64–5.

different than the United States.[69] For them, the power of Canadian courts to strike down legislation 'can only be understood as establishing strong-form judicial review'.[70] The main difference between the two constitutional rights regimes is section 33, but this difference has become formal only as 'the notwithstanding clause is unused, and all but unusable',[71] an irrelevance, giving courts the de facto final word. Furthermore, the existence of legislative sequels under section 1 does not mean that Canada has a weak form of judicial review where (as Hogg and Roach insist) the judiciary is the final, authoritative interpreter of the Charter and the SCC can choose, by structuring its section 1 analysis accordingly, 'to preclude any legislative response other than enactment of the Court's decision'.[72] That is, the SCC has the power to decide what is a reasonable limit and how deferential it chooses to be, including whether or not to let Parliament have the last word. For this position, the main function of dialogue theory is 'to rationalize judicial supremacy over the interpretation of the Charter ... by exaggerating the power of the democratic branch of government to respond to judicial decisions'.[73] On this view, it is no wonder, then, that the SCC has embraced the metaphor.

The third position lies in between these other two. It is not sceptical of dialogue theory per se, but holds that, as currently formulated, it fails to demonstrate the relative weakness of judicial review under the Charter regime, and can and should be reformulated in order to do so more successfully. Christopher Manfredi has long argued that Hogg's empirical criterion of dialogue – that judicial invalidation of a law is followed by 'some action' by the legislature – is too weak or broad for meaningful assessment, that the narrower definition of reversing, modifying or avoiding a court decision is more useful analytically but relatively rarely satisfied in practice, and that it is essential to encourage genuine dialogue about what rights mean – which Hogg and Roach are reluctant to do because for them this is ultimately the task of the courts – perhaps

---

[69] See G. Huscroft, 'Constitutionalism from the Top Down'; A. Petter, 'Taking Dialogue Theory Much Too Seriously (or Perhaps Charter Dialogue isn't Such a Good Thing After All)' (2007) 45 *Osgoode Hall Law Review* 147. That is, substantive outcomes of judicial review may differ, but not the underlying power of the courts.

[70] Huscroft, 'Constitutionalism from the Top Down', 97.   [71] *Ibid.*, 96.   [72] *Ibid.*, 97.

[73] G. Huscroft, 'Rationalizing Judicial Power: The Mischief of Dialogue Theory' in J. Kelly and C. Manfredi (eds.), *Contested Constitutionalism: Reflections on the Charter of Rights and Freedoms* (Vancouver: University of British Columbia Press, 2009), p. 68.

through reform of section 33.[74] A different view, within the general parameters of this third position, is offered by Rosalind Dixon. In essence, she agrees with those who argue that current dialogue theory has failed to demonstrate that Canadian judicial review is weaker than the US, but presents 'new dialogue theory' as a way to weaken and distinguish it, in which the central component is a norm under section 1 analysis of SCC deference to reasonable legislative sequels in second-look cases.[75] This would both permit courts to exercise robust review in first look cases, and so satisfy the reasons for empowering judicial review at all, and yet constitute a form of dialogue that does distinguish Canadian from US practice.

For the purposes of this chapter, I am looking at the Canadian system exclusively through the lens of the new Commonwealth model, and asking whether or not its distinctive new model features are working well – in anything like the way that the ideal theory discussed in the previous chapter suggests. That is, part of my inquiry is whether the Charter regime is operating well as an instance of the specific form of judicial review that is constitutive of the new model – and not (as with the dialogue debate) whether in some other, more general or broader sense it can be said that Canada has weaker judicial review than the United States.[76] Clearly, within the general model of judicial supremacy there are particular systems that are relatively weaker than others, both in terms of formal powers and in practice, but this is not sufficient to make them weak-form systems in the new model sense. For example, as mentioned above,[77] constitutional courts in Japan and Scandinavia have rarely exercised their power to invalidate statutes, but tend to be highly deferential to legislatures, exercising extreme judicial self-restraint. The fact that, as a result, in practice legislatures usually have the final word in these systems does not mean that they have adopted the new model or its specific form of judicial review, although it does suggest that in a mean-ingful sense they have weaker judicial review than, say, Germany. In

---

[74] Manfredi, *Judicial Power and the Charter*, chapter 7; C. Manfredi and J. B. Kelly, 'Six Degrees of Dialogue: A Response to Hogg and Bushell' (1999) 37 *Osgoode Hall Law Journal* 513; C. Manfredi, 'The Day the Dialogue Died: A Comment on *Sauvé* v. *Canada*' (2007) 45 *Osgoode Hall Law Journal* 105.

[75] Dixon, 'The Supreme Court of Canada'. Both Hogg and Roach are sceptical about deference in second-look cases and argue that the SCC should take an independent view of a sequel's consistency with the Charter.

[76] It is part of my inquiry, not the whole, because I shall also be looking at the working of pre-enactment political rights review.

[77] See Chapter 4, p. 78.

other words, deference and judicial self-restraint within strong-form judicial review is not the same as the legislative power of the final word that is part of the new model. The two rely on different types or sources of weakness in the system and on a different balance of powers between courts and legislatures. In short, assessing whether judicial review is weaker in Canada than the US and assessing the success of its new model features are two separate – if not wholly unrelated – issues.

The distinctive new model features of the Charter are, as discussed above, first, the political rights review triggered by the Minister of Justice's reporting duty and, secondly, section 33. By contrast, section 1 is *not* a new model feature at all – even though all five new model bills of rights contain equivalent and, in some cases, identical provisions – but rather, as an express limitations clause, is part of the general post-war paradigm of constitutionalism, part of the standard contemporary model of strong-form judicial review.[78] The fact that, unlike several other modern limitations clauses, section 1 does not enumerate the objectives that may limit rights is of little practical significance in terms of enhancing legislative power (or dialogue) because courts in these other systems almost always defer to the government's claim to be acting for one of the specified objectives, just as the SCC almost always defers to the legislature's judgment about the importance of its objective.[79] As in Canada, most of the work is done at the means stage. And here, the principle of proportionality that the SCC adopted in *Oakes* is similarly part of the contemporary constitutional mainstream, having originated with the paradigmatically strong-form German Constitutional Court in the late 1950s and subsequently spread like wildfire.[80] Indeed, the *Oakes* test itself was largely borrowed from the German court by Chief Justice Brian Dickson, without attribution.[81] The notion that express limitation clauses in bills of rights, such as section 1, as applied through the principle of proportionality create substantial leeway for legislative choice of means in promoting conflicting public

---

[78] Such express limitations clauses are subdivided into two types: general limitations clauses applying to all rights, as with section 1 of the Charter and section 36 of the South African Constitution, and special limitations clauses applying individually to particular rights, as with the German Basic Law and the ECHR.

[79] I am responding here to Kent Roach's argument that this difference among limitations clauses establishes a more dialogic form of judicial review in Canada. See Roach, 'Dialogic Judicial Review'.

[80] See A. Stone Sweet and J. Mathews, 'Proportionality, Balancing and Global Constitutionalism' (2008) 47 *Columbia Journal of Transnational Law* 68.

[81] Although the attribution was made in later cases. See, e.g., *JTI-Macdonald Corp.* at [36].

policy objectives is a general characteristic of contemporary rights jurisprudence and judicial review around the world. It is certainly not
confined to, or distinctive of, new model jurisdictions; it is not part of
the package of constitutional innovations that define the new model
experiment.

Moreover, as dialogue critics correctly point out, section 1, like limitations clauses generally (but unlike section 33), still gives the legal
power of the final word to the judiciary contrary to one of the essential
characteristics of the new model – even where courts exercise this power
to let legislative decisions stand; even where the SCC chooses to defer to
reasonable legislative sequels in second-look cases. As Peter Hogg him-
self acknowledges:

> Who is to decide whether a law satisfies the requirements of s. 1? . . . When a
> law is challenged in the courts, the reviewing court will reach its own
> determination on the question whether s. 1 is satisfied. When appeals have
> been exhausted, it is the final decision of the courts that prevails over the
> judgment of the government and legislature that enacted the law.[82]

In fact, section 1 and section 33 embody and express a major difference
between the contemporary paradigm of judicial supremacy on the one hand
and the new model on the other. This is the difference between granting
legislatures what is, in effect, a *limited* power to override judicially interpreted
rights (section 1), and granting an *unlimited* one (section 33).[83] Most
modern legal constitutionalist systems contain the former, via their limitations clause or clauses and, accordingly, this feature must be – but rarely is in
practice – part of any general defence or critique of judicial review. What
renders the override power limited in most modern systems of judicial
supremacy is, first, that there are substantive constitutional criteria for its
valid exercise (for example, the *Oakes* test) and, secondly, that whether these
criteria are satisfied and the power validly exercised on any given occasion is
ultimately up to the courts. Now, one might argue that judicial review of
exercises of this substantively limited power should be marked by deference
and self-restraint for various reasons,[84] but, even if these arguments are
accepted, this does not eliminate the difference between a limited and an
unlimited override power. For the latter is a matter of legislative discretion,
defined by the absence of substantive legal criteria and judicial review.

---

[82] Hogg, *Constitutional Law of Canada*, Vol. 2, p. 36.
[83] See Gardbaum, 'Limiting Constitutional Rights', pp. 821–3.
[84] As, in fact, I have – for democratic reasons. *Ibid.*, pp. 829–52.

Here is where the relative parochialism of the Canadian dialogue debate, with its near-exclusive focus on the United States,[85] has distorting effects. By comparing the Charter regime mainly with the United States, section 1 is made to seem like a distinctive source of weakness, of 'dialogue', because, according to the standard picture at least, the United States is one of the very few strong-form regimes outside this contemporary constitutional paradigm – having no express limits on rights and not employing the principle of proportionality. But if we put section 33 aside, as most Canadian dialogue theorists feel constrained to do, given its recent non-use, almost everything they say about the relative weakness of judicial review compared to the US stemming from section 1 would remain true if, instead of Canada, we substituted any strong-form system adhering to the post-war paradigm, including Germany.[86] In other words, the argument really turns not on the exceptionalism of Canada – as a pioneer in experimenting with a new, intermediate model of constitutionalism – but on the conventionally understood exceptionalism of the United States in its rights jurisprudence. For on this account, almost *all* strong-form systems are similarly weaker in this respect than that of the United States.

Now, I happen to reject this conventional wisdom about the United States and believe that, labels and doctrinal terminology apart, it shares the post-war paradigm's general conception of constitutional rights and their limits.[87] Accordingly, I agree with Huscroft, Petter and Dixon that, 'on closer inspection',[88] judicial review in Canada is not generally weaker than the United States simply because of the existence of section 1. US courts have long implied limits on seemingly absolute textual rights and engaged in a similar two-step process of rights adjudication. If it is

---

[85] As has historically been the case. See J. Cameron, 'The Charter's Legislative Override: Feat or Figment of the Constitutional Imagination?' (2004) 23 *Supreme Court Law Review* (second series) 135, 165–7. Occasionally, the debate acknowledges that Canadian judicial review is not as weak as in New Zealand and the UK.

[86] See, for example, Mattias Kumm on the structure of rights in systems where proportionality is the test for justified limits. 'A rights-holder does not have very much in virtue of having a right ... An infringement of the scope of a right merely serves as a trigger to initiate an assessment of whether the infringement is justified'. M. Kumm, 'Political Liberalism and the Structure of Rights: On the Place and the Limits of the Proportionality Requirement' in S. Paulson and G. Pavlakos (eds.), *Law, Rights, Discourse: Themes of the Work of Robert Alexy* (Oxford: Hart Publishing, 2007).

[87] S. Gardbaum, 'The Myth and the Reality of American Constitutional Exceptionalism' (2008) 107 *Michigan Law Review* 391, 416–31.

[88] Dixon, 'The Supreme Court of Canada', p. 239.

weaker than the US, it is only because of the relatively deferential way the SCC conducts section 1 analysis compared to the strict and intermediate scrutiny tests for limiting rights in the US.[89]

The critical comparative issue, however, is not whether – section 33 aside – judicial review in Canada is weaker than in the United States, but whether it is weaker than in other countries with a judicial invalidation power, express limits on rights and the proportionality test. Yet the Canadian dialogue debate never really focuses on this more important comparison. If it isn't weaker, this is unlikely to rebut the critics' claim that Canada has judicial supremacy and strong-form review. If it is, it is likely the result not of section 1 per se, but rather (once again) the SCC's current and controversial practice of relative deference to the government in applying the various prongs of the proportionality test, as compared with such other countries – a judicial practice that a future SCC majority might easily change. In any event, any weakness deriving from the application of section 1 by the SCC is a weakness in the strong-form part of the Charter system, not the new model part. In other words, it is akin to the relative weakness of judicial review in Japan or Scandinavia compared to Germany: a difference within strong-form judicial review, not between strong-form review and something else.

More generally (that is, now putting section 1 aside), legislative sequels are not unique to the Charter, but are fairly common occurrences in strong-form systems. As in Canada, sometimes they reflect legislative attempts to implement a judicial decision, sometimes they reflect outright legislative disagreement with the court, and sometimes something in between. Here, it is instructive to compare both (1) the continuing absence of any duly enacted legislative sequel following the SCC's invalidation of the federal criminal code provisions on abortion in *Morgentaler* and (2) the legislative sequel dutifully implementing the SCC's 'guidelines' in *RJR-Macdonald* with the German Parliament's sequels implementing the Federal Constitutional Court's (FCC) decisions in its well-known 1975 and 1993 abortion decisions. Not only were there enacted legislative sequels in Germany on both occasions, but on the second it took two years of 'very controversial political and social debate'[90] before Parliament was able to agree on amendments to the

---

[89] Although note that where, in the US, the rational basis test applies, judicial review is arguably weaker than under section 1 analysis in Canada.

[90] D. Reitz and G. Richter, 'Currrent Changes in German Abortion Law' (2010) 19 *Cambridge Quarterly of Healthcare Ethics* 334.

1992 statutory provisions invalidated by the FCC. Even then, these amendments arguably departed from the FCC rulings in certain respects and there has been no second-look case.[91] Indeed, more recent legislative amendments, enacted in 2008, appear to depart even further from the FCC's 1993 position.[92] Does this mean that in Germany Parliament has the final word and there is de facto legislative supremacy on this issue? In the United States, there have been several legislative sequels in recent decades that express congressional disagreement with the Supreme Court on the relevant constitutional issues, with varying outcomes. Thus, as mentioned above, Congress enacted numerous statutes containing legislative vetoes after the USSC seemingly held the general practice unconstitutional in *Chadha*, which have not been the subject of a second-look case. Following the invalidation by the USSC of a Texas statute criminalizing flag-burning, Congress enacted a legislative sequel in essentially identical terms, which was subsequently also invalidated in the second-look case.[93] By contrast, the federal partial birth abortion statute enacted after the USSC invalidated a similar state one was upheld in the second-look case.[94]

Of course, in the case of the German and US legislative sequels, the highest court has the legal power of the final word if and when the statute comes before it as a second-look case, and may chose to exercise this power in a way that is relatively deferential to the legislature (as in the partial birth abortion case) or not (as in the flag-burning case). So, too, in Canada, absent the use of section 33. Thus, in *Mills*, the SCC deferred to Parliament's legislative sequel, but in *Sauvé II* it did not.[95] What the new model provides, that strong-form judicial review does not, is a mechanism whereby the legislature can take the final decision away from the courts. By using the distinctive new model power of section 33, Canadian legislatures have the legal power to resolve the issue themselves.

Accordingly, my position on the dialogue debate from the perspective of assessing the Charter as an instance of the new model is the following. First, the main problem with dialogue theory is that (section 33 aside) it does not identify or specify an intermediate form of constitutionalism, but rather demonstrates how judicial supremacy may and does operate in practice

[91] Kommers, *Constitutional Jurisprudence*, pp. 355–6.
[92] Reitz and Richter, 'Current Changes in German Abortion Law', p. 341.
[93] *Texas* v. *Johnson* 491 US 397 (1989); *United States* v. *Eichman* 496 US 310 (1990).
[94] *Stenberg* v. *Carhart* 530 US 914 (2000); *Gonzalez* v. *Carhart* 550 US 124 (2007).
[95] *Sauvé* v. *Canada (Chief Electoral Officer)* [2002] 3 SCR 519.

where rights are legally limitable by the political institutions. This is actually an extremely valuable contribution to general constitutional theory and comparative constitutional law, in part because the normative role of the standard limited override power has been ignored by critics of judicial review – and also by most of its (non-Canadian) supporters.[96] But it is not describing or justifying a form of constitutionalism that is an alternative to judicial supremacy. Under the Charter, only section 33 is the basis for such an alternative – and neither section 1 nor the suspended declaration of invalidity. Neither section 1 nor the suspended declaration of invalidity are unique or distinctive structural features of the Charter as equivalents commonly exist in strong-form systems, and neither gives the power of the final word to the legislature.[97] Indeed, as 'dialogic' features present within many systems of judicial supremacy, they illustrate that on Kent Roach's definition of 'dialogic judicial review' as 'any constitutional design that allows rights, as contained in a bill of rights and as interpreted by the courts, to be limited or overridden by the ordinary legislation of a democratically elected legislature',[98] there really is almost no *non*-dialogic judicial review anywhere. The danger of this over-inclusive term lies in blurring what I hope to have shown is a valuable and instructive distinction: between the new Commonwealth model and judicial supremacy. Similarly with the attempt of 'new dialogue theory' to weaken judicial review in Canada compared to the United States by establishing a norm of judicial deference under section 1 to reasonable legislative sequels in second-look cases. Judicial self-restraint and deference to legislative decisions is a different source or type of weakness (a weaker form of weakness, if you will) than the distinctive new model mechanism of giving legislatures the power of the final word, and is comfortably accommodated within systems of judicial supremacy – from the Thayerian strand in the US, to the text of the Swedish constitution.[99]

---

[96] Kumm, 'Political Liberalism and the Structure of Rights: On the Place and the Limits of the Proportionality Requirement', is one exception.

[97] The South African constitution expressly grants the power of suspended invalidity to the courts, in section 172(b)(ii), and the German Constitutional Court has developed a range of equivalent techniques, including finding statutes unconstitutional but not void (*unvereinbar* versus *nichtig*) – meaning they are in force during a transition period pending correction by the legislature – and upholding statutes but warning they will be invalidated in future if not amended or repealed.

[98] Roach, 'Dialogic Judicial Review', p. 55.

[99] Courts may only exercise the power of judicial review if the inconsistency is 'manifest'. Swedish Constitution, chapter 11, section 14.

Secondly, I believe that section 33 is not only one of the two distinctive new model features of the Charter, but remains an important one, so that claims of its unusability or irrelevance are somewhat overstated. Whilst obviously its current non-use is a practical problem for the working of the model, section 33 is not yet the equivalent of the Royal Assent: a purely and exclusively formal power. Even now, as a legally authorized outlet for popular and/or legislative disagreement with the courts, it arguably renders exercises of judicial review a little less prone to some of the normative concerns discussed in Chapter 3. Moreover, if in the future, judicial decisions raise the amount or degree of controversy that they have in numerous strong-form jurisdictions, section 33 is likely to be revived. Here, I agree with Peter Hogg's assessment in his 2007 response to his critics:

> There is no reason to suppose that the current political reluctance to use section 33 is a permanent feature of the Canadian legal system, which will prevail no matter what the Court does, or how public opinion changes, or which political parties come into power ... Make no mistake about it: if conflict between the judicial and legislative branches in Canada ever approached the intensity and duration of the conflict that occurred in the United States during the Lochner era or ... the Warren Court ..., the current reluctance by Canadian politicians to use the override would disappear.[100]

Indeed, the Alberta government seriously considered using the override in response to the SCC's decision in *Vriend*,[101] which read into its provincial human rights statute sexual orientation as a prohibited basis of discrimination when the legislature had expressly decided to omit it, but ultimately did not. Alberta *did*, however, subsequently use the override pre-emptively in enacting its 2000 statute banning same-sex marriage: the Marriage Amendment Act.[102]

IV   Overall assessment of the Charter as an institutionalization of the new model

The strengths of the Charter as the second instantiation of the new model are best appreciated by comparing it with the first one, the

---

[100] P. W. Hogg, A. A. B. Thornton and W. K. Wright, 'A Reply on "*Charter* Dialogue Revisited"' (2007) 45 *Osgoode Hall Law Journal* 193, 201.

[101] *Vriend* v. *Alberta* [1998] 1 SCR 493.

[102] The Act itself was of questionable constitutionality on federalism grounds as Parliament has the exclusive jurisdiction to legislate in relation to marriage under section 91 of the Constitution Act 1867. Alberta's use of the override was not renewed when it lapsed after five years.

ill-fated CBOR. If the very general criteria of success are effective protection of rights and a greater balance of power between courts and
legislatures than under either judicial or legislative supremacy, then the
Charter is operating fairly successfully in terms of the first. Pre-enactment rights review by the executive in particular appears to be quite
systematic and the courts have generally taken their rights-interpreting
and enforcing functions seriously at the judicial review stage. Here, the
comparison with the CBOR in terms of interpretive methodology and
frequency of exercise of the invalidation power is very clear and marked.
There is no real argument that granting the legal power of the final word
to the legislature in section 33 has resulted in the under-enforcement of
rights, or that the Charter is unstable in the direction of reverting to
traditional parliamentary sovereignty.

On the general attitude of the courts towards prior legislative deliberation about rights and their limits, where it has occurred, the record is
more mixed and complicated by the fact that the SCC is split on whether
'dialogue' requires deference to legislative decisions in second-look
cases. Thus, it exhibited an appropriately respectful attitude in *Mills*:

> Courts do not hold a monopoly on the protection and promotion of
> rights and freedoms; Parliament also plays a role in this regard and is
> often able to act as a significant ally for vulnerable groups . . . If constitu-
> tional democracy is meant to ensure that due regard is given to the voices
> of those vulnerable to being overlooked by the majority, then this court
> has an obligation to consider respectfully Parliament's attempt to
> respond to such voices.[103]

On the other hand, even where upholding a legislative sequel in the
second-look case of *JTI-Macdonald*, the SCC was arguably somewhat
patronizing towards legislative deliberation,[104] and the majority in *Sauvé
II*, which invalidated Parliament's sequel, was downright hostile to it.[105]

From the new model perspective, the Charter's main weaknesses have
been in both stages of political rights review – pre-enactment and post-
enactment – leading to the concern that the increases in judicial power
and the scope of legal constitutionalism have not in practice been balanced by the new model's mechanisms for legislative input on rights and
political constitutionalism. At the pre-enactment stage, too much of the

---

[103] *Mills* at [58].   [104] As Huscroft claims in 'Rationalizing Judicial Power', p. 78.
[105] Chief Justice McLachlin described the debate in Parliament as offering 'more fulmina-
tion than illumination'. *Sauvé* v. *Canada (Chief Electoral Officer)* [2002] 3 SCR 519 at
[21].

review has been undertaken by the executive and not the legislature, in correspondingly opaque and secretive rather than transparent and public discussions, and in the form of narrowly legal rather than broader political and moral deliberation. The exceptions have mostly been just a handful of legislative sequels to judicial invalidations, in which the government has deliberately encouraged and choreographed parliamentary participation in the belief that permitting disagreement with the courts to be aired and debated in the legislative forum would be strategically helpful in the eventual second-look case.[106] This type of legislative deliberation (minus the government choreography) should, but does not, routinely occur during passage of original bills, where disagreement is more likely to be with the executive rather than the courts. To this end, the rationale for the Attorney General's decision not to report, including all supporting documents produced during executive rights vetting, should routinely be made available to Parliament, and its committee system should be strengthened by increasing specialization, resources and independence from partisan politics.

Similarly, post-enactment, obviously section 33 has not been a sufficiently active mechanism of political rights review. It has been too rarely used or contemplated – especially in a reactive way – so that the judicial function is almost always to make the final decision rather than to alert and trigger legislative deliberation. As the sole and distinctive source of new model-style judicial review under the Charter, potential employment of section 33 and (even more importantly) the deliberation that precedes it must be encouraged and normalized by developing the norm of legitimate use discussed in Chapter 4. The new model does not depend on courts exercising their power of the final word to defer to reasonable legislative disagreements, but on legislatures exercising theirs. Accordingly, where after serious deliberation on the merits, Parliament or a provincial legislature reasonably disagrees either that legal reasoning suffices to resolve a rights issue or with a court's legal reasoning on that issue, it should be understood that the Charter authorizes employment of section 33. Once again, it is the deliberation itself that is the most important product of the Charter engineering and if, as influenced and informed by broader public opinion, it results in a conclusion that the judicial decision should stand, the values underlying that engineering are well served. The legislature will have had the final word, just as a court does when it decides to defer to a legislature. But, of course, the

---

[106] Hiebert, *Charter Conflicts*, pp. 96–113.

seriousness of that deliberation turns on the possibility of its direct legal and practical effect.[107] Accordingly, as Hiebert and Waldron among others have argued, steps might usefully be taken to try to ease its use.[108] If not already too late, these should attempt to reframe popular conceptions of section 33 from overriding or disregarding the rights themselves to legitimating reasonable legislative disagreement on the resolution of rights issues. If a formal change of wording is required, then either Manfredi's suggestion[109] or something along the lines of the VCHRR version of section 33 might be helpful.[110] The focused public discussion on the nature of the Charter regime that such an amendment process would presumably trigger might well be a salutary exercise in itself.

Non-use of section 33 is one problem, but another has been the added disincentive to use it resulting from the practice of legislative sequels attempting to overrule a court decision without recourse to section 33. We have noted above that the desired type of legislative rights review and deliberation have occasionally taken place in the context of enacting legislative sequels – and just suggested that this is a form of pre-enactment review that should occur during the passage of original bills and not only certain sequels. But they were also responses to judicial decisions with which Parliament disagreed. It is, of course, a central component of the new model and its intermediate character that legislatures are empowered to disagree with judicial decisions about rights and ultimately resolve the issue themselves, and under the Charter version the authorized and distinctive mechanism for such disagreements and resolutions is section 33. It is distinctive in two ways. First, section 33 expresses the *empowerment* of the legislature; it has the discretionary

---

[107] See Kahana, 'Understanding the Notwithstanding Mechanism', p. 250.

[108] See J. Hiebert, 'Is it Too Late to Rehabilitate Canada's Notwithstanding Clause?', (2004) 23 *Supreme Court Law Review* (second series) 169; Waldron, 'Some Models of Dialogue'; J. Goldsworthy, 'Judicial Review, Legislative Override, and Democracy' (2003) 38 *Wake Forest Law Review* 451.

[109] 'Parliament . . . may expressly declare . . . that the Act . . . shall operate notwithstanding *a final judicial decision that the legislation or a provision thereof abrogates or unreasonably limits* a provision included in section 2 or sections 7 to 15 of this Charter'. Manfredi, *Judicial Power and the Charter*, p. 193. The italicised words constitute the proposed amendment of section 33, which 'emphasizes the fact that, by invoking the notwithstanding clause, legislatures would not be overriding Charter rights *per se*, but judicial interpretations of those rights'. It also prevents pre-emptive use of the override. *Ibid.*

[110] VCHRR, section 36.

legal power and right to insist on its position, whereas absent the use of section 33 the SCC has the final word on whether it chooses to defer: yes in *Mills*, no in *Sauvé*.[111] Legislative sequels can and do express disagreement with courts wherever there is constitutional review, what the new model provides is the legal mechanism for the legislature to resolve the disagreement itself. It is one thing for a legislature to ask a court to reconsider its previous decision, to test the court's commitment to it – and this is the only option within judicial supremacy – but another for the legislature to have the power to override that decision. Once again, the new model relies on legislative power, not on judicial self-restraint and deference.

But, secondly, section 33 gives greater transparency, visibility and legitimacy to legislative disagreements than occurs without such a mechanism. Contrary to the main thrust of dialogue theory, such disagreements may not be about section 1/reasonable limits at all, but about the SCC's interpretation of the Charter and the resolution of conflicting rights, so that forcing them into this box as the only legal one available to justify a sequel will be disingenuous. This was in fact the case in the two major examples thus far under the Charter. In *Daviault*, there was barely a reference to section 1 in either the majority or dissenting opinions and the preamble to the legislative sequel reinstating the rule declared unconstitutional by the SCC expressed clear disagreement with what it viewed as the SCC's undervaluing of the section 15 right to equality.[112] In the second-look decision in *Mills* upholding the legislative sequel to *O'Connor*, there was no discussion of section 1 at all and, again, Parliament's disagreement with the court was plainly based on gender equality concerns under section 15 of the Charter.[113] Nonetheless, 'the preamble [to the statute at issue in *Mills*] had obviously been inserted with a view to supporting a section 1 justification in the event of a constitutional challenge'.[114] Moreover, absent use of section 33, both

---

[111] Of course, *Sauvé* involved section 3 of the Charter, which is expressly outside the scope of the section 33 override power; but the point here is to illustrate that without use of section 33, the key issue is whether the SCC chooses to defer or not.

[112] See preamble to Bill C-72, an Act to Amend the Criminal Code (Self-Induced Intoxication): 'Whereas the Parliament of Canada recognizes that violence has a particularly disadvantaging impact on the equal participation of women and children in society and on the rights of women and children to security of the person and to the equal protection and benefit of the law as guaranteed by sections 7, 15 and 28 of the [Charter]'.

[113] The identical paragraph as in *ibid.*, was inserted into the preamble.

[114] Hogg, Thornton and Wright, 'Charter Dialogue Revisited', p. 21.

legislatures and courts are forced into questionably legitimate conduct in terms of general rule of law values when they enact or uphold sequels that express disagreement with, rather than merely implement, the original judicial decision. Legislatures are relying either on there being no second-look case, as so far with the sequel to *Daviault*,[115] or on the SCC effectively overruling itself and permitting what is, until that point, an unconstitutional act to stand. Courts must state that the law is X in Case 1, but not-X in Case 2, and yet they are not really acknowledging that they made a mistake the first time, as is typical with judicial over-rulings of prior decisions, but rather that reasonable legislative disagreement is sufficient to uphold the law the second time. But if the second, why not the first? Alternatively, courts may engage in disingenuous attempts to distinguish the two cases, as arguably in the second US partial abortion case of *Gonzales* v. *Carhart*.[116] By contrast, within the Charter framework, section 33 provides a legitimate, authorized and transparent mechanism for legislative disagreement and a cleaner and clearer division of authority between courts and legislatures that does not pose awkward problems of this sort.

Accordingly, the better and more transparent practice is that where a legislature disagrees with a judicial decision (1) about the interpretation of rights or the resolution of a conflict of rights, as with *Daviault* and *O'Connor*, or (2) about the reasonableness of its limits on a right under section 1, if it wishes to enact a sequel incorporating the disagreement then it should use section 33 – thereby eliminating the possibility of a second-look case, at least until it expires.[117] By contrast, where a legislative sequel essentially implements, or at least is not intended to be inconsistent with, the court's decision invaliding the original law under section 1, as in *JIT-Macdonald*, then section 33 need not be used

---

[115] At least at the SCC level, see n. 47 above.   [116] 550 US 124 (2007).

[117] Here I agree with Kent Roach (and others) and disagree with Tsvi Kahana, who argues that Parliament was right not to use section 33 in reinstating by statute the common law rule held to be unconstitutional in *Daviault*. Kahana's argument seems to turn on (1) the claim that use of section 33 should be a last resort, where Parliament has no other legal option, and so limited to re-enacting invalidated statutes, whereas the law at issue in *Daviault* was a common law rule which Parliament did not need section 33 to reinstate, and (2) an underlying concern to reduce the number of uses of section 33 to a minimum. At this point, I think the latter concern is unwarranted. K. Roach, 'Editorial: When Should the Section 33 Override be Used?' (1999) 42 *Canada Law Quarterly* 1, 2; K. Roach, 'Constitutional and Common Law Dialogues between the Supreme Court and Canadian Legislatures' (2001) 80 *Canadian Bar Review* 481, 525; Kahana, 'Understanding the Notwithstanding Mechanism', pp. 270–2.

and the possibility of a second-look case remains. That is, there should be a clearer understanding that *Mills*-type sequels are different from *RJR*-type ones and one of the points of section 33 is to clarify and institutionalize this difference, to ensure that greater public visibility and awareness surround attempted legislative overrulings.

And here, arguably, is where the courts are to blame, for it is their willingness to consider legislative disagreements without use of section 33 (perhaps for their own institutional reasons) combined with the strong desire of legislators to avoid it if possible that has led to its further marginalization. Under current circumstances at least, if legislatures need not use section 33 in order to challenge the SCC, they surely will not. Why use section 33 and incur the associated political costs if the same goal can be achieved without, as in *Mills*? And then we are back into the conventional, strong-form terrain of judicial deference and self-restraint rather than the new model's focus on legislative power. To counter this, courts should presume that section 33 is the proper mechanism for reasonable legislative disagreement and that sequels enacted without using it are intended to correct the constitutional invalidity found in the first case, as in *RJR*, or at most to ask that the court reconsider its decision, and they should give no additional deference to the legislature in the second-look case but once again give its best view of the merits. Of course, like any highest court, the SCC may change its mind but not because some new, higher degree of deference is due. Had the SCC not deferred in *Mills*, Parliament might have ended up using section 33.[118] Here, too, dialogue theory and the SCC's references to it have also perhaps helped to blur the distinction between sequels expressing legislative disagreement with a judicial decision and ones designed to implement a judicial decision, thereby handing legislatures an additional excuse for avoiding section 33.

In sum, the Charter institutionalizes the new model through the pre-enactment reporting duty and section 33, and not section 1 or the suspended declaration of invalidity. However, neither is operating satisfactorily or distinctly. Section 33, which is unique to the Canadian version of the new model and always places the burden of inertia on the legislature in order to exercise its power of the final word, is suffering from a serious practical problem due to its near non-use. The problem is

---

[118] It could not use section 33 following the decision in *Sauvé II*, because, as noted in n. 95, the case involved section 3 of the Charter, which is expressly exempted from the section 33 power.

less that the override power is rarely exercised per se than that this practice seems largely to exclude the sort of political deliberation about rights called for by the ideal working of the new model. The same exclusion also occurs at the pre-enactment stage, where executive (rather than legislative) and legal (rather than political) review tend to predominate. Overall, as its formal features might have predicted, the Charter system is currently operating in a way that is too close to judicial supremacy for it to be the most distinct or successful version of the new model. From the perspective of seeing the Charter operate in a genuinely intermediate manner, there needs to be a shift in power towards the legislature and the political – a greater blending of political with legal constitutionalism.

6

New Zealand

Although Canada was the pioneer in institutionalizing the new model as a whole, it is the New Zealand version of it – the New Zealand Bill of Rights Act 1990 – that has proven to be the most influential in terms of direct borrowing. For all three subsequent versions – in the UK, the ACT and Victoria – have self-consciously adopted (and adapted) its basic form and strategy, rather than that of the Canadian Charter. At the federal level in Australia, too, the recent debate over whether or not to create a national bill of rights was conducted in terms of the choice between enacting a New Zealand-style measure and adhering to the status quo. The Canadian Charter was not a viable candidate.

I Central features of the NZBORA

In terms of structure and status, there are two key differences between the NZBORA and the Charter. First, the NZBORA is a statutory rather than a constitutional bill of rights. It was very deliberately enacted as an ordinary statute through the ordinary legislative process after the original 1985 White Paper proposal for a constitutional bill of rights along the lines of the Charter met with overwhelming opposition. As such, it is not superior to other legislation and, as a formal matter, can be amended or repealed by this same ordinary process. Secondly, although the NZBORA applies to acts of the legislature,[1] section 4 expressly states that courts have no power to invalidate, disapply or treat as ineffective legislation that is inconsistent with the NZBORA.[2] Although this second difference might be thought to follow from the first – if a bill of

---

[1] NZBORA, section 3(a).

[2] NZBORA, section 4: 'Other enactments not affected – No court shall, in relation to any enactment (whether passed or made before of after the commencement of this Bill of Rights) –

(a) Hold any provision of the enactment to be impliedly repealed or revoked, or to be in any way invalid or ineffective; or

rights is not higher law so as to render subsequent inconsistent statutes (in the words of the Charter) 'of no force or effect', then surely courts do not have the power to invalidate or disapply such statutes[3] – pre-existing jurisprudence in both Canada and the UK strongly suggested that even a statutory rights regime can be given limited priority over subsequent inconsistent statutes under a form of 'clear statement rule', contrary to the normal doctrine that the later in time prevails.[4] Accordingly, with these examples in mind, section 4 expressly ousted this possibility and mandated the rule that courts are to resolve inconsistencies between a protected right and a subsequent statute by applying the inconsistent statute. Indeed, by also including prior inconsistent legislation within its ambit, section 4 gives *less* than ordinary statutory protection to the rights it contains because it also ousts the normal rule that earlier statutes are impliedly repealed by a later inconsistent one (i.e., the NZBORA). In other words, not only is the NZBORA not superior to other statutes, but it is subordinate to any other inconsistent statute regardless of when enacted. As Paul Rishworth notes, in prescribing 'anti-primacy', the drafters of section 4 'plainly pulled out all the stops to preclude every judicial technique that might elevate the Bill of Rights over other enactments'.[5] By contrast, the judicial technique of rights protection that the NZBORA does rely on in the legislative context is statutory interpretation, directing the courts in section 6 to interpret statutes consistently with rights whenever such a meaning 'can

---

(b) Decline to apply any provision of the enactment – By reason only that the provision is inconsistent with any provision of this Bill of Rights.'

[3] This is, of course, the inverse of Chief Justice Marshall's argument for judicial review in *Marbury* v. *Madison*.

[4] This jurisprudence was *R.* v. *Drybones* (holding that the SCC was empowered to 'not apply' a statute that was inconsistent with the CBOR where Parliament had not expressly declared that it was to apply under section 2); *Winnipeg School Division No. 1* v. *Craton* [1985] 2 SCR 150 (holding that a subsequent statutory rule in conflict with the Manitoba Human Rights Code was correctly 'not applied', even absent a 'notwithstanding formula', which is to be deemed implicit in the Code). In the UK, the courts had strongly suggested in dicta that the effect of the European Communities Act 1972 was to import the supremacy of EU law over subsequent conflicting UK statutes, unless Parliament expressly states to the contrary. This was affirmed in *R.* v. *Secretary of State Ex p. Factortame Ltd* [1990] 2 AC 85, in which the House of Lords denied effect to the Merchant Shipping Act 1988. For an excellent discussion of this jurisprudence, see Rishworth, 'The Inevitability of Judicial Review under "Interpretive" Bills of Rights: Canada's Legacy to New Zealand and Commonwealth Constitutionalism?', pp. 239–58.

[5] Rishworth, *ibid.*, pp. 258–9.

be given'.[6] Where it cannot, however, courts are required to apply the statute under section 4. In this context, the NZBORA is an interpretative rather than an overriding bill of rights.[7] It creates a statutory duty (augmenting the common law presumption) of rights-consistent judicial interpretation of statutes where possible, but also of judicial application of inconsistent statutes where not.

Section 5 contains a general limitations clause, the wording of which is directly borrowed from section 1 of the Charter: 'Subject to section 4 of this Bill of Rights, the rights and freedoms contained in this Bill of Rights may be subject only to such reasonable limits prescribed by law as can be demonstrably justified in a free and democratic society.' 'Subject to section 4' means that, unlike the Charter, unreasonable limits on rights may still be applied by the courts.[8] Finally, among the general provisions at the beginning of the NZBORA, section 7 establishes the second, non-judicial technique of rights protection, the political mechanism of pre-enactment rights review by requiring the Attorney-General to issue a report on a bill's introduction where it 'appears to be inconsistent' with any of the protected rights.

The content of the protected rights, which begin in section 8, is described by the general heading as 'civil and political rights', but they are not identical to the rights in the ICCPR which the NZBORA aims to 'affirm'.[9] They are subdivided into the following: 'life and security of the person' (sections 8–11); 'democratic and civil rights' (sections 12–18), including electoral rights and the freedoms of thought, conscience, religion, expression, peaceful assembly and association; 'non-discrimination and minority rights' (sections 19–20); and 'search, arrest and detention' (sections 21–7). The list of rights is comparatively both narrow and specific: there is no general right to liberty or security of the person, as under section 7 of the Charter or the ICCPR, but only the right not to be arbitrarily arrested or detained; no general right to privacy (unlike the ICCPR) and no right to property or any socio-economic rights. Apart from several of the criminal procedure rights, they are mostly succinctly stated. Most of the rights that

---

[6] 'Interpretation consistent with Bill of Rights to be preferred – wherever an enactment can be given a meaning that is consistent with the rights and freedoms contained in this Bill of Rights, that meaning shall be preferred to any other meaning'.

[7] In the context of executive action, by contrast, the NZBORA is an overriding bill of rights.

[8] 'May', not must, because, according to the now-governing approach, it will only be applied if no alternative, rights-consistent meaning can be given to the statutory provision under section 6. See section II below.

[9] 'An Act – . . . (b) To affirm New Zealand's commitment to the International Covenant on Civil and Political Rights' NZBORA, preamble.

are present correspond to rights in the ICCPR, to which affirmation of New Zealand's commitment is stated to be one of the two purposes of the NZBORA, but they are far from identical to these international rights. Broadly speaking, the rights in the NZBORA are mostly far briefer versions of ICCPR rights and lack the special, customized limitations placed on the latter in favour of the general limitations clause in section 5.

In sum, the rights contained in the NZBORA are protected through (1) a non-judicially enforceable legal obligation on Parliament to act consistently with them, (2) the political mechanism of mandatory rights review within the legislative process itself, (3) the judicial mechanism of rights-consistent statutory interpretation where possible, and (4) the judicial power to quash and remedy rights infringing executive action. The NZBORA also establishes a form of constitutional review, in that courts are empowered to determine the consistency of a statute with the protected rights under sections 5 and 6 (does it impose a reasonable limit on a right, can it be interpreted consistently with the right?),[10] although they are required to apply an inconsistent one. Moreover, if the legislature overrules a judicial interpretation of consistency made under section 6, the courts must also apply the new statute under section 4. In short, the NZBORA is the prototype of an interpretative rather than an overriding or supreme bill of rights.

II   The NZBORA in operation

The general function of pre-enactment political rights review under the new model is to build into the legislative process itself a counter against any tendency towards under-enforcement of rights in legislative outputs. Stemming from section 7, this stage under the NZBORA can be chronologically subdivided into (1) executive review prior to a bill's introduction in Parliament, (2) Attorney-General reporting under section 7 on introduction, and (3) parliamentary scrutiny after the bill's introduction and during the remainder of the legislative process.

Starting with executive review, or what is generally referred to as 'rights-vetting' in New Zealand, the specialist Human Rights Unit in the Ministry of Justice evaluates all draft bills for consistency with the NZBORA, except those bills it is sponsoring. These are vetted by the separate Crown Law Office (headed by the Attorney-General), thereby ensuring external assessment in all cases. The Attorney-General is advised if an inconsistency is

---

[10] A minority view, which includes Chief Justice Elias among its proponents, holds that the courts do not have a mandate to employ section 5. See text accompanying nn. 34–6 below.

identified. In addition, the sponsoring departmental legal advisor provides an evaluation to aid his or her minister, who is required by Cabinet guidelines to submit a statement identifying any inconsistencies with the NZBORA and the steps taken to address them or available justifications in papers accompanying a draft bill.[11] The Cabinet Manual also endorses the guidelines developed by the Legislation Advisory Committee for the drafting of bills to be submitted to the Cabinet, which emphasize the approach to reasonable limits on rights in *R v. Oakes*.[12] The concern about possible inconsistent legal advice from the various sources has been addressed by the publication of still another set of guidelines for the development of legislation consistent with NZBORA[13] and the practice of contact and cooperation between departmental and Ministry of Justice lawyers. As Grant Huscroft characterizes this stage:

> Governments are risk averse, and as a result have considerable incentive to formulate policy in such a manner as to avoid a report from the Attorney-General. Herein lies the main significance of the reporting duty: it has formalized the place of the Bill of Rights in the policy development process, at least where the government's legislative agenda is concerned ... Thus, Bill of Rights concerns are likely to be identified and addressed long before a bill reaches Parliament.[14]

How many draft bills are eliminated before introduction as a result of this process is unknown due to its confidentiality, but presumably some, with others being amended or reworded.

If bureaucratic review procedures, criteria for assessing the reasonableness of limits and reporting duties are all broadly similar under the NZBORA to those in Canada, despite the different legal statuses of their bills of rights, the practices of respective Attorneys General in issuing reports to Parliament could not be more different. Whereas in Canada, it will be recalled, the Attorney General/Minister of Justice has never issued a report of inconsistency between a bill and the Charter, the New Zealand Attorney-General has tabled fifty-nine such reports since

---

[11] See www.cabguide.cabinetoffice.govt.nz/procedures/legislation-and-regulations/check ing-human-rights-issues.

[12] Cabinet Office, *Cabinet Manual 2008* (Wellington: Cabinet Office, 2008), p. 93 [7.60].

[13] *The Guidelines on the New Zealand Bill of Rights Act: A Guide to the Rights and Freedoms in the Bill of Rights Act for the Public Sector* (Wellington: Ministry of Justice, 2004).

[14] G. Huscroft, 'The Attorney-General's Reporting Duty' in P. Rishworth, G. Huscroft, S. Optician and R. Mahoney (eds.), *The New Zealand Bill of Rights Act* (Melbourne: Oxford University Press, 2003) 196.

1990.[15] Twenty-eight of these have related to government bills and thirty-one to non-government ones. This radical difference in reporting practices has been explained by differing political cultures about the appropriateness of pursuing bills requiring a report, different legal consequences of a report given the judicial invalidation power in Canada and its absence in New Zealand, the resulting greater influence of Canadian Ministers of Justice within Cabinet discussions of legislative priorities, and a greater reliance on lawyers' opinions about consistency and less on independent political judgment in New Zealand than in Canada.[16] It has also been attributed to New Zealand Attorneys-General choosing to err on the side of reporting in close cases.[17] For those who believe there have been too many reports,[18] the main consequence is to dilute their seriousness.[19] In practice, the reports reproduce the advice furnished to the Attorney-General by the Ministry of Justice or Crown Office lawyers. Although Attorneys-General only report when they conclude that a bill is inconsistent with the NZBORA, the government has since 2003 chosen to make available the advice provided to the Attorney-General on all bills.

The major function of the reporting duty is to alert and inform Parliament about rights issues for discussion and scrutiny in the remainder of the legislative process. A section 7 report itself has no formal implications for the proposed legislation's status. No special process ensues and Parliament is free to attach what importance it chooses to the report. Of the first twenty-two government bills to receive section 7 reports, nineteen became law without any amendments to change the apparent NZBORA inconsistency.[20] Thus, with regard to such bills, Parliament as a whole has either disagreed with or simply ignored the Attorney-General's advice and legislated despite a section 7 report for 90 per cent of the time. Given that reports consist mainly

[15] As of September 2012; www.justice.govt.nz/policy/constitutional-law-and-human-rights/human-rights/domestic-human-rights-protection/about-the-new-zealand-bill-of-rights-act/advising-the-attorney-general/section-7-reports-published-before-august-2002/section-7-reports-published-before-august-2002.

[16] J. Hiebert, 'Rights-Vetting in New Zealand and Canada: Similar Idea, Different Outcomes' (2005) 3 *New Zealand Journal of Public and International Law* 63, 90–3.

[17] Huscroft, 'Reconciling Duty and Discretion', p. 14.

[18] Which is by no means the universal view. Indeed, some believe that, to the contrary, New Zealand Attorneys General have been guilty of under-reporting. See Archer, 'Section 7 of the Bill of Rights Act', p. 323.

[19] Huscroft, 'The Attorney-General's Reporting Duty', p. 215.

[20] A. Geddis, 'The Comparative Irrelevance of the NZBORA to Legislative Practice' (2009) 23 *New Zealand Universities Law Review* 465, 477.

of legal advice based on what courts have said in previous cases, this figure suggests that a majority of legislators (like government ministers) are willing to depart from judicial decisions on rights.[21] By contrast, non-government bills with section 7 reports attached have not fared so well.[22] In New Zealand, unlike either Canada or the UK, there is no separate standing committee to consider section 7 reports or the rights implications of proposed legislation generally; rather this falls within the purview of the ordinary, subject-matter select committee. Although neither specialised nor expert, select committees receive public submissions from interested groups, including submissions on NZBORA concerns, and occasionally recommend amendments based on these submissions – sometimes even where there was no section 7 report. Tessa Bromwich concludes her study of parliamentary rights-vetting as follows: 'On occasion, parliament has lived up to [the ideal of squarely confronting the rights implications of proposed legislation], but too often it has ignored the rights implications raised by the Attorney-General'.[23] This record also perhaps supports the claim that the consequence of the frequency of reports is the diminished seriousness with which they are taken.

Turning to judicial rights review, despite its ordinary statute status and the requirements of section 4, the courts have played a significant role in ensuring that the NZBORA has emerged from its inauspicious, almost stillborn, birth to be viewed nearly universally as part of the country's constitutional canon. Within the existing constitutional arrangements in New Zealand – the near unique lack of a formal, entrenched codified constitution – this is the highest status available and is shared with a handful of other 'constitutional statutes' together with certain conventions, common law principles and the Treaty of Waitangi. From soon after its enactment, the Court of Appeal, then the highest domestic court,[24] regularly and consistently attributed constitutional

---

[21] This suggestion is not inconsistent with the fact that individual MPs have on occasion strenuously raised rights concerns where there are section 7 reports. See Butler, 'It Takes Two to Tango – Have They Learned their Steps', available at ssrn.com/abstract=2022681. Also, many of the court decisions used in the reports are foreign ones, particularly Canadian, given the relative paucity of domestic case law in some areas. Finally, it is of course possible that at least some legislators disagree with the analysis of previous court decisions contained in the section 7 report, and not with the decisions themselves.

[22] Geddis reports that twenty-one of the first twenty-six non-government bills with section 7 reports were either defeated in the House of Representatives or passed after amendment. See 'The Comparative Irrelevance of the NZBORA'.

[23] T. Bromwich, 'Parliamentary Rights-Vetting Under the NZBORA' (2009) *New Zealand Law Journal* 189, 192.

[24] Under the Supreme Court Act 2003, the Supreme Court of New Zealand was created as the highest court and court of last resort in New Zealand, replacing the right of appeal from the Court of Appeal to the Judicial Committee of the Privy Council in London. The

significance to the NZBORA based on its subject-matter, both in affirming a 'generous', 'constitutional' mode of rights interpretation[25] and in vigorously applying these rights against the police, in particular, in the criminal procedure context.[26] These early cases culminated in the establishment of both a prima facie exclusionary rule for evidence obtained in violation of the NZBORA and an implied public law remedy of damages where the exclusionary rule could not redress a violation.[27]

One thorny structural issue under the NZBORA has been the tension between, and the proper respective weight to attach to, sections 4 and 6. To the extent that courts apply the interpretative duty in section 6 robustly, in a way that modifies or distorts statutory language and/or parliamentary intent, this appears to violate section 4's prohibition on courts declining to apply the legislature's inconsistent statutes. The enacted line between judicial interpretation or construction and judicial law-making is a fine one in practice. This issue inheres in all interpretative bills of rights, at least those without greater specification of the duty, and has been a major source of contention both in New Zealand and, even more, in the UK. It is also the source of the claim that – through radical use of the interpretative power to rewrite legislation – statutory bills of rights can, and indeed have, come to resemble fully constitutional ones in practice, leading to de facto judicial supremacy.[28]

Overall, the New Zealand courts are widely thought to have taken a reasonably moderate and restrained position on this issue, particularly by comparison with courts in the UK under a similar interpretive duty.[29] Within this overall picture, however, there have been clear differences among judges as to the appropriate strength of the duty to interpret statutes

---

Supreme Court has five judges and began work in June 2004. The Court of Appeal remains as the intermediate appellate court.

[25] *Ministry of Transport* v. *Noort* [1992] 3 NZLR 260 at 268–9 (Cooke P.), 277 (Richardson J., McKay J., concurring), 286 (Hardie Boys J.).

[26] For a list of these cases, see P. Rishworth, 'The New Zealand Bill of Rights' in P. Rishworth, G. Huscroft, S. Optician and R. Mahoney (eds.), *The New Zealand Bill of Rights Act* (Melbourne: Oxford University Press, 2003), pp. 10–11.

[27] *R.* v. *Kirifi* [1992] 2 NZLR 8 (CA) (exclusionary rule); *Simpson* v. *Attorney-General* [1994] 3 NZLR 667 (CA) (*'Baigent's Case'*). The prima facie exclusionary rule was subsequently abolished by the Court of Appeal in 2001. *R.* v. *Shaheed* [2002] 2 NZLR 377.

[28] This claim has been made both by those who approve and disapprove of the convergence in practice. For the former (in the UK context), see Kavanagh, *Constitutional Review*, pp. 416–19; for the latter, see J. Allan, 'Portia, Bassano or Dick the Butcher? Constraining Judges in the Twenty-first Century' (2006) 17 *King's College Law Journal* 1, 9.

[29] See, for example, A. Geddis and B. Fenton, '"Which is to be Master?" – Rights-Friendly Statutory Interpretation in New Zealand and the United Kingdom' (2008) 25 *Arizona Journal of International & Comparative Law* 733.

in a rights-friendly way, differences over when such an interpretation 'can be given', resulting in at least two strands of cases and dicta. Among the leading examples of interpretative restraint is the unanimous decision of the Court of Appeal in the 1998 case of *Quilter*[30] declining to interpret the gender-neutral language of the 1955 Marriage Act as embracing same-sex marriage, despite not only section 6 but also section 19 of the NZBORA, as amended by the 1993 Human Rights Act to prohibit discrimination on grounds of sexual orientation. Such an interpretation, said the court, would be to act contrary to Parliament's intent and to assume the role of lawmaker.[31] Similarly, soon after the NZBORA went into effect, the Court of Appeal came to the opposite conclusion from the UK's House of Lords in interpreting essentially identical statutory language imposing a reverse onus of proof on criminal defendants found in possession of a controlled drug, with the House of Lords giving the more rights-consistent but arguably strained meaning, and the New Zealand Court of Appeal refusing to do so.[32]

On the other hand, although no New Zealand case has gone quite so far as the most 'adventurous'[33] of the UK ones in interpreting statutory provisions in ways that Parliament seemingly did not intend, some New Zealand judges have espoused more expansive statements of the judicial power to give merely possible, rather than plausibly intended, meanings to statutes, and there are dicta to this effect in majority opinions in a few cases.[34] Thus, in *Poumako*, although the case was decided on other grounds, the majority opinion stated: 'It is not a matter of what the legislature . . . might have intended. The direction [in section 6] is that wherever a meaning consistent with the Bill of Rights can be given, it is to be preferred.'[35] And in *Pora*, three members of the Court of Appeal were prepared to employ section 6 to interpret the language in an earlier statute that its rule against retrospective punishments applied 'notwithstanding any other enactment or rule to the contrary' as controlling a subsequent statute imposing retrospective punishment, absent a clear statement in the latter of intent to restrict a fundamental right, thus rejecting the orthodox view that the latter impliedly repeals the former.

---

30 *Quilter* v. *Attorney-General* [1998] 1 NZLR 523 (CA).
31 *Ibid.* at [178], *per* Gault J., at [223], *per* Tipping J.
32 *R.* v. *Phillips* [1991] 3 NZLR 175 (CA); *R.* v. *Lambert* [2001] UKHL 37.
33 A. Butler and P. Butler, *The New Zealand Bill of Rights Act: A Commentary* (Wellington: LexisNexis, 2005), p. 169.
34 *Flickinger* v. *Crown Colony of Hong Kong* [1991] 1 NZLR 439 (CA); *R.* v. *Poumako* [2000] 2 NZLR 695 (CA); *R.* v. *Pora* [2001] 2 NZLR 37 (CA).
35 *Poumako*, 702.

As these three judges deemed this a tenable interpretation of the earlier statute that would avoid the inconsistency with the NZBORA right against retrospective punishment in section 25(g), they felt obliged to prefer this meaning under section 6 so that section 4 did not apply.[36] Indeed, two of the judges argued that section 6 adopts a general principle of 'legality' requiring express words when Parliament legislates contrary to human rights.[37] Arguably, this is precisely the sort of judicial technique for elevating human rights over other enactments that section 4 was framed to oust. As Andrew and Petra Butler concluded in 2005: 'There is little consistency of approach or application [to section 6] . . . One can find support in the case law for almost any view relevant to s 6 . . . In this respect, [NZ]BORA case law is no different from the case law that has developed in respect of s 3(1) of the HRA (UK).'[38]

More recently, this inconsistency and variation has diminished and a clearer resolution reached as a result of the 2007 decision in *R. v. Hansen*.[39] In this case, the NZSC unanimously affirmed the original 1991 Court of Appeal decision in *Phillips* that no alternative to the plain meaning of the statutory reverse onus of proof provision in the 1975 Misuse of Drugs Act was possible under section 6, despite the subsequent opposite conclusion in the UK interpreting the provision as evidentiary only and so consistent with the right to be presumed innocent until proven guilty.[40] The NZSC expressly and self-consciously discussed and rejected the 'broader' use of the equivalent and textually similar interpretive duty of UK courts in favour of the narrower requirement of 'reasonably possible' meanings – versus what Tipping J. characterized as 'unreasonably possible' ones in the UK.[41]

In terms of the specific application (versus the general scope or strength) of section 6, courts have employed it to read down statutes in several areas, including the various seemingly relevant statutory immunities from liability of the police and the Crown in *Baigent's Case*, retrospective punishment in

---

[36] Three other judges in *Pora* applied the orthodox rule that because the two enactments could not be reconciled, the later in time prevails despite its inconsistency with a NZBORA right.

[37] *Pora* at [53] and [56], *per* Elias, C.J. and Tipping, J. The principle of legality was acknowledged by Lord Hoffman in the UK case of *R. v. Secretary of State for the Home Department, ex parte Simms* [2000] 2 AC 115, 131 the previous year.

[38] Butler and Butler, *The New Zealand Bill of Rights Act*, p. 183.

[39] [2007] NZSC 7 (SC). [40] *Lambert*.

[41] 'So far as it is possible to do so, primary legislation . . . must read and given effect in a way which is compatible with the Convention rights'. HRA, section 3(1). *Hansen* 158.

Poumako and *Pora*,[42] and notably in the context of freedom of expression. In *Moonen*,[43] the Court of Appeal held that section 6 required the relevant statutory language in the Films, Videos, and Publications Classification Act 1993 permitting censorship of 'objectionable' publications to be given 'such available meaning as impinges as little as possible on freedom of expression'. In two important public protests cases, the NZSC held that lower courts had insufficiently taken into account the right to freedom of expression under section 14 of the NZBORA in interpreting 'disorderly' and 'offensive' conduct respectively under the Summary Offences Act 1981.[44]

Returning to *R. v. Hansen*, having first found that the statute's limit on the right to be presumed innocent was unreasonable under section 5 and that no reasonably possible alternative meaning of the reverse onus provision was available under section 6, three of the five judges relied on section 4 to apply the rights-violating statute, and dismissed the defendant's appeal. This makes *Hansen* one of only a handful of cases in which the actual decision turned on what Paul Rishworth has referred to as 'considered reliance' on section 4;[45] that is, applying section 4 only after engaging in the now mostly accepted methodology of first finding that the limit on a right is unreasonable (under section 5) and then that no alternative, rights-consistent meaning is possible (under section 6). If a limit is reasonable or an alternative meaning is available, then there is no inconsistency with the NZBORA and no need to rely on section 4. Most previous reliances on section 4 were based on the alternative, and now mostly rejected '*Moonen*' methodology, of eschewing section 5 analysis and moving directly from a finding that no rights-consistent interpretation is possible to application of section 4.[46] Accordingly, in addition to establishing the 'reasonably possible' meaning standard under section 6, *Hansen* also affirmed that the generally accepted methodology in NZBORA cases is to apply sections 5, 6 and 4 in that order. At least for now, this appears to have resolved what had been a long-standing problem of the proper application of these three sections.[47]

---

[42] A majority of the Court of Appeal read down the retrospective penalty provision of the 1999 statutory as applying only to offences committed during the fifteen-day period after enactment of the separate 'home invasion' definition statute and before the new minimum penalty came into effect, rather than any time between offence and sentencing.

[43] *Moonen v. Board of Film and Literature Review* [2000] 2 NZLR 9 (CA).

[44] *Brooker v. Police* [2007] NZSC 30; *Morse v. Police* [2011] NZSC 45.

[45] Rishworth, 'Interpreting Enactments: Sections 4, 5, and 6', pp. 156–7.

[46] Although this was still the analysis of Chief Justice Elias in *Hansen*.

[47] On the now largely solved so-called '4–5–6 problem', see Rishworth, 'Interpreting Enactments', pp. 118–20.

A second issue that is still playing itself out in the case law is whether courts impliedly have the power to issue formal declarations of incompatibility (or their equivalent) once, as in *Hansen*, they have found a statute to be inconsistent with the NZBORA and applied section 4. Unlike the UK's HRA and the more recent Australian bills of rights, the NZBORA does not expressly grant such a declaratory power to the courts. Soon after the HRA came into effect, and perhaps not coincidentally, it seemed as if the Court of Appeal had taken the fairly bold step of implying such a power.[48] However, not only has this power never clearly been used in the years since, but the NZSC has consistently narrowed the jurisdictional scope of this maybe yes/maybe no power.[49] If *Hansen* helped to resolve two other long-standing issues – the so-called '4–5–6 problem' and the scope of the interpretive power under section 6 – it only clouded this issue of the implied declaratory power. Justice McGrath stated that 'a New Zealand court must never shirk its responsibility to indicate, in any case where it concludes that the measure being considered is inconsistent with protected rights, that ... it has been necessary for the court to revert to s 4 of the Bill of Rights and uphold the ordinary meaning of the other statute'.[50] But then he appeared to authorize such shirking by adding immediately afterwards: 'Normally that will be sufficiently apparent from the court's statement of its reasoning' (i.e., without the need for a formal declaration or indication). And that is what happened in *Hansen*. In Claudia Geiringer's words, the Court 'stopped at describing the inconsistency without taking the further step of making a formal declaration'.[51] The effect was largely to bury the judicial finding of a rights violation as almost a detail within the Court's overall and more emphasized conclusion that the defendant's appeal was dismissed. Perhaps, not surprisingly, the 'informal' indication of inconsistency attracted little or no media attention.[52] Geiringer suggests that judges are wary of establishing a formal declaratory power because they are not comfortable with being placed in the role of critic of the legislature.[53]

---

[48] In *Moonen*. The Court of Appeal, however, used the term 'indication' rather than 'declaration' of inconsistency.

[49] Among these limitations are that the subject-matter of the declaration must have been raised before the court of first instance, and there is no jurisdiction to make declarations in criminal cases or with respect to freestanding, abstract claims. See C. Geiringer, 'On a Road to Nowhere: Implied Declarations of Inconsistency and the New Zealand Bill of Rights Act' (2009) 40 *Victoria University Wellington Law Review* 612, 623–40.

[50] *Hansen* at [253].   [51] Geiringer, 'On a Road to Nowhere', p. 639.   [52] *Ibid.*, p. 642.

[53] *Ibid.*, p. 646.

Now moving to the third stage, how have the government and Parliament responded to judicial rights decisions? Has the legal power to disagree with the courts been exercised in practice? Has there been space for independent political judgment on rights issues? In almost every case, the political branches have responded to judicial decisions in one way or another, with an overall mixed record of accepting and not accepting these decisions. Following the landmark decision of the Court of Appeal in *Baigent's Case*, which established a cause of action for public law damages against the Crown for violations of the NZBORA despite the existence of several seemingly relevant statutory immunities, the government referred the issue of whether to legislate to remove, limit or regulate such damages to the independent Law Commission.[54] The Commission's report recommending against such legislation was considered by the Ministry of Justice, which took no further action on the issue, leaving development of the cause of action and the scope of the remedy to the courts.[55] By contrast, when the High Court subsequently awarded a relatively high amount of damages to five maximum security prisoners whose treatment was held to have violated section 23(5) of the NZBORA,[56] there was a public outcry to which Parliament responded by enacting the Victims' Compensation Act of 2005. This statute gives inmates' victims the right to share in any compensation award and so can be thought of as a partial acceptance and partial modification of the judicial decision.[57]

In *Quilter*, discussed above, the Court of Appeal made clear its view that changing the law on same-sex marriage was not legitimately within its section 6 interpretive power, but was a matter for the legislature to address if it saw fit.[58] This decision received some media attention, and

---

[54] The Law Commission is an independent Crown entity funded by government to review areas of the law that need updating, reforming or developing. It makes recommendations to Parliament, which are published in its report series.

[55] New Zealand Law Commission, *Crown Liability and Judicial Immunity: A Response to Baigent's Case and Harvey v. Derrick*, NZLCR 37 (Wellington, 1997); Ministry of Justice, *Corporate Plan 1997–99: Public Law*.

[56] *Taunoa v. Attorney-General* [2004] 7 HRNZ 379 (HC). Section 23(5) of the NZBORA states: 'Everyone deprived of liberty shall be treated with humanity and with respect for the inherent dignity of the person.' The High Court's decision was somewhat tentatively affirmed by the Court of Appeal in *Attorney-General v. Taunoa* [2006] 2 NZLR 457 (CA).

[57] The statute was initially enacted for a two-year period and was renewed for a further three years in 2007, and again for a further two in 2010.

[58] At the same time, the majority in *Quilter* did not find that the Marriage Act of 1955 was inconsistent with section 19 of the NZBORA, which incorporates the right to freedom from discrimination on the grounds (including sexual orientation) contained in the 1993 Human Rights Act.

was followed two years later by both a Ministry of Justice discussion paper and a Law Commission study on the treatment of same-sex couples under the law.[59] Between 2001 and 2004, the Attorney-General issued section 7 reports on six government bills for being inconsistent with the prohibition on sexual orientation discrimination under section 19 of the NZBORA, as amended by the 1993 Human Rights Act.[60] And in 2004, the Civil Union Act was enacted by Parliament. Along somewhat similar lines, the retrospective increase in penalty provision of the 1999 Criminal Justice Amendment Act, which the Court of Appeal had invited Parliament to reconsider in the course of its decision in *Poumako*,[61] was amended by Parliament in 2002.[62]

By contrast, not only has Parliament not yet repealed the reverse onus of proof provision of the 1975 Misuse of Drug Act that was found to be inconsistent with the right to be presumed innocent in *Hansen* but applied under section 4, it amended the Act to extend the scope of this provision shortly after that judicial decision. In response to the government's Expert Advisory Committee on Drugs' recommendation that Benzylpiperazine (BZP) be classified as an illegal drug under the 1975 Act and thereby subject to its reverse onus provision, the government introduced the Misuse of Drugs (Classification of BZP) Bill into the House of Representatives two months after the NZSC's decision in *Hansen*. In light of this ruling, the Attorney-General attached a section 7 report to the bill, which set out the majority reasoning in the case and concluded that the law would be an unreasonable limit on section 25(c) of the NZBORA, but also argued that the public health risk of BZP use made it necessary to reclassify it without delay. The report stated that the government had requested the Law Commission to undertake a comprehensive review of the 1975 Act, which might lead to future changes.[63] The section 7 report played little role in the remainder of the legislative process. The select committee report on the bill noted its existence and summarized its content, but the majority expressed confidence that the

---

[59] Ministry of Justice, *Same-Sex Couples and the Law* (Wellington, 1999); Law Commission, *Recognising Same Sex Relationships*, NZLC SP4 (Wellington, 1999).

[60] See Butler and Butler, *The New Zealand Bill of Rights Act*, pp. 205–6.

[61] R. v. *Poumako* (2000) 5 HRNZ, 652, 665 [42], 672 [67], 683 [107] *per* Richardson P., Gault, Keith, Henry, Thomas JJ.).

[62] Section 6 of the Sentencing Act 2002 clarifies that an offender has the right, if convicted of an offence in respect of which the penalty has been varied between the commission of the offence and sentencing, to the benefit of the lesser penalty.

[63] Report of the Attorney-General under the New Zealand Bill of Rights Act 1990 on the Misuse of Drugs (Classification of BZP) Amendment Bill 2007, AJHR, J.4.4, 2007.

Law Commission would address any NZBORA issues in the future.[64] Only the Green Party minority view engaged these issues, concluding that '[w]e are alarmed that Parliament is allowing this significant breach of the New Zealand Bill of Rights Act 1990 on the basis of such flimsy evidence. In our view, setting a presumption of supply at 5 grams – or possession of 100 tablets – is arbitrary and low, and cannot be justified rationally.'[65] There was a single reference to the NZBORA in the subsequent parliamentary debates before the bill's enactment without amendment by a vote of 109 to 11.[66]

A second post-*Hansen* bill along the same lines, reclassifying ephedrine and pseudoephedrine as controlled drugs, and so within the reverse onus provision of the 1975 Act, was introduced in 2010 also with a section 7 report concluding that the bill was an unreasonable limit on the right to be presumed innocent.[67] This bill, the Misuse of Drugs Amendment Bill 2010, was introduced after the Law Commission had submitted its tentative position paper suggesting the reverse onus provision should not be retained, and was enacted into law by a vote of 104–14 in August 2011, three months after the Law Commission published its final report definitively recommending its repeal together with the creation of a new offence of 'aggravated possession' based on quantity, along with many other proposed changes to the 1975 Act.[68] There was essentially no discussion of the reverse onus issue in either the select committee report on the bill or the subsequent parliamentary debates. One month after the bill's enactment, the government issued its official response to the Law Commission report, in which it pledged to generally overhaul the 1975 Act during the next parliament but was noncommittal on the specific issue of repealing the reverse onus provision.[69]

In addition, in several immigration cases, including one decided in 2010 by the NZSC, Parliament responded to pro-plaintiff judgments of

---

[64] Misuse of Drugs (Classification of BZP) Amendment Bill, 146–1, Report of the Health Committee, p. 7.

[65] *Ibid.*, p. 8.

[66] This episode is discussed in Geddis, 'Comparative Irrelevance', pp. 486–7; J. B. Kelly, 'Judicial and Political Review as Limited Insurance: the Functioning of the New Zealand Bill of Rights Act in "hard" cases' (2011) 49 *Commonwealth & Comparative Politics* 295, 310–13.

[67] The introduction of this bill, prior to its final enactment, is also discussed in Kelly, *ibid.*

[68] The Law Commission report, *Controlling and Regulating Drugs – A Review of the Misuse of Drugs Act*, was issued on 3 May 2011. The report recommended repealing the reverse onus provision, see *ibid.*, pp. 191–6.

[69] www.beehive.govt.nz/release/next-government-will-overhaul-misuse-drugs-act.

the courts based on rights-consistent interpretations of relevant provisions of the Immigration Act 1987 by swiftly amending these provisions and overruling those decisions.[70]

III   The stability of the NZBORA

Twenty-two years after its enactment as an ordinary statute, there is little support within New Zealand for converting the NZBORA into a constitutional bill of rights.[71] A few academic commentators have called for lesser forms of strengthening, such as establishing an express judicial declaratory power[72] and replacing section 4 with a section 33-type legislative override mechanism to reduce 'plaintiff disincentivising' effects.[73] At the same time, there does not appear to be much support for abolishing the NZBORA.[74]

There is broad consensus that the NZBORA is in practice, as well as formally, a 'weaker' rights regime than the Canadian Charter in terms of the scope of judicial power and the constraints on the legislature. This consensus includes those who view the NZBORA as successfully blending legal and political constitutionalism,[75] and also, at least for the moment, the handful of commentators who argue that under the

---

[70] *Tavita v. Minister of Immigration* [1994] 2 NZLR 257 (CA); *Mohebbi v. Minister of Immigration* [2003] NZAR 685 (HC); *New Zealand Association for Migration and Investments Inc. v. Attorney-General* [2006] NZAR 45 (HC); *Ye v. Minister of Immigration* [2010] NZSC 76. These cases are discussed in Butler, 'It Takes Two to Tango', pp. 41–4.

[71] For a powerful argument against conversion, see G. Huscroft and P. Rishworth, '"You Say You Want a Revolution": Bills of Rights in the Age of Human Rights' in D. Dyzenhaus, M. Hunt and G. Huscroft (eds.), *A Simple Common Layer: Essays in Honour of Michael Taggart* (Oxford: Hart, 2009), p. 123.

[72] See Geiringer, 'On a Road to Nowhere', pp. 646–7 (arguing that if more robust dialogue between the legislature and the courts is desired, an express declaratory power is necessary).

[73] Butler and Butler, 'The New Zealand Bill of Rights Act', pp. 1115–16.

[74] The NZBORA is, uniquely among the new model bills of rights, supported by both major political parties (although both major parties also voted in favour of the extensions in the reverse onus of proof, discussed below). Within academic circles, John Smillie is one clear exception, see J. Smillie, 'Who Wants Juristocracy?' (2006) 11 *Otago Law Review* 183, 191. James Allan is perhaps a second, see Allan, 'Portia, Bassano or Dick the Butcher?'.

[75] See, for example, P. Butler, 'Human Rights and Parliamentary Sovereignty in New Zealand' (2004) 35 *Victoria University Wellington Law Review* 341; P. Joseph, 'Parliament, the Courts and the Collaborative Enterprise' (2004) 15 *King's College Law Journal* 321.

NZBORA judges in New Zealand have started down the (inevitable) road to de facto judicial supremacy.[76] The growing, and so I think more pressing, assessment of the NZBORA from the overall perspective of the new model is rather the opposite one: that it is reverting towards traditional parliamentary sovereignty and operating far more like the ill-fated Canadian Bill of Rights than is generally acknowledged. In this way, it is suggested the NZBORA is living refutation of the claim that it embodies a new or intermediate model.

Andrew Geddis argues that 'the impact of the NZBORA on Parliament's behaviour is so minimal in nature as to be almost irrelevant',[77] so defying the expectations of *both* proponents of inter-institutional dialogue on rights and members of the inevitability-of-judicial-supremacy school of criticism. Accordingly, for him, New Zealand 'partly vindicates' Mark Tushnet's hypothesis that weak-form judicial review will generally prove to be unstable, in this case by reverting to parliamentary sovereignty.[78] Geddis is careful to qualify his claim ('partly vindicates'), however, which addresses only the relationship between Parliament and the courts. He does not suggest that the NZBORA has had no impact on New Zealand law as a whole, and he specifically mentions its effects on judicial oversight of the executive in particular.[79] James Kelly argues that in 'hard cases' – those involving 'law and order' provisions restricting the liberty of an unpopular segment of society – the NZBORA operates as an 'under-insured' bill of rights.[80] Its mechanism of political rights review has largely failed to act as a constraint on Parliament, resulting in 'very limited insurance for rights protection'.[81] In so doing, Kelly concludes, the NZBORA 'may confirm Tushnet's position that "weak-form" bills of rights place marginal limitations on the principle of parliamentary supremacy and do not represent a middle ground between judicial supremacy and parliamentary supremacy, as suggested by defenders of parliamentary bills of rights'.[82] As with Geddis, Kelly's argument focuses specifically on the impact of the NZBORA on Parliament, acknowledging that NZBORA has resulted in important judicial safeguards in the area of police action and criminal procedure.[83]

For the purpose of a more general assessment of whether the NZBORA is operating in an intermediate manner, it does seem necessary to take the full, global picture into account and not only that

---

[76] Allen, 'Portia, Bassano or Dick the Butcher?'; Smillie, 'Who Wants Juristocracy?'.
[77] Geddis, 'Comparative Irrelevance', p. 471. [78] *Ibid.* [79] *Ibid*, p. 467.
[80] Kelly, 'Judicial and Political Review', p. 296. [81] *Ibid.*, p. 297. [82] *Ibid.* [83] *Ibid.*

important slice consisting of parliamentary responses to the NZBORA, as I think Geddis and Kelly acknowledge. Moreover, even within this slice, for the reasons discussed in the previous chapter, the presence or absence of inter-institutional 'dialogue' should not distract or monopolize our thinking about the greater balance between judicial and legislative power that is constitutive of the new model. With these two thoughts in mind, there appear to be strong grounds for concluding that the NZBORA is generally functioning in ways that are distinct from traditional parliamentary sovereignty as previously practised in New Zealand and the UK, and as still operating at the national level in Australia. Once again, the vigour of the recent debate in Australia between the supporters of an NZBORA-like national bill of rights and of maintaining the status quo does not suggest that participants were persuaded of their practical equivalence.

As discussed above, there is almost universal acknowledgement that the NZBORA has attained constitutional status in New Zealand, which was not generally true of the CBOR in pre-Charter Canada.[84] Although obviously such status means something different in a legal system lacking a codified, supreme law constitution, the fixed text, reasonably specific and comprehensive nature of the bill of rights (compared to common law rights) together with the commitment to the protected rights that constitutional status entails push and challenge the neat legal formulations of traditional parliamentary sovereignty, as perhaps best exemplified in the *Pora* case.[85] Moreover, as affirmed by the majority in *Hansen* and alluded to by the dissenting chief justice on this point,[86] New Zealand courts engage in precisely the same sorts of analyses as courts operating under a constitutional bill of rights, in determining whether a statute is consistent with the NZBORA. The only difference – and this is what makes judicial review in New Zealand 'soft' or 'weak' – is the consequence of finding an inconsistency.[87] Such a judicial power of

---

[84] At least in some part, this is due to the differences in scope of the two bills, as well as their judicial application. Although most relevant law-making takes place at the provincial level, the CBOR covered only federal law.

[85] That is, with respect to the doctrine of implied repeal.

[86] '[Considering section 5 as a necessary step in determining whether an enactment is consistent with a right] would set up a soft form of judicial review which seems inconsistent with s4 of the Act'. *Hansen*, Elias, C. J., at para. [6].

[87] Rishworth, 'The Inevitability of Judicial Review'; Butler and Butler, 'The New Zealand Bill of Rights Act', p. 195.

constitutional review is, of course, not part of the orthodox position within the model of parliamentary sovereignty.

Similarly, courts in New Zealand use the NZBORA to subject discretionary executive action to full-blooded substantive rights review just like courts in systems with constitutional bills of rights, and unlike the more limited judicial review grounds of unreasonableness or *ultra vires* within traditional parliamentary sovereignty. As both Geddis and Kelly acknowledge, New Zealand courts have employed the NZBORA to increase their oversight of the executive branch in general, and the police in particular, substantially reworking the law and practice of criminal procedure.[88]

At the bureaucratic level, we have seen that the NZBORA has had a significant impact on the government's pre-legislative procedures. To repeat Grant Huscroft's words, 'it has formalized the place of the Bill of Rights in the policy development process, at least where the government's legislative agenda is concerned'.[89] Even if the impact on the legislature is more minimal, this is significant within a government-dominated parliamentary system[90] and is a new development resulting directly from section 7 of the NZBORA.

Returning to the judiciary, although overall New Zealand courts have not been as 'adventurous' as UK ones in applying the similar interpretive duty, the relevant question here is whether they have interpreted statutes in a more rights-consistent way than under previous, common law principles and presumptions. Are statutes more likely to be read in a manner that is consistent with rights and freedoms under the NZBORA than before? Only if the answer is no has the NZBORA reverted to the traditional practices of parliamentary sovereignty in this area. The very first NZBORA judgment of the Court of Appeal answered this question in the affirmative. For seventy-seven years, New Zealand courts had interpreted section 66 of the Judicature Act 1908 as not conferring appellate jurisdiction on the Court of Appeal in 'criminal' habeas corpus cases, such as extradition. As late as 1985, the Court of Appeal held that an interpretation of section 66 as containing such a right of appeal was 'plainly untenable [and] altogether inconsistent with statutory patterns and New Zealand legal history'.[91] Nonetheless, a year after the

---

[88] Geddis, 'Comparative Irrelevance', p. 467; Kelly, 'Judicial and Political Review', p. 297.
[89] See n. 11.
[90] The government domination of Parliament tends to be greater in New Zealand than elsewhere, because it is unicameral.
[91] *R. v. Clarke* [1985] 2 NZLR 212, 214 (CA).

NZBORA's enactment, the same court was prepared to depart from this case law on the basis of the mandate in section 6 (and the right to habeas corpus in section 23(1)(c) of the NZBORA), and embraced appeals in criminal habeas cases. The Court noted that a different interpretation had been given in previous cases because the 'statutory context and history [of the provision] led to a different conclusion', but continued that in light of section 6, 'if s 66 of the [1908 Act] can be given a meaning consistent with the rights and freedoms contained on the Bill of Rights, that meaning must be preferred'.[92]

As we saw in *Pora*, three Court of Appeal judges were prepared to say that section 6 of the NZBORA can operate to effectively overrule the orthodox constitutional principle under parliamentary sovereignty that later statutes impliedly repeal earlier inconsistent ones. More recently, in the two important freedom of expression cases mentioned above, the NZSC employed section 6 to overrule pre-NZBORA statutory interpretations as insufficiently taking into account free speech values. In *Brooker* v. *Police*,[93] decided in 2007, the NZSC considered the meaning of 'behaves in [a] disorderly manner' under section 4(1)(a) of the Summary Offences Act 1981, in the context of a conviction under the Act for a public protest that fell within the freedom of expression protected by section 14 of the NZBORA. In upholding the conviction on appeal, both the High Court and Court of Appeal had relied on the pre-NZBORA precedent of *Melser* v. *Police*,[94] which had interpreted 'disorderly' behaviour as conduct 'of a character which is likely to cause annoyance to others who are present'.[95] The NZSC set aside the conviction on the basis that *Melser* was no longer good law in light of the NZBORA, and replaced it with the freedom of expression-consistent meaning that 'disorderly behaviour' requires 'a clear danger of disruption [of public order] rising far above annoyance'.[96] As Chief Justice Elias put it: 'I consider that the meaning of disorderly behaviour adopted in *Melser* v. *Police* does not comply with s6 of the New Zealand Bill of Rights Act. It is more restrictive of freedom of expression than is necessary in protection of public order'.[97] In reaching the same conclusion, Blanchard J. wrote: '[l]ittle guidance can now be obtained from pre-Bill of Rights cases.'[98] In *Morse* v. *The*

---

[92] *Flickinger*, 439–40. This part of the judgment was obiter dicta as the Court, making the assumption that it had jurisdiction, dismissed the appeal on its merits.
[93] [2007] NZSC 30.   [94] [1967] NZLR 437 (CA).   [95] *Ibid.* at 443, per North, P.
[96] *Brooker* at [42], per Elias, C. J.   [97] *Ibid.*   [98] *Brooker* at [63], per Blanchard, J.

Police,[99] decided in 2011, the NZSC similarly overturned a conviction for burning the New Zealand flag based on pre-NZBORA interpretations of behaving 'in an offensive manner in a public place' under the same provision of the Summary Offences Act 1981. The NZSC found that just as in *Brooker*, it was necessary to reconsider the meaning of 'disorderly' behaviour in the light of the purpose and statutory context of section 4(1)(a), including the context of the NZBORA, so too the meaning of 'offensive' must be reconsidered. The result of the NZBORA-informed reconsideration was to reject the previous interpretation that 'behaviour is offensive within the meaning of s4(1)(a) simply on the basis that it is capable of wounded feelings or arousing outrage in a reasonable person, irrespective of objectively assessed disruption of public order'.[100]

In sum, section 6 of the NZBORA has not been irrelevant to, or had little impact on, the courts. It has significantly augmented their rights-protecting functions as compared to the common law principles and presumptions of statutory interpretation of the pre-NZBORA era. As Paul Rishworth concludes: 'The outcome [of the NZBORA] is that enactments are more likely [than before] to be read in a manner that is consistent with rights and freedoms.'[101]

Finally, on the specific issue of the NZBORA's impact on Parliament in terms of its responses to judicial decisions, as detailed above the overall record is sufficiently mixed to belie the claim of irrelevance. Parliament has not simply ignored judicial rights concerns across the board, in the way that it has often disregarded, or at least failed to act on, section 7 reports. To the contrary, it has responded in some way to almost all judicial decisions. Thus, the legislature eventually accepted the judicial invitations to amend or repeal the relevant statutes at issue in the *Quilter* and *Poumako* judgments, enacting the Civil Unions Act 2004 and the Sentencing Act 2002 respectively. Even the two seemingly opposite legislative responses to the judgments in *Baigent's Case* (accepting the judicial decision) and *Hansen* (rejecting it) both resulted in referring the respective rights issues identified by the courts to the Law Commission. The ultimate result of the latter referral remains to be seen, but its having been made refutes the notion that Parliament completely disregarded the court's decision, even if its delegation of the issue to an outside body is hardly the ideal mode of legislative deliberation. And although Parliament responded to a lower court decision with which it

---

[99] [2011] NZSC 45.   [100] *Ibid.* at [38], *per* Elias, C. J.
[101] Rishworth, 'Interpreting Enactments', p. 120.

disagreed by narrowing the scope of future public law damages in the specific situation of awards to prison inmates where there are identifiable victims, it obviously could have scaled them back far more or even rejected any compensation altogether.[102] Accordingly, judicial-legislative relationships do not appear to be unchanged since the advent of the NZBORA. The political costs of legislative disagreement with the courts may be lower than in Canada (and the UK), and perhaps too low overall, but they are not zero – and the very fact that such inter-institutional disagreement over rights exists and is aired at all goes beyond what is typically part of traditional parliamentary sovereignty.

Moreover, taken in context and not in isolation, far from undermining the claim that the NZBORA is a distinct, intermediate model, the *Hansen*/BZP episode bolsters it as a fairly clear case of legislative independence from judicial rights decisions that the new model supports – as does the series of legislative overrulings of judicial interpretations of the 1987 Immigration Act mentioned above. It is certainly true that the *Hansen*/BZP episode is not an instance of 'inter-institutional rights-dialogue'[103] in any qualitative or deliberative sense, but what is central to the new model is the practical ability of legislatures occasionally to say no to the courts and exercise their power of the final word. Again, from the perspective of ideal theory, that the legislature should exercise its power without robust debate of the rights issues involved and arguably in the absence of a reasonable basis for rights disagreement means the episode falls short of what the new model aspires to. But, particularly from the comparative perspective of Canada, and in light of some of the other legislative responses detailed above, the entire *Hansen* episode supports rather than detracts from the new model's claim to distinctness. Here, the courts have identified and prioritized a rights issue raised by a piece of legislation, setting out their reasons for finding an inconsistency with section 25(c) of the NZBORA and causing the government to refer the matter to the Law Commission, and at the end of the day the issue will be resolved politically, by the government deciding whether to propose and Parliament whether to approve repeal of the reverse onus provision, as recommended by the Law Commission report. This ultimate political decision appears to be a genuinely open one, not merely

---

[102] Indeed, the NZSC itself recently narrowed the scope of compensation by holding that the public law damage remedy does not apply to judicial – as distinct from executive – violations of the NZBORA. *Attorney-General* v. *Chapman* [2011] NZSC 110.
[103] Geddis, 'Comparative Irrelevance', p. 487.

formal or made with 'hands tied' by legal or practical constraints, and seemingly could go either way. As such, overall the episode is a decent example of how the new model is supposed to work.

In sum, even if the impact of the NZBORA on Parliament as a whole during the legislative process has been fairly minimal,[104] its impact on the executive during this same process, its impact on the courts generally, its impact on criminal procedure and on substantive law in several areas, and its impact on Parliament following the courts' exercise of their rights-protecting powers has not been minimal or irrelevant. In combination, these other impacts have brought about significant change to the New Zealand legal system, changes that show no obvious signs of instability, and changes that all depart from the traditional system of parliamentary sovereignty.

IV   Overall assessment of the NZBORA from the new model perspective

The strength of the NZBORA as an instantiation of the new model lies in the greater balance of power it has achieved between the legislature and courts. Although the NZBORA has undoubtedly augmented the powers of courts – and significantly impacted their conduct – by enabling them to assess the consistency of statutes with protected rights for the first time and to give more rights-friendly interpretations to statutes than previously, judicial power is still quite constrained, certainly compared to Canada. Indeed, if anything, the balance could afford to shift a little more in the direction of the courts, in ways to be discussed below. The legislature still decides most significant and contested issues and, equally importantly, the courts still believe that it should. There is ample room for legislative decision-making where rights issues are in play, with courts giving rights-consistent interpretations to their finished products where reasonably possible but not overly straining to do so, and applying them where not without creating almost insuperable pressure for change in the process. In this way, the NZBORA seems to have established a court-influenced but not court-centred approach to resolving rights issues: judicial review without judicial supremacy.

The weakness of the NZBORA from the new model perspective is arguably less clear-cut than this strength, but there is a lingering sense

---

[104] As distinct from its impact on certain individual MPs, who have forcefully made NZBORA-based arguments. See Butler, 'It Takes Two to Tango'.

that the rights of unpopular groups – such as drug users, prison inmates and immigrants – are sometimes under-enforced in terms of legislative outputs, so that the distinctive new model solution of addressing or attempting to minimize this within the legislative process itself, political rights review, is not working adequately.[105]

Nonetheless, for the reasons discussed in the previous sections, the NZBORA does appear to be currently operating in a more clearly intermediate manner than the Canadian Charter, which, as we have seen, has the reverse strengths and weaknesses, but in a far more lopsided way with respect to the twin overarching goals of the new model. The NZBORA has been better able to balance political and legal constitutionalism. Soon after its inception, the NZBORA came to be applied in a manner that moved it somewhat away from the traditional Westminster-style parliamentary sovereignty pole, where many thought its ordinary statute status had terminally consigned it, and it has remained in this newly conceived space without basic reversion since that time. As will already be obvious, this overall stability has not been achieved without certain problems or concerns from the perspective of the ideal working of the new model discussed in Chapter 4. So let me turn to identifying these and discussing possible practical reforms to address them, taking the three stages in order.

As far as pre-enactment political rights review is concerned, the key weakness is the institutional role of the legislature. As we have seen, the various strands of pre-introductory executive review taken together generally mean that the NZBORA implications of proposed bills are taken seriously in the policy development process, albeit with some risk of inconsistent advice among the various rights-vetting entities, and over-emphasis on the purely legal dimension of the process at the expense of the political. How much this latter is compensated for at Cabinet level discussions of legislative priorities is, of course, hard to discover. At the parliamentary level, the problems begin with both the quantity and the content of section 7 reports by the Attorney-General. As Huscroft argues, the comparative frequency of such reports conveys an ambivalent message to Parliament about the seriousness with which the Attorney-General's Cabinet colleagues, at least, take the NZBORA as a constraint on legislation, a message that may well influence Parliament into taking a similar view. Moreover, the common pattern for section 7

---

[105] As discussed, this is the essence of James Kelly's critique. See Kelly, 'Judicial and Political Review'.

reports to consist more or less exclusively of the government lawyers' concerns may also have the effect of making them appear as merely technical obstacles for politicians – whether in Cabinet or Parliament – to surmount. Accordingly, the number of reports should be reduced (though not to the Canadian zero) to increase their individual and political significance and to counter any sense of routinization. This could be achieved by Attorneys-General becoming less legally risk-averse, especially concerning the reasonableness of limits on rights, by relying on reasonable alternative legal views to those of previous judicial majorities and by including potentially countervailing political judgments. The reporting task could also be transferred from the Attorney-General to the relevant sponsoring minister to further reduce the sense that this is avoidable law-talk.[106]

Beyond section 7 reports, the absence of a specialized human rights committee is a major weakness of the parliamentary rights-vetting process. Such a single-tasked committee needs to be established to consider the rights implications of all bills, whether or not a section 7 report is filed, and with sufficient funding to enable it gain access to independent information and expertise, and employ its own legal advisor. As a result, it is to be hoped and expected that this more expert and specialized committee would also plug a major symptom of weakness in the current parliamentary review process, which (as Geddis and Kelly note) is that too few amendments and objections are made to bills with section 7 reports; too many are enacted as is. With fewer reports and a specialized committee to consider them, a more focused review process would be enabled, culminating in the like-lihood of more frequent proposed amendments and expressed rights concerns. And by providing a greater number of specific proposals and alternatives for subsequent debate, this in turn might help to resolve the final current weakness of too little NZBORA-focused parliamentary delib-eration at the post-committee stage of the legislative process. The goal of bolstering the parliamentary rights review process is, of course, to increase the 'rights insurance' provided by the legislature itself without calling in the judiciary.

In a nutshell, the ideal of judicial rights review under the new model is for courts (1) to take the protected rights seriously; (2) to treat legislative rights judgments respectfully but not in a formally deferential manner; (3) to engage in rights-friendly but not strained statutory interpretations, where relevant, leaving open the possibility of legislatures acting

---

[106] As is the case under both the HRA and the VCHRR.

inconsistently with judicial rights judgments; and (4) where there is such an inconsistency, to alert and inform for potential remedial action by the legislature but again not in practice to foreclose it from maintaining its position. Matched against these standards, the New Zealand judiciary is performing reasonably well. The two main areas of weakness are the second and fourth, and they are connected. That is, the hesitancy and reluctance of the Court of Appeal and now the NZSC to imply and exercise the power to formally declare/indicate an inconsistency between the NZBORA and another statute before applying section 4 both *reflects* a highly – perhaps too – respectful attitude towards the legislature in not wishing to act as critic, and *results* in too little focused attention on the judicially determined inconsistency. As discussed, *Hansen* is paradigmatic in this regard. Rather than formally declaring the inconsistency that its analysis had found between the reverse onus provision and the right to be presumed innocent under section 25(c) of the NZBORA, the NZSC effectively buried its finding in the details of the judgments, with its major apparent conclusion being simply that the defendant's appeal was dismissed. As such, the judicial determination of inconsistency was an insufficiently important and heralded event. The decision received no media attention, and the government and Parliament were able to partly (though not wholly) ignore it, as detailed above. Accordingly, a little less judicial respect for Parliament and a little more attention and importance for findings of inconsistency seem to be called for. Whether an expressly granted declaratory power is the best solution is uncertain. Whilst on the one hand it would likely help to overcome the 'tentative and self-effacing'[107] nature of the courts' interactions with the political branches and likely ensure greater attention and importance to judicial inconsistency rulings, on the other, certain comparative experience (as we will see) suggests the possibility that an express declaratory power might just be a tipping point beyond which the legislative power to disagree is rendered too politically costly for the norm of legitimate use to apply in practice. Accordingly, perhaps the clear confirmation and exercise of the implied power, with its subtly different constraints and implications, would be a preferable step, if the courts are up to taking it.

Finally, regarding the third stage of post-enactment political rights review, we have seen that the problem is not that judicial rights decisions have had no impact on Parliament. In terms of outcomes or results, Parliament has not simply ignored the courts across the board but has a

---

[107] Geiringer, 'On a Road to Nowhere', p. 616.

strong record of responding to their NZBORA judgments by way of affirming, modifying and rejecting them, which at least some commentators have referred to as instances of dialogue.[108] Putting this vexed latter term to one side, a mixed record here is hardly prima facie evidence that the new model is not working as it should. The problem has been more at the level of process than outcome: the overall quality of parliamentary engagement with the rights issues and concerns identified by the courts has not been sufficiently high. Bills responding to judicial decisions in one way or another have suffered from the same weaknesses in the pre-enactment parliamentary rights review process as other pieces of legislation discussed above. Again, the *Hansen*/BZP episode may, in its result, support rather than undermine the new model's claim of distinctness, as I have argued, but the lack of both robust parliamentary debate about the rights issues involved and, arguably, a reasonable disagreement with the courts means that the process was far from the model's ideal.

In large part, this procedural problem is likely the consequence, or fruit, of those identified in the previous two stages, especially the diminished seriousness attaching to rights-inconsistent legislative action resulting from both the frequency of section 7 reports and the absence of formal judicial declarations/indications. It is also reflected in, and aggravated by, the common practice of the government referring judicial rights concerns to the Law Commission, and Parliament delegating its responsibilities for identifying and resolving such issues to that body, whose reports too often replace rather than trigger legislative debate. Perhaps the suggested changes to section 7 practice and the clear establishment and exercise of the implied declaratory power would be sufficient to increase the attention paid to, and perceived seriousness of, legislative rights inconsistencies so that parliamentary deliberative responses become richer and more engaged. Failing that, establishing a practice or requirement that the Attorney-General (or sponsoring minister) issue a written response to a formal judicial declaration/indication and report it to Parliament within a fixed time period, as enacted under the two Australian bills of rights, might help to provoke the desired parliamentary deliberation.

---

[108] For example, P. Butler and A. Butler, '16 Years of the New Zealand Bill of Rights', Paper presented at Southern Currents: Australian and New Zealand Law Librarians Conference, University of Melbourne Law School, 27–29 Sept. 2006, p. 16.

7

The United Kingdom

The HRA, which came into force on 2 October 2000, was the centrepiece of the former Labour Government's 1997 election manifesto commitments for constitutional reform.[1] Its enactment was also the culmination of a decades-long debate in the United Kingdom about the merits and legal possibility of some form of codified bill of rights in general, and the incorporation of the country's international obligations under the ECHR into domestic law in particular. This debate had taken place in the context of the traditional conundrum posed by the British constitution: on the one hand, ordinary statutory protection of the rights would likely prove insufficient; on the other, more protection than this was problematic if not impossible under its central doctrine of parliamentary sovereignty. The novelty of the HRA's approach to this conundrum lies in the manner in which the ECHR was incorporated into, or rather (to use the words of its preamble) given 'further effect' in, domestic law, which was to adopt a third variation of the new model, albeit one far closer to the NZBORA version that the Canadian Charter. Despite its general popularity among lawyers, the HRA did not during its first decade succeed in achieving broad political appeal and its future remains uncertain. At the general election in May 2010, the Conservative Party had pledged to repeal the HRA and replace it with a 'British bill of rights', of undisclosed content and status. After the election, the new Cameron government was forced into a compromise by its staunchly pro-ECHR Liberal-Democrat coalition partner, and an independent commission, the Commission on a Bill of Rights, was established in March 2011 'to investigate the creation of a British Bill of Rights that incorporates and builds on all our obligations under the European Convention on Human Rights, ensures that these rights continue to be enshrined in British law, and protects and

---

[1] The other main components were devolution of power from Westminster to Scotland and Wales, reform of the House of Lords and establishing an elected mayor and a new local authority for London.

extends British liberties'.[2] The Commission is still meeting as of the time of writing, and is expected to issue its report by the end of 2012.

I Central features of the HRA

The HRA is a variant on the interpretative bill of rights first established by the CBOR and again by the NZBORA. Its central provisions are as follows. A statute enacted through the ordinary legislative process 'to give further effect to the rights and freedoms guaranteed under the European Convention on Human Rights', section 1 of the HRA defines as 'Convention rights' Articles 2 to 12 and 14 (Articles 1 and 13 are excluded) of the ECHR and refers to a schedule to the Act in which these articles are reproduced verbatim. Section 2 requires UK courts to take ECtHR jurisprudence into account in HRA cases, but does not say they are bound by it.[3] Sections 3 and 4 contain the two new rights-protecting judicial powers, the former similar to the interpretive duty/power under section 6 of the NZBORA – as well as under EU law[4] – and the latter a novel one when enacted.[5] Section 3(1) states that 'so far as it is possible to do so, primary legislation and subordinate legislation must be read and given effect in a way which is compatible with the Convention rights'. Section 3(2) makes this applicable whenever the legislation in question was enacted and affirms that this section 'does not affect the validity, continuing operation or enforcement of any incompatible primary legislation'. Rather, section 4 empowers, but does not require, the higher courts to make a declaration of incompatibility with respect to such

---

[2] HM Government, *The Coalition: Our Programme for Government* (London: Cabinet Office, May 2010), p. 11.

[3] 'A court or tribunal determining a question which has arisen in connection with a Convention right must take into account any – (a) judgment, decision, declaration or advisory opinion of the European Court of Human Rights ... whenever made or given, so far as, in the opinion of the court or tribunal, it is relevant to the proceedings in which that question has arisen'. HRA, section 2(1).

[4] In the EU, the *Marleasing* case imposed a duty on all national courts to interpret domestic law in line with untransposed directives wherever possible to do so: Case C-106/89 *Marleasing SA v. La Comercial Internacionale de Alimentacion SA* [1990] 1 ECR 4135. *Marleasing* itself arguably had its roots in German constitutional law. In the famous *Lüth* decision of 1958, the Federal Constitutional Court stated that: 'Constitutional rights form an objective order of values ... This value system ... must be looked upon as a fundamental constitutional decision affecting the entire legal system ... It naturally influences private law as well; no rule of law may conflict with it, *and all such rules must be construed in accordance with its spirit*'. *Lüth*, BverfGE 7, 198 (1958) (emphasis added).

[5] See Chapter 2, n. 30 above.

legislation, repeating in section 4(6) that such a declaration has no effect on the validity or continuing operation of the provision in respect of which it is given and adds that it is 'not binding on the parties to the proceedings in which it is made'. Section 10, in turn, empowers the relevant minister to amend legislation subject to a declaration of incompatibility (or an adverse ECtHR judgment) by a 'fast-track' remedial order as an alternative to the ordinary legislative process, but there is no obligation to respond to the courts. Accordingly, the HRA unbundles or separates the judicial power to review legislation for compatibility with protected rights from the power to invalidate or disapply legislation deemed incompatible, granting only the former in contrast to the contemporary constitutional paradigm.

Section 6, which has been referred to as 'the most significant provision' of the HRA,[6] makes it unlawful for all public authorities (defined to exclude Parliament but as including the courts) to act incompatibly with Convention rights – unless mandated to do so by primary legislation that cannot be interpreted consistently with the rights. By creating 'a new type of illegality in domestic public law',[7] such that any public act or decision incompatible with Convention rights is rendered *ultra vires*, section 6 has become the most frequent basis for litigation under the HRA. Both the Scottish Parliament and the Northern Ireland Assembly, created with limited competences by the 1998 devolution legislation, are public authorities under section 6, so that their legislative acts must be compatible with Convention rights. As expressly stated in the Scotland Act and Northern Ireland Act, courts have the power to make an order declaring incompatible statutes invalid.[8] In this way, the HRA sets up a separate system of strong-form judicial review of legislative acts of these two devolved assemblies alongside the weak-form review of acts of the UK Parliament at Westminster.

Finally, the trigger for pre-enactment political rights review under the HRA is section 19, which requires the responsible minister in charge of a

---

[6] D. Feldman, 'Extending the Role of the Courts: The Human Rights Act 1998' (2011) 30 *Parliamentary History* 65, 68; Lord Bingham described section 6 as 'the central provision' of the HRA. T. Bingham, 'The Human Rights Act' (2010) 6 *European Human Rights Law Review* 568, 571.

[7] T. Hickman, *Public Law After the Human Rights Act* (Oxford: Hart Publishing, 2010), p. 27.

[8] Scotland Act 1998, sections 28, 29, 100, 101, 102, Schedule 6; Northern Ireland Act 1998, sections 6, 71, Schedule 10. By contrast, the Welsh Assembly, created by the Government of Wales Act 1998, was not given power to enact legislation.

bill to make a statement before second reading to the effect that in the minister's view either the bill is compatible with the Convention rights ('a section 19(1)(a) statement') or that 'although he is unable to make a statement of compatibility the government nevertheless wishes the House to proceed with the bill' ('a section 19(1)(b) statement').[9]

Accordingly, like the Charter and the NZBORA, the HRA mandates pre-enactment political rights review and grants to courts enhanced powers to protect rights whilst retaining the legal power of the final word on whether primary legislation is the law of the land for the legislature. Although far closer to the NZBORA as an interpretative bill of rights than the supreme law Charter, the major differences in general or structural provisions between the two are: (1) that unlike the NZBORA, the rights under the HRA are textually identical to the international human rights it is designed to affirm; (2) Parliament is not legally bound by the rights contained in the HRA, unlike the case under the NZBORA;[10] (3) the HRA's express judicial power to make a declaration of incompatibility in section 4; (4) its express judicial power to award damages (or such other remedy as the court thinks just and appropriate) for unlawful acts of public authorities in section 8; and (5) the duty imposed on the relevant minister (rather than the Attorney-General) to make a statement to Parliament *whether or not* the proposed legislation is deemed compatible under section 19. The major difference in the context of operation between the NZBORA and the HRA is that although both are stated to affirm or give effect to the countries' pre-existing international human rights obligations, only the HRA functions in the shadow of a powerful international court which is the final and authoritative interpreter of those rights, to which disappointed domestic litigants may still in effect appeal,[11] and whose decisions in individual cases in which the state is a party impose a legal duty of compliance.[12]

---

[9] HRA, section 19.

[10] Compare HRA, section 6(1), expressly excluding Parliament from the public authorities bound to act compatibly with Convention rights, with NZBORA, section 3(1).

[11] Technically, domestic litigants do not appeal a decision of a UK court to the ECtHR but make a separate application to it.

[12] That is, an international (rather than a domestic) legal duty of compliance. ECHR, Article 46 states: 'The High Contracting Parties undertake to abide by the decision of the Court in any case to which they are parties.' By contrast, the procedure for individual complaints under the First Optional Protocol to the ICCPR authorizes the Human Rights Committee to forward its (non-legally binding) 'views' to the relevant state. Article 5(4).

Two distinct, if not entirely unconnected, issues concerning the general nature and constitutional status of the HRA have provoked a certain amount of disagreement. The first is whether the substantive rights in the HRA are to be understood (primarily or ultimately) as domestic rights or as international law rights given effect in domestic law. Again, this issue derives to a significant extent from the textual identity of HRA and ECHR rights. Seemingly at stake here are (1) whether HRA rights are to be interpreted and applied independently by UK courts or effectively as subordinates of the ECtHR, (2) whether causes of action and remedies should exactly parallel, and be limited by, what a claimant would have available in Strasbourg and (3) whether HRA rights are effectively subject to override by subsequent international law obligations of the UK.[13] On this issue, reflecting the inherent tension in the text and purpose of the HRA, there has been a marked division of opinion, especially among judges.[14]

The second issue is the constitutional status of the HRA within the UK legal system and, in particular, whether it is superior to 'ordinary' statutes and/or partially entrenched, notwithstanding that Parliament is legally entitled to legislate incompatibly with Convention rights, that courts are required to apply such legislation, and that there is no provision making it harder to amend or repeal than other statutes. The disagreement is not in the subject-matter, substantive or 'small-c' sense of the term that views certain statutes – as well as conventions and common law rules and principles – as constitutional in nature because of their importance or centrality to the political/legal system as a whole. Because it (potentially) affects the meaning of all other legislation and the legality of all public authority decision-making, there is broad consensus that the HRA has constitutional status in this sense, as is similarly true of the NZBORA in New Zealand. The more controversial issue engages the 'big-C' meaning of constitutional and the possible superiority and/or entrenchment of the HRA vis-à-vis ordinary statutes. It is controversial because on one view any such hierarchy of statutes is inconsistent with the traditional overarching constitutional principle of parliamentary sovereignty and its conventional implication that the one

[13] See *R. (Al-Jedda)* v. *Secretary of State for Defence* [2007] QB 621 [96] in which the Court of Appeal upheld the Divisional Court's finding that if Article 5 of the ECHR is qualified as a matter of international law by subsequent UN Security Council Resolutions, it is also qualified under the HRA.

[14] For an excellent discussion of the various positions, see Hickman, *Public Law After the Human Rights Act*, pp. 30–46.

thing Parliament cannot do is bind its successors. Indeed, this discussion over the status of the HRA is part of a more general, pre-existing debate about whether there are such things as 'constitutional statutes' in this sense in the UK. In *Thoburn*, Laws L. J. stated that constitutional statutes have superior status to ordinary statutes, in that they are not subject to the normal doctrine of implied repeal by later conflicting statutes, but can only be amended or repealed expressly.[15] As such, they are entrenched in a way or to a degree that ordinary statutes are not. Accordingly, this second issue has tended to revolve around the specific claim that the HRA is immune from implied repeal. Proponents of the claim argue that, unlike ordinary statutes, provisions of the HRA are not impliedly repealed by subsequent conflicting statutes, because section 3 mandates that such statutes be given an HRA-compatible interpretation if possible – and, if not, courts may issue a declaration of incompatibility under section 4.[16] Those opposing or sceptical of the claim argue that the HRA is subject to implied repeal like any other statute because, regardless of whether Parliament expressly addresses the issue, if the provision of a later statute cannot be interpreted consistently with the HRA under section 3, the courts must apply it. In effect, section 3 is the functional equivalent of the conventional principle of statutory interpretation that implied repeal is the last resort, employed only where courts first attempt to, but cannot, interpret the later statute consistently with the earlier one.[17]

II   The HRA in operation

Once again, let us review the working of the new model's three stages in order. The general function of pre-enactment political rights review, of course, is to reduce reliance on courts by introducing earlier, alternative modes and sites of review that help to ensure either that laws violating protected rights are not enacted or, if they are, that the process is undertaken deliberately and deliberatively, with eyes wide open. As with the

---

[15] *Thoburn* v. *Sunderland City Council* (2003) QB 151. Laws L. J. stated that only 'express words in the later statute, or … words so specific that the inference of an actual determination to affect the result contended for was irresistible' can repeal a provision of a constitutional statute. *Ibid.* at [63].

[16] See, e.g., Kavanagh, *Constitutional Review*, pp. 293–303. Although, unlike an ordinary statute, the HRA does not impliedly repeal an inconsistent earlier statute under section 4(2), the argument is that section 3 achieves the same result through interpretation.

[17] See Hickman, *Public Law After the Human Rights Act*, pp. 46–8; Young, *Parliamentary Sovereignty*, ch. 2.

Charter and the NZBORA, the reporting duty placed on the specified government minister in the early stages of a bill's passage through the legislature is the legal trigger for various strands of pre-enactment political rights review under the HRA. As we have seen, the HRA differs from these two by imposing a duty to make a statement in all cases, rather than only in cases of incompatibility, and by placing it on the responsible minister rather than the Attorney General. Section 19's requirement that the minister make either a compatibility statement or a 'nevertheless statement' before second reading has resulted in four chronological stages of review. These are: (1) pre-introductory executive review; (2) section 19 statement practice; (3) scrutiny by the specialized parliamentary committee, the Joint Committee on Human Rights (JCHR); and (4) subsequent parliamentary deliberation.

The impact of the requirement that the minister state his or her understanding of a bill's compatibility with Convention rights before second reading begins at the policy development stage, at least as a matter of procedure. Current Cabinet Office guidelines state that standard practice when preparing policy initiatives is for officials to consider the impact of the proposed policy on people's Convention rights. 'Such consideration must not be left to legal advisors . . . or to a last-minute "compliance exercise".'[18] It was decided that rather than delegate the task of assessing compatibility of all bills to a specialist bureaucratic body, as in Canada and New Zealand, it was preferable to broaden awareness of rights by spreading responsibility among departments. Before a bill is formally drafted, the guidelines specify that departmental lawyers are required to prepare an ECHR Memorandum, which must be cleared with the Law Officers and presented with the proposed bill to the Cabinet's Legislation Committee when approval is sought for inclusion in the government's legislative programme.[19] This memorandum:

> Should cover the human rights raised, with a frank assessment by the department of the vulnerability to challenge in legal and policy terms . . .
> [It] should address the weaknesses as well as the strengths in the department's position. It need not, however, be a compendious discussion of the case law. What is needed is a clear and succinct statement of the human rights considerations and the justification in ECHR terms for any interference . . . Departmental legal advisors should prepare the Memorandum with input from policy officials.[20]

---

[18] Legislation Secretariat, *Guide to Making Legislation* (London: Cabinet Office, 2010), 12.6.
[19] *Ibid.*, 12.8.   [20] *Ibid.*, 12.9–12.11.

The 2006 review of the implementation of the HRA by the Department of Constitutional Affairs concluded that 'the HRA had had a significant, but beneficial, effect upon the development of policy by central Government'.[21] According to Lord Lester, a former member of the JCHR, 'few, if anyone, in Whitehall or Westminster appreciated just how significant the practical impact of [the section] 19 procedure would be upon the preparation and interpretation of proposed legislation'.[22] How much of this impact is substantive – in terms of changing or defeating policy proposals – and not only procedural is hard to determine, given the norms of confidentiality. It is clear, however, that legal advice and the issue of what will likely succeed before the courts, domestic and the ECtHR, predominates over other considerations, although the current guidelines reflect a clear attempt to reduce the primacy of this perspective.[23] There is also a widespread perception that governments are most amenable to substantive amendment on rights grounds at this early stage of the legislative process before they have already committed themselves to the bill.[24]

In terms of section 19 statements, previous versions of the Cabinet Office guidelines provided that ministers are to form their view 'on the basis of appropriate legal advice' and that a bill can only be deemed compatible if, 'at a minimum, the balance of [legal] argument supports the view that the provisions are compatible' or if 'it is more likely than not that the provisions of the bill will stand up to challenge on Convention grounds before the domestic courts and the Strasbourg Court'.[25] The current version, however, contains no such specific criteria for the ministerial assessment of compatibility, stating that although 'departmental legal advisors will take the lead in

---

[21] Department of Constitutional Affairs, *Review of the Implementation of the Human Rights Act* (London: Department of Constitutional Affairs, 2006), p. 1.

[22] A. Lester and K. Taylor, 'Parliamentary Scrutiny of Human Rights', in A. Lester and D. Pannick (eds.), *Human Rights Law and Practice*, Second Edition (London: LexisNexis, 2004), p. 600.

[23] J. Hiebert, 'Parliament and the HRA: Can the JCHR Facilitate a Culture of Human Rights?' (2006) 4 *International Journal of Constitutional Law* 1; J. Hiebert, 'Governing Under the Human Rights Act: The Limitations of Wishful Thinking' (2012) *Public Law* 27, 35; F. Klug and H. Wildbore, 'Breaking New Ground: the Joint Committee on Human Rights and the Role of Parliament in Human Rights Compliance' (2007) *European Human Rights Law Review* 231.

[24] See Hiebert, 'Governing Under the Human Rights Act'. This is one major reason the JCHR changed its practice to consider legislative proposals at an earlier stage, see text below accompanying nn. 33–4.

[25] Cabinet Office Constitution Secretariat, *Human Rights Act 1998: Guidance for Departments* (London: Home Office, 2000), para. 36.

providing the formal advice required to justify such statements', it is the minister's 'personal assurance' that is called for.[26]

Thus far, only once has the responsible minister issued a section 19(1)(b) 'nevertheless statement' of incompatibility on introducing a government bill – reflecting a strong presumption against doing so.[27] This was in December 2002 regarding the Communications Bill, and was issued only with respect to clause 309, the provision maintaining the blanket ban on paid political advertisements on television and radio that had been in place since 1927. The responsible minister, Tessa Jowell, stated that the reason for being unable to certify compatibility was a 2001 ECtHR decision in a case against Switzerland, finding that a blanket ban violated Article 10 of the ECHR.[28] After several rounds of correspondence with ministers and in the course of two reports on the bill, the JCHR was eventually satisfied that the government had shown proper respect for human rights and that its action was legitimate. The bill was duly enacted with clause 309 intact and eventually adjudged compatible with Article 10 of the ECHR by the House of Lords Judicial Committee in proceedings for a declaration of incompatibility.[29] Their Lordships unanimously found that the blanket ban was 'necessary in a democratic society' and proportionate, despite the prior ECtHR decision, in which Lord Bingham did 'not think the full strength of this argument [the pressing need to maintain a level playing field and protect against the mischief of 'partial' political advertising] was deployed'.[30]

It has been suggested that this small number of incompatibility statements reflects the more partisan nature of the reporting procedure in the UK than New Zealand, as the responsible minister has a conflict of interest – given that a compatibility statement will ease the bill's passage – as compared with the more independent Attorney-General.[31] On the other hand, it may be that the responsible minister has greater political clout in the Cabinet than the chief legal advisor, and more at stake personally to ensure that identified

---

[26] *Guide to Making Legislation*, 12.14 and 12.15.

[27] Janet Hiebert cites two other section 19(1)(b) statements with respect to amendments proposed by the House of Lords to the previously introduced Civil Partnership Bill (2004) and the Local Government Bill (2000). Hiebert, 'Governing Under the Human Rights Act', n. 49.

[28] *VgT Verein gegen Tierfabriken* v. *Switzerland* (2001) EHRR 159.

[29] *R. (on the application of Animal Defenders International)* v. *Secretary of State for Culture, Media and Sport* [2008] UKHL 15. After this decision, the appellant lodged an application with the ECtHR and a Grand Chamber decision is imminent at the time of writing.

[30] *Ibid.* at [29].

[31] I. Leigh and R. Masterman, *Making Rights Real: The Human Rights Act in its First Decade* (Oxford: Hart Publishing, 2008), pp. 31–2.

rights concerns are addressed before a bill is introduced. Moreover, the task is handled by the Attorney General in Canada, where there has never been even a single incompatibility statement.

The initial practice of the government in making its otherwise invariable compatibility statement was the minimalist one of stating compatibility without giving reasons, which are not required by section 19, on the basis of concerns over the confidentiality of legal advice. However, following early practice of the JCHR in probing the reasons through correspondence with departments and publishing its conclusions, as well as the committee's direct requests that it do so, the government has, since 2002, routinely included fuller statements of reasons in the explanatory notes published with bills. More recently still, it has become increasingly common for departments to supply the JCHR with even more detailed human rights memoranda.[32]

The clearly distinctive feature of pre-enactment review under the HRA is the role of the JCHR. Established as a rare, permanent joint committee of both Houses of Parliament in January 2001, four months after the HRA came into effect, the characteristics that distinguish the JCHR from the parliamentary committees with rights responsibilities in Canada and New Zealand are that it is (1) fully and exclusively specialized on human rights,[33] (2) mostly non-partisan and relatively independent of the government, and (3) aided in its work by a high-quality, full-time legal adviser. The general perception of the JCHR's independence results from the fact that the government does not have an automatic majority on the committee due to its composition of equal numbers of MPs and peers, the tradition of joint parliamentary committees being used to handle bipartisan questions and acting mostly by consensus, and the seniority and experience of some of its members. Further enhancing its perceived independence, stature and effectiveness has been the employment of a highly regarded, full-time legal adviser: initially Professor David Feldman and, since 2004, public law barrister Murray Hunt.

During its first six years, the JCHR made a decision to focus primarily on scrutinizing bills introduced into Parliament and examining the

---

[32] M. Hunt, 'The Impact of the Human Rights Act on the Legislature: a Diminution of Democracy or a New Voice for Parliament?' (2010) 6 *European Human Rights Law Review*, 601, 607.

[33] The JCHR is a specialized select committee with terms of reference that limit it exclusively, albeit broadly, to matters concerning human rights, and not to legal/constitutional affairs generally (as in Canada). In New Zealand, the task is assigned to an ordinary subject-matter select committee.

justification for the government's section 19 statements, as well as assessing its responses to judicial declarations of incompatibility and adverse ECtHR judgments. Typically, the legal adviser screened all bills to flag rights issues, the JCHR would enter into correspondence with the relevant minister in an attempt to evaluate the basis for the section 19 statement and issue one or more reports on the rights implications of the bill, including suggested amendments, to aid subsequent parliamentary deliberations. The seriousness of the JCHR's scrutiny has also undoubtedly acted as an incentive to enhance the quality of the government's section 19 and pre-legislative rights review. Apart from initial reluctance by the government to disclose the reasons for its compatibility statements, the JCHR has faced the twin problems that the government's often hurried legislative timetable does not provide sufficient time for Parliament to digest its reports and the reality that the government is rarely willing to significantly change the content of its bills after the section 19 stage unless it faces substantial political opposition.[34] Consequently, the direct or quantifiable influence of its reports on bills has generally not been great. The Klug-Wildbore study conducted for the JCHR in 2006 found that during the 2005–6 session of Parliament, there were fifty-nine references to the work of the committee in House of Commons debates, of which 45 per cent had 'significant impact' on the debate. The numbers in House of Lords debates were 118 and 60 per cent respectively. Of approximately 500 bills considered by the JCHR since its inception, the study calculated that eighteen were amended as a likely result of its reports. The study, however, found exceptions to this general picture, with the JCHR having greater substantive impact on three important bills in particular: the Anti-Terrorism, Crime and Security Act 2001, the Civil Partnership Act 2004 and the Equality Act 2006.[35]

Since this study was conducted, the JCHR has concluded in its reports that both the increased limit on pre-charge detention of terrorist suspects to ninety days under the 2006 Terrorism Bill and to forty-two days under the 2008 Counter-Terrorism Bill were incompatible with Convention rights,[36] and both extensions were ultimately defeated in the parliamentary process – although the JCHR was clearly not the only source of opposition to these measures. Moreover, a recent empirical study has shown a 'dramatic increase' in the number of references to

[34] Hiebert, 'Governing Under the Human Rights Act', p. 40.
[35] As described by the authors in Klug and Wildbore, 'Breaking New Ground'.
[36] The JCHR issued six reports on the 2008 bill.

JCHR reports in parliamentary debates, from twenty-three over the course of the 2000–5 Parliament to 1,006 during 2005–10.[37] These were made by 241 members of Parliament, although a disproportionate number came from the House of Lords and from ten 'high- and medium-frequency users' in the Commons.[38] At least sixteen of these references resulted in the government offering or agreeing to offer amendments to a bill based on recommendations in JCHR reports.[39]

Based in part on the Klug-Wildbore study's recommendations for solving the two identified problems, the JCHR announced a change in its working practices in July 2006.[40] Since that time, the committee has taken a more selective approach to scrutinizing current bills, focusing and reporting only on those raising the most significant human rights issues, while spending more time and resources on the government's future legislative programme over which it may have more direct influence, especially White Papers and Green Papers. The JCHR has also responded to another of the study's criticisms, that it was too focused on legal views and second-guessing what the courts will do, rather than expressing its own independent judgment on some of the underlying political and moral issues involved and thereby helping Parliament to do likewise. As a result, it has tended to spend more time on the proportionality part of the rights analysis than before.[41] Finally, the JCHR adopted a policy of proposing specific amendments to bills based on its stated concerns and recommendations, which have been moved and debated on the floor of both Houses, accounting for some of the increased references to its reports.[42]

In terms of subsequent parliamentary debate and action, whilst it is true that the HRA did not prevent the enactment of several draconian, post- 9/11 and 7/7 national security statutes,[43] there have been a few notable examples of successful parliamentary opposition to provisions in such government bills that raised particularly clear and obvious rights concerns, although no section 19(1)(b) statements were made by the responsible ministers. In each case, the concerns had been raised by the JCHR, although, again, attributing causal effect is difficult because it was

---

[37] Hunt, Hooper and Yowell, 'Parliaments and Human Rights: Redressing the Democratic Deficit', pp. 19–22.

[38] Ibid., pp. 24–6.   [39] Ibid., p. 43.   [40] Klug and Wildbore, 'Breaking New Ground'.

[41] Ibid.; Hunt, 'The Impact of the Human Rights Act', p. 603.

[42] Hunt et al., 'Parliaments and Human Rights', p. 22.

[43] Keith Ewing makes this point as part of his claim that the HRA has been futile. See Ewing, The Futility of the Human Rights Act'.

hardly the only voice in opposition.[44] In its Asylum and Immigration Bill of 2003/4, the Blair Government included the highly controversial clause 11, which ousted the jurisdiction of the courts to review or hear appeals from decisions of the new Asylum and Immigration Tribunal.[45] The bill met with outrage from lawyers and judges, with the Lord Chief Justice, Lord Woolf, stating that the courts would refuse to apply it if enacted. Relying on its huge majority, the bill passed the House of Commons, but the government withdrew the provision when it became clear that it would likely be voted down in the House of Lords.

Although the 2005 Prevention of Terrorism Bill, introduced in response to the House of Lords' decision in *A and others*,[46] was enacted in an extremely swift eighteen days (due to the imminent expiration of the 2001 Act under which A and others were being detained), it produced the longest session in House of Lords' history (thirty hours) and was passed only with a commitment from the government to review the control order regime in a year's time. The following year, in its Terrorism Bill, the government attempted to increase the limit on pre-trial detention of terrorism suspects from the existing fourteen days to ninety. The JCHR report found that this was 'clearly disproportionate' and so in violation of Article 5 of the ECHR and, indeed, that the case for *any* extension had not been made.[47] A rebellion by Labour MPs resulted in a rare defeat for the government in the House of Commons,[48] which eventually agreed to a compromise extension to twenty-eight days.

Finally, in 2008, Gordon Brown's Government again sought an extension, this time to forty-two days. In one of its six full reports on the Counter-Terrorism Bill, the JCHR found the government had not made the necessary compelling case required by Article 5 for any additional

---

[44] Indeed, this applies equally to the HRA itself, for it could certainly be argued – and is impossible to disprove – that such opposition would have occurred anyway, absent the HRA.

[45] The proposed clause 11(7) of the Asylum and Immigration (Treatment of Claimants, etc.) Bill 2003 stated, *inter alia*: '(1) No court shall have any supervisory or other jurisdiction ... in relation to the [Asylum and Immigration] Tribunal. (2) No court may entertain proceedings for questioning (whether by way of appeal or otherwise) – any determination, decision or other action of the Tribunal'.

[46] *A and others* v. *Secretary of State for the Home Department* [2004] UKHL 56 ('the *Belmarsh* case').

[47] JCHR, Counter-Terrorism Policy and Human Rights: Terrorism Bill and related matters (Third Report of Session 2005–6), 5 December 2005, p. 4.

[48] The Labour Government suffered only six defeats on the floor of the House of Commons after the HRA's adoption. 'Government Defeats on the Floor of the House of Commons', available at: www.election.demon.co.uk/defeats.html.

extension.[49] Another Labour rebellion followed a five-hour House of Commons debate, with the Government narrowly avoiding defeat only because of the likely bargained-for votes of the Ulster Unionists, and the extension was eventually defeated in the Lords, with the Government opting to drop it rather than face another difficult vote in the Commons. Overall, this bill spent ten months in Parliament, during which it was subject to numerous critical reports – not only from the JCHR but also from other committees in each House – and detailed scrutiny. Pre-enactment parliamentary consideration of this bill, along with that of the Communications Act 2003, praised by the House of Lords Judicial Committee,[50] was a model of rights-conscious legislative deliberation, given the twin general constraints of government control and political partisanship of House of Commons proceedings, that sets the standard for all bills.[51]

How has judicial rights review operated under the HRA? Not surprisingly, there has been a range of views on the judicial record.[52] In this section, my aim is to report the most salient facts from the perspective of the new model before discussing and assessing them in the next two. Despite not being bound by general ECtHR jurisprudence in HRA cases but only to take it into account under section 2, the House of Lords established a general policy of following the 'clear and constant' jurisprudence of the ECtHR.[53] In the best-known dicta on this issue, Lord Bingham stated that 'the duty of the national courts is to keep pace with the Strasbourg jurisprudence as it evolves over time: no more, but certainly no less'.[54] His reasons were that under section 6, the courts are required to act compatibly with Convention rights and that as an international instrument the Convention should be uniform throughout the states party to it.[55]

Although certain more recent cases might appear to cast doubt on the Supreme Court's continuing commitment to either half of this 'mirror principle',[56] it seems unlikely that it will be discarded as a general or

---

[49] JCHR, Counter-Terrorism Policy and Human Rights: 42 days (Second Report of Session 2007–08), 14 December 2007, p. 4.

[50] *Animal Defenders International* at [13]–[21].

[51] This view is also expressed in A. Tomkins, 'The Role of Courts in the Political Constitution' (2011) 60 *University of Toronto Law Journal* 1, 3, 19.

[52] These are reported in the following section, as is my own.

[53] *R. (Alconbury Developments Ltd)* v. *Secretary of State for the Environment* [2001] UKHL 23 at [26].

[54] *R. (on the application of Ullah)* v. *Special Administrator* [2004] UKHL 26 at [20].

[55] *Ibid.*

[56] The term is used in J. Lewis, 'The European Ceiling on Human Rights' (2007) Public Law 720.

starting presumption. On the 'certainly no less' side, in the context of the admissibility of hearsay evidence where the victim died before trial and so could not be called to give evidence, the Supreme Court held that it need not apply a recent ECtHR decision under Article 6 announced in a case against the UK where it had concerns as to whether the Strasbourg Court sufficiently appreciated the particular protections within the common law criminal trial.[57] But it only did so after extended justification for its departure. Moreover, the House of Lords' judgment a few months earlier in the control order case of *AF* strongly suggested that it considered its hands tied by a decision of the ECtHR granting greater minimum procedural rights under Article 6 than their Lordships had previously indicated that Article to require.[58] On the 'no more' side, the House of Lords held that unmarried couples seeking to adopt will be able to claim rights against discrimination under the HRA that have not yet been recognized explicitly by the ECtHR, which views them as falling within the margin of appreciation.[59] More recently, the Supreme Court held that the state's duty to protect the life of an individual under Article 2 ECHR was owed to a voluntarily admitted, mentally ill hospital patient, despite the absence of any specifically relevant Strasbourg jurisprudence.[60] At least in this context where no opposing rights appear to be in play, a more liberal domestic interpretation of Convention rights is unlikely to result in a subsequent ECtHR judgment against the UK.

Unsurprisingly, the majority of HRA litigation has involved section 6 and claims that one public authority or another – from government ministers to school principals – has violated an individual's Convention rights in a decision affecting the claimant. Where the courts agree, they have the power to quash the decision, except where mandated by primary legislation that cannot be interpreted consistently with the rights.[61] With respect to such cases, and particularly regarding the

---

[57] *R. v. Horncastle* [2009] UKSC 14 (rejecting the test that hearsay evidence cannot be the 'sole or decisive' basis for a conviction announced by the ECtHR a few months earlier in a different case against the UK, *Al-Khawaja and Tahery* v. *United Kingdom* (2009) 49 EHRR 1, which at the time was under appeal to the Grand Chamber). Subsequently, the Grand Chamber accepted some of the criticism in *Horncastle* and overturned the decision of the initial chamber, [2011] ECHR 26766/05 (15 December 2011).

[58] *Secretary of State for Home Department* v. *AF (No. 3)* [2009] UKHL 28, applying the ECtHR decision in *A and others* v. *United Kingdom* (Application No 3455/05) and reconsidering its previous decision in *Secretary of State for the Home Department* v. *MB* [2007] UKHL 46.

[59] *Re P* [2008] UKHL 38.

[60] *Rabone & Anor* v. *Pennine Care NHS Trust* [2012] UKSC 2.   [61] HRA, section 6(2).

proportionality part of the analysis, the House of Lords established that the object of review is the substance of the decision, rather than the procedure by which it is made – except, of course, where there is an independent claim to a fair hearing under Article 6 of the ECHR – thereby resolving a previously outstanding issue.[62]

Turning to the impact of the two new judicial powers on primary legislation, they have been employed roughly equally, with approximately forty pieces of legislation effectively found in final judgments of the courts not to be compatible with Convention rights.[63] That is, where the courts have relied on either the section 3 interpretive power to render the provision compatible with a right where it was not under initial, more conventional modes of statutory interpretation, or on section 4 to make a declaration of incompatibility. The general methodology of the courts, following both the language of the HRA and the admittedly non-conclusive legislative history during its enactment, is that where the ordinary or conventional meaning of a statutory provision is incompatible with a Convention right, to use section 3 as the 'primary remedy' where 'possible' and only if it is not, to use section 4.[64]

In terms of the line between the two, for which there is of course no further guidance in the HRA itself other than the clear and immediate implication in section 3(2) that there are limits to the interpretive power,[65] a certain amount of stability appears to have taken hold in the applicable principles over the past several years following a flurry of divergent and not easily reconcilable viewpoints in the earlier cases. This is not to deny that there are still differences among judges as to the proper strength of the interpretive duty or, of course, on its application in particular cases,[66] but there seems to be more of a judicial consensus

---

[62] *R. (on the application of Begum)* v. *Headteacher and Governors of Denbigh High School* [2006] UKHL 15; *Belfast City Council* v. *Miss Behavin' Ltd* [2007] 1 WLR 1420.

[63] There have been nineteen final declarations of incompatibility, see text below. I have not seen or calculated the precise number of uses of section 3, but Sedley L. J. stated there had been 'not more than a dozen cases' in the first five years of the HRA, the 'same number as declarations of incompatibility', and Aileen Kavanagh wrote that section 3 has been used 'in a small number of cases in the first ten years of the HRA's existence'. Accordingly, I am estimating roughly twenty uses in total. S. Sedley, 'No Ordinary Law,' *London Review of Books*, 5 June 2008, 20. Kavanagh, 'Constitutional Review', pp. 116–17.

[64] See *R.* v. *A (No. 2)* [2002] 1 AC 45; *Ghaidan* v. *Godin-Mendoza* [2004] UKHL 30; *Sheldrake* v. *Director of Public Prosecutions* [2004] UKHL 43.

[65] By referring to the continuing validity of incompatible legislation, section 3(2) implies that some legislation cannot be interpreted compatibly with Convention rights.

[66] See Samuels, 'Human Rights Act 1998 Section 3: A New Dimension to Statutory Interpretation?', p. 138.

on the extent and limits of the mandatory section 3 duty/power than before. As influentially summarized by Lord Bingham in *Sheldrake*,[67] the leading case remains *Ghaidan* v. *Godin-Mendoza*,[68] in which the majority opinions affirmed that the 'interpretative obligation under section 3 is a very strong and far reaching one, and may require the court to depart from the legislative intention of Parliament'.[69] They also set out two limits to section 3, situations in which a Convention-consistent interpretation is not possible: (1) where such an interpretation is incompatible with a 'fundamental feature', 'cardinal principle' or the 'underlying thrust' of the legislation, or (2) where it would go beyond modification of the particular statutory language at issue and require the court to engage in broader, effectively legislative deliberation or law reform that is the province of Parliament.[70] In his summary, Lord Bingham also made clear that in his view, the decision in *Ghaidan* had narrowed the arguably still broader and more controversial view of the section 3 power in the 2001 case of *R* v. *A*,[71] which had suggested that only a *'clear* limitation in Convention rights ... stated *in terms'* would render use of section 3 impossible.[72] Accordingly, the test is not really one of 'possibility' *per se*, but rather the overall appropriateness of using section 3 bearing in mind the difference between judicial and legislative law-making.[73]

One case in which the House of Lords explicitly discussed the merits of using section 3 versus section 4 and decided on the former – although not without reservation by Lord Bingham and condemnation by the JCHR[74]– was *Secretary of State for the Home Department* v.

---

[67] [2004] UKHL 43 at [28].   [68] [2004] UKHL 30.   [69] *Sheldrake* at [28].

[70] *Ghaidan* at [33], [49], [110]–[113], [116], summarized in *Sheldrake, ibid.*

[71] 'This opinion [*R.* v. *A*] must now be read in the light of the later decision of the House in *Ghaidan* v. *Godin-Mendoza'. Sheldrake* at [24].

[72] 'A declaration of incompatibility is a measure of last resort. It must be avoided unless it is plainly impossible to do so. If a *clear* limitation of Convention rights is stated *in terms*, such an impossibility will arise'. *R.* v. *A (No.2)* at [44], *per* Steyn L.J. (emphases in original). The implication here, is that *only* such an express limitation will render the use of section 3 impossible.

[73] Kavanagh, 'Constitutional Review', p. 90.

[74] The JCHR sharply criticized the House of Lords for using section 3 rather than section 4, claiming it had ignored both the deliberate mandatory language of the control order legislation and the HRA's scheme of 'democratic human rights protection', giving Parliament 'a central role in deciding how best to protect' ECHR rights. According to the JCHR, it would have been more consistent with this scheme to have used section 4, requiring Parliament to think again about the balance it struck in the legislation between national security and civil liberties. JCHR, *Counter-Terrorism Policy and Human Rights*, Ninth Report of Session 2007–8, 7 February 2008, pp. 17–19.

MB,[75] one of the three first-round control order cases. Here, the majority judgment read into the 2005 Prevention of Terrorism Act procedural provisions for judicial review a qualification that closed evidence is not to be used where this would deprive the controlee of a fair hearing under Article 6 of the ECHR. One example of the reverse situation, where the House of Lords explicitly rejected the use of section 3 in favour of section 4, is *R. (Wright)* v. *Secretary of State for Health*.[76] Here, their Lordships concluded that the interpretative solution devised by the Court of Appeal to the incompatibility with Article 6 – reading into the statute a provision giving care workers the right to make representations before being placed on a provisional list of persons unsuitable to work with vulnerable adults – would only partially solve the incompatibility, and so required a new legislative scheme.[77] Overall, as already mentioned, despite the strength of the section 3 duty, it has been used on roughly the same number of occasions as section 4, and there are certainly commentators who have criticized the House of Lords/Supreme Court for not using section 3 more vigorously,[78] just as there are with respect to section 4.[79]

On this latter power, as of the time of writing, twenty-seven declarations of incompatibility have been issued by the higher courts, of which nineteen have become final (i.e., not subject to further appeal) and eight were overturned on appeal. The most recent declaration made or upheld by the Supreme Court was on 22 April 2010, declaring section 82 of the Sexual Offences Act 2003 incompatible with Article 8 of the ECHR,[80] and the most recent by any higher court was made by the Administrative Court on 10 November 2010.[81] Six of the nineteen final declarations concerned provisions in primary legislation enacted by the Labour

---

[75] [2007] UKHL 46.   [76] [2009] UKHL 3.   [77] *Ibid.* at [29].

[78] See, e.g., G. Phillipson, '(Mis)-Reading Section 3 of the Human Rights Act' (2003) 119 *Law Quarterly Review* 183; G. Phillipson, 'Deference, Discretion, and Democracy in the Human Rights Era' (2006) *Current Legal Problems* 40. Tom Hickman describes the House of Lords' non-use of section 3 in *Bellinger* v. *Bellinger* as 'weak and deferential'. Hickman, 'Public Law', p. 94.

[79] See, e.g., D. Nicol, 'Law and Politics after the Human Rights Act' (2006) *Public Law* 722.

[80] *R. (on the application of F and Angus Aubrey Thompson)* v. *Secretary of State for the Home Department* [2010] UKSC 17 (upholding declaration made by the Court of Appeal).

[81] *R. (on the application of Royal College of Nursing)* v. *Secretary of State for Home Department* [2010] EWHC 2761.

Government that established the HRA, four of which have been issued since the *Belmarsh* case.[82]

Turning to the third stage, under the HRA, of course, Parliament retains the legal authority to have the final word in response to both judicial interpretative decisions under section 3, which it can override,[83] and declarations of incompatibility under section 4, which it can leave 'unremedied'. As yet, Parliament has not overridden a section 3 interpretation per se, although it has overruled what it perceived to be judicial error in the interpretation of the HRA itself when it enacted section 145 of the Health and Social Care Act 2008 in direct response to the House of Lords' decision in *YL* v. *Birmingham City Council*.[84] That case had held that a private care home was not exercising 'functions of a public nature' under section 6 of the HRA and so was not bound by the Convention rights. As of the time of writing, eighteen of the nineteen final declarations of incompatibility have resulted in amendment or repeal of the relevant provision of primary legislation,[85] and one remains unremedied since it was issued on January 2007. In this case, relying directly on the ECtHR's 2005 judgment in *Hirst* v. *UK (No. 2)*[86] on the same point, the Registration Appeal Court (Scotland) declared the blanket ban on all convicted prisoners voting in parliamentary elections under section 3 of the Representation of the People Act 1983 incompatible with Article 3 of

---

[82] These six are: (1) the penalty scheme contained in Part II of the Immigration and Asylum Act, 1999, declared incompatible with Article 6 and Article 1 of the First Protocol by the Court of Appeal in *International Transport Roth GmbH* v. *Secretary of State for the Home Department* [2002] EWCA Civ 158; (2) section 23 of the Anti-terrorism, Crime and Security Act 2001 in the *Belmarsh* case; (3) section 19(3) of the Asylum and Immigration Act 2004 declared incompatible with Articles 12 and 14 of the ECHR in *R. (on the application of Baiai and others)* v. *Secretary of State for the Home Department* [2008] UKHL 53; (4) section 82(4) of the Care Standards Act 2000 declared incompatible with Articles 6 and 8 in *R. (on the application of June Wright and others* v. *Secretary of State for Health* [2009] UKHL 3; (5) section 82 of the Sexual Offences Act 2003 declared incompatible with Article 8 in *Thompson*; (6) Schedule 3 to Part 1 of the Safeguarding Vulnerable Groups Act 2006 (SVGA) declared incompatible with Article 6 (and potentially also Article 8) ECHR in *Royal College of Nursing*.

[83] As Lord Steyn stated with respect to section 3 in *Ghaidan*: 'If Parliament disagrees with an interpretation by the courts under Section 3(1), it is free to override it by amending the legislation and expressly reinstating the incompatibility.' *Ghaidan* at [63].

[84] [2007] UKHL 27.

[85] Most recently, the Sexual Offences Act 2003 was amended by the Sexual Offences Act 2003 (Remedial) Order 2012 and the SVGA by the Protection of Freedoms Act 2012.

[86] [2005] ECHR 681.

the First Protocol to the ECHR.[87] The former Labour Government responded to the declaration and the ECtHR decision by expressing general, if somewhat equivocal, willingness to amend the law and publishing a second-stage consultation paper on voting rights in 2009.[88] The current government indicated in December 2010 that it was actively considering the issue of prisoners' voting rights, and specifically the introduction of a ban only on those serving terms of four years or more, but subsequently announced it would wait for the ECtHR Grand Chamber judgment in the case of *Scoppola* v. *Italy*,[89] reviewing the Second Section decision of January 2011 that a ban on all three-plus year prisoners was impermissible.[90] The UK sought and was granted authorization to intervene in the Grand Chamber proceedings, in which it invited the court to reconsider its decision in *Hirst*. Although in its 22 May 2012 final judgment the court overturned the chamber decision, finding the Italian three-year ban acceptable and within the margin of appreciation, it reaffirmed that the UK's 'general, automatic and indiscriminate' ban on all prisoners violated Article 3.[91]

Of the eighteen remedied declarations, three have been resolved by remedial orders under section 10 of the HRA;[92] three had already been resolved by legislation at the time the declaration was made[93]; and twelve have been resolved by subsequent primary legislation.[94] Despite the

[87] 'The High Contracting parties undertake to hold free elections at reasonable intervals by secret ballot, under conditions which ensure the free expression of the opinion of the people in the choice of the legislature.'

[88] Ministry of Justice, *Voting Rights of Convicted Prisoners Detained within the United Kingdom, Second Stage Consultation*, Consultation Paper CP6/09 (2009).

[89] Ministry of Justice, *Responding to Human Rights Judgments: Report to the JCHR* (London: HMSO, September 2011), p. 43.

[90] Case 126/05, judgment of the Second Section of 18 January 2011.

[91] *Scoppola* v. *Italy (No, 3)*, judgment of the Grand Chamber of 22 May 2012. The ECtHR had also postponed the date by which the UK was required to introduce legislation to implement the *Hirst* decision and subsequent pilot judgment in *Greens and MT* v. *UK* [2010] ECHR 1826, until six months from the date of its decision in *Scoppola*, which now expires on 22 November 2012.

[92] These are the declarations made in: (1) *R. (on the application of H) v. Mental Health Review Tribunal for the North and East London Region & the Secretary of State* [2001] EWCA Civ 415, on 28 March 2001; (2) *Baiai*; and (3) *Thompson*.

[93] These were: (1) *R. (on the application of Wilkinson) v. Inland Revenue Commissioners* [2005] UKHL 30; (2) *R. (on the application of Hooper and others) v. Secretary of State for Work and Pensions* [2005] UKHL 29; (3) *R. (Clift) v. Secretary of State for the Home Department* [2007] 1 AC 484; *Secretary of State for the Home Department v. Hindawi and another* [2005] 1 WLR 2004. See *Responding to Human Rights Judgments*.

[94] Most recently by the Protection of Freedoms Act 2012.

official record of remedied declarations, several of the parliamentary responses appear 'minimal' or questionable as to whether they sufficiently address the incompatibility found by the courts. Although there has as yet been no 'second-look' case in which a court has issued a declaration with respect to legislation enacted to remedy a prior declaration,[95] there is published disagreement between the JCHR and the government as to whether legislation fully resolves a declared incompatibility in at least one case.[96]

What of parliamentary responses to declarations of incompatibility? Have there been instances of high-quality, principled debates on the underlying rights issues, regardless of the outcome, or does Parliament appear to be ceding the territory of rights decision-making to the courts? The first thing to be said here is that although there have been nineteen final declarations of incompatibility and so, seemingly, nineteen opportunities for Parliament to debate whether or not to respond and change the law, the reality is that seven of these involved provisions of primary legislation that had either already been (1) adjudged by the ECtHR to violate the ECHR in cases against the UK so that there was a legal obligation to respond, unlike under the HRA itself,[97] or (2) amended or

---

[95] The closest is *Royal College of Nursing*, in which the Administrative Court declared the procedures established in Schedule 3 of the Safeguarding Vulnerable Groups Act 2006 incompatible with Article 6 of the ECHR. The legislation which preceded the SVGA had also been declared incompatible, although only after it had been replaced. *R. (on the application of June Wright and others v. Secretary of State for Health* [2006] EWHC 2886.

[96] *Morris v. Westminster CC* [2005] EWCA Civ 1184. See Ministry of Justice, *Responding to Human Rights Judgments: Government Response to the Joint Committee on Human Rights' Thirty-first Report of Session 2007–08* (London: HMSO, 2009), p. 25.

[97] Again, although under the ECHR this is an international legal duty to respond rather than a domestic one, in the case of a statute found in violation of the Convention by the ECtHR, the result is usually the same in practice: a legal obligation to amend or repeal the statute, as exemplified by both *Dudgeon v. United Kingdom* (1980) 3 EHRR 40 and *Hirst*. The government cannot lawfully remedy the violation and permit Hirst to vote whilst the statute imposing a blanket ban on all voting by prisoners remains unamended. The four declarations in this category are (1) *Bellinger v. Bellinger* [2003] UKHL 23, involving section 11 of the Matrimonial Causes Act 1973, part of the domestic law held to violate Articles 8 and 12 of the ECHR in *Goodwin v. United Kingdom* (1996) 22 EHRR 123; (2) *McR's Application for Judicial Review* [2002] NIQB 58, involving section 62 of the Offences Against the Person Act 1861 (attempted buggery) held to violate Article 8 ECHR in *Dudgeon*; (3) *R. (on the application of M) v. Secretary of State for Health*, involving sections 26 and 29 of the Mental Health Act 1983 held to violate Article 8 ECHR in *JT v. United Kingdom* (2000) ECHR 133, and which the UK promised the ECtHR to amend; (4) *Smith v. Scott* (2007) CSIH 9, involving section 3 of the Representation of the People Act 1983 held to violate Article 3, First Protocol ECHR in *Hirst v. UK*.

repealed by the time the declaration was made.[98] Accordingly, the number of open, undecided, 'hands untied' cases has been relatively small. And of these, few involved the sort of controversial issues about which ordinary voters care very much and so some parliamentary resistance is to be expected. Moreover, at least one of the remaining declarations, the one made in the *Belmarsh* case, involved a fairly clear violation of Convention rights on the specific question at issue, with respect to which parliamentary disagreement would not have been reasonable.[99]

Although Parliament eventually responded to the *Belmarsh* declaration by fully accepting the discrimination point and making the new control order regime applicable regardless of nationality, this new regime, adopted after vigorous (if expedited) debate and the longest session in House of Lords history, reflected something of a pre-emptive compromise on the underlying and broader substantive issue of the permissibility of indefinite detention without trial under Article 5. This compromise was subsequently litigated and substantially accepted by the Judicial Committee in the 'second-look' control order cases.[100]

Undoubtedly the most controversial issue that has been the direct subject of a declaration of incompatibility is prisoners' voting rights, and it is surely no coincidence that this remains the one unremedied declaration, the fate of which cannot (at the time of writing) be taken for granted.[101] More than five years after it was made, no specific bill or remedial order has yet been introduced, and the government's willingness to amend the blanket ban on all prisoner voting to a more limited one, as demanded by the ECtHR and reaffirmed in its recent Grand Chamber decision in *Scoppola* v. *Italy*, is far from certain. On 10 February 2011, three senior

---

[98] See the list in n. 82.

[99] That is, the necessity and proportionality of subjecting only non-UK terrorist suspects to the indefinite detention without trial regime under section 23 of the 2001 Act.

[100] That is, two of the three specific control orders at issue were upheld by the House of Lords in 2007. The most drastic of the three, involving an eighteen-hour curfew, was invalidated as a deprivation of liberty and, in *MB*, the House of Lords used section 3 to read a fair trial limitation into the statutory provision prohibiting the Secretary of State from revealing evidence contrary to the public interest. Since these original control order cases, and prodded into doing so by the ECtHR, the courts have continued to add to the fair trial requirements under Article 6, see *AF No. 3* (2009) and *Secretary of State for the Home Department* v. *AP* [2010] UKSC 24.

[101] A November 2010 public opinion poll reported that 62 per cent of respondents oppose allowing prisoners to vote and 24 per cent support this notion. 'Most Britons Believe Prisoners Should Not Vote in Elections', Angus Reid public poll available at www.angus-reid.com/wp-content/uploads/2010/11/2010.11.22_Prisoner_BRI.pdf.

backbench MPs, including Jack Straw (the Home Secretary when the HRA was enacted), tabled a motion in the House of Commons to retain the existing blanket ban despite the *Hirst* judgment.[102] Following a six-hour debate, in which 'parliamentarians made their own thoughtful constitutional assessment as to whether prisoner voting was a human right'[103] and the overwhelming sense was that the issue should be decided by Parliament and not the courts (domestic or the ECtHR), the non-binding free vote was 234 to 22 in favour of the motion and the status quo of not changing the Representation of the People Act 1983. Given the Prime Minister's stated aversion to seeing prison inmates voting and apparent pledge not to 'succumb' to the ECtHR immediately after its May 2012 decision in *Scoppola*,[104] it remains to be seen whether this will be the first declaration that Parliament chooses to leave unremedied. There seems little doubt that, but for the direct legal obligation and the potential financial and political costs of defiance resulting from the ECtHR's judgments in *Hirst* and, more recently, *Greens and MT*,[105] no action would be taken. And had the Grand Chamber in *Scoppola* ruled in a more ambiguous way, the domestic declaration in *Smith* v. *Scott* would almost certainly now be largely irrelevant.

In addition to the issue of *whether* to respond to a declaration of incompatibility, there have been several principled, high-quality legislative debates on *how* to resolve judicially determined incompatibilities, with Parliament generally fulfilling the expectations of the courts in not using section 3 that it was better placed than they to deliberate on specific procedures/remedies or the required broader 'legislative' change in the law. Thus, for example, the extensive debates on the Mental Health Bill 2007 about the specific procedure to be used to remedy the declared incompatibility with Article 8 (and the prior judgment of the ECtHR in *JT* v. *UK*[106]) of not

---

[102] The debate was partially a response to the ECtHR's point in *Hirst* that no substantive discussion about the continued justification for the blanket ban had taken place in Parliament.

[103] D. Nicol, 'Legitimacy of the Commons Debate on Prisoner Voting' (2011) *Public Law* 681, 691.

[104] 'David Cameron: Britain will decide on votes for prisoners, not a "foreign court"', *Daily Telegraph*, 23 May 2012.

[105] *Greens and MT*, in which the ECtHR affirmed its decision in *Hirst* and applied its 'pilot judgment' procedure to give the UK six months from the date of the decision to introduce legislation removing the blanket ban. This deadline has now been extended to six months following its judgment in *Scoppola*.

[106] Case 26494/95 (2000) ECHR 133.

permitting those detained to challenge unsuitable appointments as their 'nearest relative' were a model of rights-conscious policy-making, taking all relevant and complex factors into account.[107] Similarly deliberative were the parliamentary discussions of the Gender Recognition Act 2004, following the adverse 2002 ECtHR judgment in *Goodwin* v. *UK* and the 2003 declaration of incompatibility in *Bellinger* v. *Bellinger*.[108]

III   Academic commentary on the stability and distinctness of the HRA

Although evaluations of the HRA by academic commentators have ranged across the full spectrum of possible positions – from futility to utility, from too weak to too strong – two critical strands of commentary have emerged as perhaps the most influential. As these two claims about how the HRA is operating in practice directly implicate my general case for the new model, it seems necessary and important to consider them first before presenting my own assessment of the HRA in the next section.

The first claim, an outright critique of how the HRA has operated, is that the record discloses there has been ineffective protection of rights. As expressed by one of its most prominent critics, the HRA has failed to prevent the enactment of rights-violating legislation, and judges have failed to oppose it.[109] Although on the basis of the general debate about the merits of judicial review, considered in Chapter 3, one might have expected that this critique would be voiced by proponents of strong-form judicial review – as underenforcement of rights is the standard concern claimed to justify it – it has in fact mostly been made by sceptics of judicial power. In any event, the basic and fairly familiar story behind the critique is that since the HRA came into effect, civil liberties have been undermined in a way previously unimaginable by a wave of post-9/11, post-7/7 national security legislative measures, notwithstanding the efforts of the JCHR, and a few backbench rebellions here and there. And with essentially the single exception of the *Belmarsh* case, the courts have done a poor job of protecting rights against claims of national security, in particular, both before and since that case. Examples of

---

[107] For details of these parliamentary debates, see Young, 'Is Dialogue Working', pp. 781–5.

[108] [2003] UKHL 21. For details, see *ibid.*

[109] Ewing, 'The Futility of the Human Rights Act'; K. Ewing, *The Bonfire of the Liberties* (Oxford University Press, 2010).

post-*Belmarsh* decisions of the House of Lords/Supreme Court rejecting rights claims under the HRA in the national security context are *Gillan* on police powers of stop and search,[110] two of the three first-round control order cases,[111] *Al Jedda* on British military detention in Iraq,[112] and *RB* on deportation, unfair trials and evidence derived from torture.[113] For Ewing, this record is the result of a culture of deference to the government on the part of the courts and the continuing pull of traditional parliamentary sovereignty, so that it would seem to confirm Mark Tushnet's instability/reversion thesis in this direction, although others have provided different explanations.[114] In addition to specific decisions, there have been complaints of disappointing judicial 'minimalism' in the methodology employed by the courts in binding themselves to the 'mirror principle', rather than the 'generous' and 'purposive' judicial interpretation of rights in Canada and New Zealand.[115]

The second influential claim is that in practice, the HRA has proven to be less distinctive from US-style constitutionalism than initially claimed or hoped; that it has created de facto judicial supremacy. If justified, this claim would confirm Mark Tushnet's prediction of instability and reversion in the opposite direction from Ewing's futility thesis, and also from the argument discussed in the NZBORA context. This second assessment posits a major gap between form and substance, theory and practice, or between how the HRA seems and what it really is. In

---

[110] R. (on the application of Gillan and another) v. Commissioner of Police for the Metropolis and another [2006] UKHL 12.

[111] MB; Secretary of State for the Home Department v. E and another [2007] UKHL 47.

[112] R. (on the application of Al-Jeddah) v. Secretary of State for Defence [2007] UKHL 58 (holding that UN Security Council Resolutions authorized British military detention without trial in Iraq and limited the application of Article 5 ECHR).

[113] RB and another v. Secretary of State for the Home Department [2009] UKHL 10 (ruling that the UK could deport RB to Jordan where he was convicted *in absentia* allegedly on the basis of evidence obtained by torture). See Ewing, Bonfire of the Liberties; A. Tomkins, 'National Security and the Role of the Court: A Changed Landscape?' (2010) 126 Law Quarterly Review 543, 544. Most of these cases are the subject of applications to the ECtHR.

[114] See A. Tomkins, 'The Rule of Law in Blair's Britain' (2007) 26 University of Queensland Law Journal 255 (suggesting that judges have generally been assertive rather than deferential with their new powers, just not in a particularly rights-protective way).

[115] E.g., I. Leigh, 'Concluding Remarks' in H. Fenwick, G. Phillipson and R. Masterman (eds.), Judicial Reasoning under the UK Human Rights Act (Cambridge University Press, 2007) at 443 ('Minimalism is the dominant mode of (judicial) reasoning. An interim term report [of the judiciary's performance] would be along the lines of "tries hard, could do better".'). See also Masterman, 'Aspiration or Foundation? The Status of the Strasbourg Jurisprudence and the "Convention Rights" in Domestic Law'.

particular, it suggests that the formal restraints on the judiciary have become largely illusory. As a result, the theoretical distinction between strong-form judicial review, as in Germany and the US, and the HRA's weak-form judicial review has proven itself to be just that: a theoretical distinction without much of a difference in the real world.

According to Ian Leigh and Roger Masterman, 'the governmental responses to . . . declarations of incompatibility have uniformly endorsed and implemented the judicial readings of compatibility put forward. If this is a dialogue at all, it is one in which the judicial voice is beginning to be heard the loudest.'[116] Janet Hiebert states that:

> the conceptual differences between this parliamentary model and the American approach are muted by pervasive doubts about the legitimacy of political rights judgments that differ from judicial perspectives . . . [T]he emerging British assumption that parliamentary sovereignty does not mean that governments should act in a manner inconsistent with judicial interpretations of rights . . . suggests that, for practical purposes, what most distinguishes these bills of rights from the American model is the concept of [pre-enactment] political rights review.[117]

Aileen Kavanagh concludes that '[t]he real distinctiveness of statutory Bills of Rights like the HRA lies in the fact that they seem to give Parliament the last word, whilst nonetheless giving the courts powers of constitutional review, not hugely dissimilar from those possessed by the US Supreme Court.'[118]

For those who supported the HRA as institutionalizing an intermediate model, rendering or accepting this practical verdict amounts to a major source of disappointment that raises serious questions about the possibility of cabining judicial power once released from the bottle of traditional parliamentary sovereignty.[119] By contrast, to those for whom strong-form judicial review is normatively appealing as necessary for the adequate protection of rights, this shedding of the outer skin of weak-form review is a welcome and justified development, and points to the success, not the failure, of the HRA. In other words, the HRA is successful largely because it is not distinctive in practice.[120]

---

[116] Leigh and Masterman, *Making Rights Real*, p. 118.
[117] Hiebert, 'New Constitutional Ideas', p. 1985.
[118] Kavanagh, *Constitutional Review*, p. 418.
[119] See, e.g., Nicol, 'The Human Rights Act and the Politicians'.
[120] Kavanagh, *Constitutional Review*, pp. 416–21.

The evidence adduced in support of this second thesis is mostly twofold. First, all final declarations of incompatibility have either already been remedied by the government, or are expected to be. Accordingly, challenging courts in the UK seems to be as politically impossible as under the section 33 legislative override provision in Canada.[121] Secondly, as a result of treating the section 3 interpretive duty as a very strong one and the primary remedy for rights violations under HRA, courts have (1) not relied on section 4 declarations – the main structural vehicle for the legislative final word – as much as some expected or hoped, (2) effectively subjected Parliament to the Convention rights despite the express wording of section 6; and (3) used section 3 in a way that goes beyond interpretation to the rewriting of statutes. In this way, as essentially the functional equivalent of a strike-down power, it has become the truly distinctive judicial rights-protecting technique under the HRA.[122]

Each of the two assessments just described obviously poses a direct challenge to the HRA as a successful instantiation of the new model. Let me begin by considering the first. On whether there is now a better regime for the protection of rights than before the HRA, 9/11 and its aftermath have undoubtedly complicated the direct comparison by changing the political and regulatory context, so that the new era of global terrorism threat and policy was seen to require permanent, general and more drastic national security responses in place of the temporary and particular ones of the earlier, IRA-focused period. Moreover, it is extremely difficult to assess the complex counterfactual of what protection of rights/liberties would now look like, absent the HRA. Nonetheless, overall it seems to me hard to deny that rights are better protected under the HRA in the following specific ways. There is clearly now greater rights-awareness than before – among citizens, courts, public officials, Parliament and government – and the rights that exist are generally better and more widely known and understood than under the pre-HRA regime of common law rights supplemented by various specific statutory protections and the externally enforced ECHR. Part of this is due, of course, to the HRA's mandatory pre-enactment political rights review, part to the enforced awareness of public authorities bound to act in accordance with Convention rights under section 6, and part to the publicity that certain HRA cases in the courts have attracted. As we have seen, rights also have greater direct impact on the pre-legislative

---

[121] Hiebert, 'New Constitutional Ideas', p. 1984; Kavanagh, *Constitutional Review*, p. 419.
[122] Kavanagh, *ibid.*, p. 418.

and legislative process, certainly in terms of procedure and arguably in terms of substance. There are also more legally recognized rights than before. Pre-HRA, there would likely have been no plausible legal claim for the UK courts to consider in the *Belmarsh* case, as there was no obvious relevant domestic right against statutory discrimination on the basis of citizenship, any more than there was on the basis of sexual orientation in *Fitzpatrick*,[123] the pre-HRA case applying the same statute as in *Ghaidan* with the opposite result. Similarly, it is only since, and under, the HRA that a new tort of 'misuse of private information' has been established.[124] Finally, what you have in virtue of having a right, the nature of the protection it affords, has been enhanced by the HRA. As stated extra-judicially by Lord Bingham, the HRA has brought about:

> a subtle but significant re-calibration of the relationship between the individual and the state ... [Prior to the HRA,] the individual enjoyed no rights which could not be curtailed or removed by an unambiguously drafted statutory enactment or subordinate order, and in important areas, such as freedom of expression and assembly, the individual's right was no more than to do whatever was not prohibited: the right would shrink if the prohibition were enlarged.[125]

As to whether the general regime of rights protection is not only better than pre-HRA, but also adequate or sufficient overall, part of any meaningful analysis here must be comparative and not purely domestic, looking at both strong-form systems of judicial review, and systems without any rights-based judicial review. Although it is true that the subsequent House of Lords/Supreme Court cases noted above have not shown as much commitment to the protection of liberty in the face of the government's national security claims, the *Belmarsh* case was of the highest importance[126] and compares favourably with the fact that the United States Supreme Court would be unlikely to rule in the same way on similar facts,[127] and

---

[123] *Fitzpatrick v. Sterling Housing Association Ltd* [2001] 1 AC 27.

[124] Compare *Kaye v. Robinson* [1991] FSR 62 (UKCA) with *Campbell v. MGN Ltd* [2005] UKHL 61.

[125] Bingham, 'The Human Rights Act', p. 569.

[126] As Aileen Kavanagh explains, part of its importance was the clear rejection for the first time that national security claims are non-justiciable. Kavanagh, 'Constitutionalism, Counterterrorism, and the Courts: Changes in the British Constitutional Landscape'.

[127] By contrast with the *Belmarsh* case, the US Supreme Court stated in 2003 that on the issue of preventative detention, the Constitution permits discrimination against aliens living in the United States. *Denmore v. Hyung Joon Kim* 538 US 510, 522 (2003). See also D. Cole, 'English Lessons: A Comparative Analysis of UK and US Responses to Terrorism' (2009) 62 *Current Legal Problems* 136, 159.

has not yet clearly and unequivocally held that any constitutional rights have been violated by post-9/11 government action – executive or legislative.[128] And if we turn to the bill of rights-free political constitution of Australia at the federal level, the sacrifice of rights and liberties there to national security concerns in more than forty pieces of legislation since 9/11 – including the introduction of control orders, preventative detention orders, and stop and search police powers[129] – has been compared unfavourably to both the UK and Canada in two separate academic studies.[130] Moreover, as we have seen, Parliament did force the government to drop some of the most draconian provisions from its various national security/ terrorism bills. And in an important recent article, Adam Tomkins demonstrates how the relevant courts of first instance – the Administrative Court, the Special Immigrations Appeals Commission and the Proscribed

---

[128] *Boumedienne* v. *Bush*, 553 US 723 (2008) and *Hamdi* v. *Rumsfeld*, 542 US 507 (2004) have come the closest. In *Boumedienne*, the US Supreme Court held that aliens detained at Guantanamo Bay are protected by the constitutional right to habeas corpus and so can raise constitutional claims against their detention by the US government. Cases raising the merits of these claims are making their way through the US federal court system, with several detainees ordered released by the lower courts. Although in *Hamdi* the Supreme Court held that in the case of a US citizen, the due process clause requires some opportunity to challenge the factual basis of the government's determination of enemy combatant status, only the dissenting justices clearly found a constitutional violation in the case.

[129] See N. McGarrity and G. Williams, 'Counter-Terrorism Laws in a Nation without a Bill of Rights: The Australian Experience' (2010) 2 *City University of Hong Kong Law Review* 45.

[130] On the UK, see A. Green, N. Johns and M. Rix, 'Liberty, National Security and the Big Society' 16(2) *Sociological Research Online* 19 ('As in Britain, Australia adopted a raft of counter-terrorism laws that, nevertheless, outstripped the Mother Country's in volume and harshness ... The size and severity of Australia's counter-terrorism regime are completely out of proportion to its level of threat.'), at 4.1–4.2, available at www.socresonline.org.uk/16/ 2/19. But *cf.* Allen, 'Statutory Bills of Rights', p. 121 (comparing maximum seven-day detention of suspected terrorists without charge under Australian federal legislation with twenty-eight-day maximum in the UK). For what it is worth, Allen does not factor in that certain states, including New South Wales, permit detention for an additional seven days, making a fourteen-day maximum. See K. Nesbitt, 'Preventative Detention of Terrorist Suspects in Australia and the United States: A Comparative Constitutional Analysis' (2007) 17 *Public Interest Law Journal* 39, at 75. On Canada, Kent Roach concludes that: 'Although both Australia and Canada responded to 9/11 with broad new anti-terrorism laws, new provisions for the protection of national security information and new police powers, the Canadian response has generally been more restrained and more reflective of rights concerns while the Australian response has generally been more robust and reflective of security concerns'. K. Roach, 'A Comparison of Australian and Canadian Counter-Terrorism Laws' (2007) 30 *University of New South Wales Law Journal* 53–85, at 85.

Organisations Appeal Commission – have kept the *Belmarsh* flame alive by subjecting government actions and decisions taken in the interests of national security to intense judicial review.[131]

If we shift from what Tomkins accurately describes as (and comparative materials confirm to be) 'this most difficult of areas of public law for enforcing the rule of law and for protecting individual liberty',[132] to more general consideration of the rights record, the story of judicial timidity is somewhat belied by the bare numbers. As we have seen, in final judgments UK courts have found approximately forty statutes to be incompatible with Convention rights in the first ten years of the HRA, if uses of section 3 and 4 are combined. This is not an inconsiderable number. Even with respect to the nineteen final declarations of incompatibility alone, this means that UK courts are finding incompatibilities at very roughly the same average rate per year as the Canadian Supreme Court.[133] An increasing percentage of declarations of incompatibility have involved recent government legislation, which was to be expected given the time-lag in the appeals process but also rebuts any suggestion that the courts are choosing easy, older targets in which the ruling government has little at stake. The section 3 interpretative power has obviously been an important judicial tool for the protection of rights, both in the national security context (especially with respect to procedural rights under Article 6) and elsewhere – particularly in such areas as sexual orientation discrimination[134] and reverse onus of criminal proof provisions[135] – and it seems hard to make the general case that it has been meekly used. And, of course, quite apart from its impact on primary legislation, the most important rights-protecting provision of the HRA in practice is section 6. Clearly, the number and type of judicial quashings of rights-violating executive actions and decisions must be taken into account in any overall assessment of the effectiveness of rights protection under the HRA.

Finally, although the 'minimalist' approach of the courts under section 2 announced in *Ullah* – interpreting the HRA as providing no less but also no more protection than given by the Strasbourg Court to the same rights – was disappointing and misguided to some,[136] and (as we have seen) may no longer fully reflect the practice of the Supreme Court, it is important to

---

[131] Tomkins, 'National Security and the Role of the Courts'.   [132] *Ibid.*, p. 545.
[133] As cited above, approximately sixty statutes have been invalidated by the SCC since 1982, or roughly two per year, which is essentially the same rate as final declarations of incompatibility under the HRA.
[134] *Ghaidan.*   [135] *R. v. Lambert* [2002] 2 AC 545.
[136] Lewis, 'The European Ceiling'; Masterman, 'Aspiration or Foundation?'.

appreciate the implications of the 'no less' half.[137] Particularly if the courts chip away at it any further. For what 'no less' entails in practice is that, despite having only the legal duty to take the ECtHR's rights jurisprudence into account, and so the power to reject its interpretations of Convention rights for HRA purposes, UK courts effectively bind themselves to what is widely considered the strongest and most powerful international human rights regime in the world. In terms of adequacy of protection, 'no less' than the ECtHR's interpretation and application of Convention rights may not be perfect, but is not to be sniffed at.

Turning to the de facto judicial supremacy thesis, I believe this strand of commentary contains some important and incisive points about how the HRA has operated during its first decade. Nonetheless, as an overall assessment I think it is significantly overstated and premature, especially to the extent it suggests there is little difference in practice between the HRA and constitutional review in systems of de jure judicial supremacy. In helpfully and properly warning against the dangers of exaggerating these differences, there has been a tendency to overcompensate and unduly minimise them.

In pronouncing the legal differences formal only, those who adopt this general perspective on the HRA sometimes move a little too quickly and fail to consider the matter systemically or comparatively. The first point here is that in conceptualizing the HRA as an intermediate or hybrid form of constitutionalism, it is far from clear that 'hugely dissimilar'[138] judicial powers between it and systems of constitutional supremacy are either claimed or to be expected. Both grant powers of constitutional review with the main difference being the far more limited direct remedial authority under section 4. There is of course a significant gap between claiming that legal differences between the HRA and the model of constitutional supremacy are purely formal, have little or no practical impact, and claiming that there are not huge dissimilarities between the two. Indeed, in her own response to Keith Ewing's futility thesis, Aileen Kavanagh relies in part on the lesser powers of courts under the HRA compared to a 'strike-down power', referring to the 'more limited mechanism of the declaration of incompatibility' and explaining the practical difference this made in the *Belmarsh* case.[139] As a matter of general comparative

---

[137] These implications were noted by Lord Bingham in his speech in the case.

[138] Kavanagh, 'Constitutional Review', p. 418.

[139] A. Kavanagh, 'Judging the Judges under the Human Rights Act: Deference, Disillusionment and the "War on Terror"' (2009) *Public Law* 287, 292.

methodology, it perhaps smoothes over too much – or is too 'similarity oriented'[140] – to deny that lesser differences are significant or relevant. In some of this commentary, the bar for what counts as a genuine difference seems unnecessarily and prohibitively high. So, in this vein, whilst I think it is correct and performs a valuable service to point out that the discontinuity and radical newness of judicial powers under the HRA can and has been exaggerated,[141] any implied chain of reasoning that runs from (a) if the pre-HRA regime was not essentially different from the post-HRA, and (b) if the post-HRA-regime is not essentially different from US-style constitutionalism, then (c) even the pre-HRA regime was not so different from US-style constitutionalism, seems a little forced. For now we seem to be moving towards a discussion not only of whether there is a third, intermediate model of constitutionalism, but whether there are even two; that the legal differences between the 1998 UK version of parliamentary sovereignty and US-style constitutional review are superficial, more about emphasis and techniques than substance, and fall within one and the same model of constitutionalism. More generally, the three models of constitutionalism are – qua models – inherently formal, they are most essentially about different allocations of legal powers among institutions. So whilst it is, of course, appropriate and valuable to ask how these legal powers interact with other factors – such as political culture and context – this is a perennial and distinct issue. Even before the HRA, it was sometimes claimed that protection of rights in the UK was, in practice, not so different from the US, despite the clear – and, in a non-trivial sense, irreducibly important – legal differences between the two constitutional systems.

Secondly, the utility of difference-oriented comparativism aside, I do not think the proponents of this view have (yet) established that the legal differences between the HRA and the 'post-war paradigm' of constitutional supremacy do have little or no practical significance, i.e. that they are merely formal in this sense. This is especially so with regard to the differences in legislative rather than judicial power. Primarily, this is because of both the newness of the HRA and methodological problems in proving counterfactuals. The fact that so far Parliament has not clearly exercised its legal power to disagree with and depart from a judicial

---

[140] M. Lasser, *Judicial Deliberations: A Comparative Analysis of Judicial Transparency and Legitimacy* (Oxford University Press, 2004) 146. For interesting and helpful essays on the sameness/difference dichotomy in comparative legal theory, see P. Legrand and R. Munday (eds.), *Comparative Legal Studies: Traditions and Transitions* (Cambridge University Press, 2003).

[141] Kavanagh, *'Constitutional Review'*, pp. 115–16.

rights decision under sections 3 or 4 is not yet compelling evidence of a political inability to use it. A decade is simply too short to justify this conclusion. Unlike the case generally with constitutional supremacy, we do not yet know the full contours of the interplay between form and substance under the HRA. Although, as we have seen, the more difficult-to-use version of the legislative power in Canada under section 33 of the Charter – in which the default position lies in favour of the courts – has lain largely dormant in recent years, overall it has been employed more often than is generally thought.[142] Were the Supreme Court of Canada to decide a case that triggered the degree of controversy marked by certain judicial decisions in other countries with full constitutional supremacy, there is no reason to think the override power might not come back into play. Just as section 33 is not yet the equivalent of the Royal Assent, neither is Parliament's power to retain legislation declared incompatible with rights by the courts, as the prisoners' voting rights issue reminds us.

Indeed, moving even more fully into counterfactual territory by focusing on these types of controversial judicial decisions and looking now at the other side of the equation, it seems hard to accept that if the US or Germany revoked its judicial power to invalidate statutes and replaced it with HRA-style declaratory and interpretive powers only, this would make no practical difference to their constitutional systems. Who would wager that either the original judicial decision in *Roe* v. *Wade*[143] or its subsequent applications would have survived the final word of state or federal legislatures, or the US Supreme Court decisions protecting flag desecration under the First Amendment?[144] And how likely is it that the Bavarian legislature would not have reinstated its classroom crucifix law that was invalidated by the Federal Constitutional Court to the expressed outrage of many, even with the knowledge that this would likely trigger an application to the ECtHR?[145] The immediate political gains to a legislature might easily be calculated to outweigh such uncertain and distant costs. Indeed, in light of the recent Grand Chamber decision of

---

[142] Kahana, 'The Notwithstanding Mechanism and Public Discussion'.
[143] 410 US 113 (1973).
[144] *Texas* v. *Johnson* 491 US 397 (1989); *United States* v. *Eichman* 496 US 310 (1990). A proposed constitutional amendment to override these decisions and prohibit flag desecration failed by one vote to gain the two-thirds majority in the US Senate on June 28, 2006 (the vote was 66–34 in favour) required to send the measure for ratification by three-quarters of the states. The proposed amendment had already received a favourable two-thirds vote in the House of Representatives.
[145] German Classroom Crucifix Case II, 93 BverfGE 1 (1995).

the ECtHR in *Lautsi v. Italy*[146] that classroom crucifixes do not violate any rights under the ECHR, such legislative action would seemingly be all-but-certain, if not already taken. Would citizens in these two countries likely be persuaded to switch to an HRA-style rights regime on the basis that a legislative final word is purely formal and makes no difference in practice? My sense is that they would expect their legislatures to use, or at least seriously consider using, the power in particularly controversial cases – and so should citizens in the UK.

Moreover, Ireland did enact an HRA-like statute for its domestic incorporation of the ECHR, even though it has long had a constitutional bill of rights and full, strong-form constitutional review by its courts to enforce it.[147] Why would Ireland bother to enact this separate statutory, weak-form regime in 2003 unless it was thought to make some practical difference? The answer cannot simply be that, given the constitution's entrenchment, it was easier politically to enact a separate statute than a constitutional amendment, because Ireland could still have incorporated the judicial power to invalidate legislation inconsistent with the ECHR into the statute.[148]

What about the two more concrete pieces of evidence concerning the practical workings of the HRA relied on by those who make or suggest this evaluation? On the claimed over-compliance with declarations of incompatibility, the political branches are between a rock and a hard place. On the one hand, to the extent that the greatest substantive concern with the new model as a whole is inadequate protection of rights without a constitutionalized charter and a non-overridable judicial invalidation power, routine ignoring of declarations of incompatibility would undoubtedly be taken by some as clear evidence that HRA is too weak and that the model is unstable and reverting to traditional parliamentary sovereignty.[149] Yet, on the other hand, the record of compliance then

---

[146] Application No. 30814/06 (18 March 2011).

[147] Incorporation occurred as a result of the signing of the Belfast/Good Friday Agreement in 1998, as part of which the Irish government agreed to 'take steps to further strengthen the protection of human rights in its jurisdiction' and to 'ensure at least an equivalent level of protection of human rights as will pertain in Northern Ireland': F. de Londras and C. Kelly, *European Convention on Human Rights Act: Operation, Impact and Analysis* (Dublin: Thomson Reuters, 2010), pp. 8–9.

[148] This method of incorporation, generally referred to in Ireland as 'direct legislative incorporation', was in fact recommended by the Irish Human Rights Commission, *ibid.* pp. 10–11.

[149] Indeed, Robert Wintermute makes this argument about the *Belmarsh* case even though the declaration was not ignored and the statute amended, and Keith Ewing about the

prompts the claim that the legislature and executive are just kowtowing to the courts, afraid to exercise an independent voice, so that the model is unstable in the other direction, rolling towards judicial supremacy.

As discussed in Chapter 4, I believe the best understanding and operation of legislative final words under the new model in general is a presumption that legislatures will abide by court decisions, and not routinely ignore them – but where there is reasonable disagreement on controversial matters of principle after high-quality debate, it should be considered legitimate for legislatures to exercise their independent legal power of having the final word. Critically, the process is the most important thing, and not the outcome – so that principled and serious legislative consideration resulting in decisions to comply with the courts manifests what the new model seeks to achieve as much as decisions not to comply, as long as the latter is generally taken to be a realistic political possibility.

As we have seen, few such 'open', reasonably contestable and sufficiently controversial issues of major principle have really arisen yet in the declaration of incompatibility context, which is why it is far too soon to render final judgment. Even the *Belmarsh* case was decided on, and limited to, the largely indefensible (from a Convention rights perspective) issue of arbitrary and unnecessary discrimination against non-UK citizens, rather than the underlying issue of the permissibility of indefinite detention itself. Although Parliament remedied the specific incompatibility in the substitute control order legislation, this new regime reflected something of a pre-emptive compromise on the broader issue, which the House of Lords substantially accepted in the 'second-look' control order cases.[150] The prisoners' voting rights issue has already been the subject of one extended parliamentary debate and non-binding vote recommending retention of the statute declared incompatible with Convention rights, and may return for more authoritative resolution in the wake of the recent ECtHR Grand Chamber decision in *Scoppola*.

On the strength and frequency of judicial reliance on section 3, I think at the outset it is a category mistake to view every use of this power as a failure or rebuttal of the HRA's intermediate character. As enacted, section 3 is undoubtedly a central part of the overall balance between rights protection

---

HRA generally even though Parliament has complied, or is seemingly in the process of complying, with all final declarations of incompatibility. R. Wintermute, 'The Human Rights Act's First Five Years: Too Strong, Too Weak, or Just Right?' (2006) 17 *King's College Law Journal* 209; Ewing, 'The Futility of the Human Rights Act'.

[150] See n. 69 above.

and democratic decision-making under the HRA, part of its complex institutional design and distribution of powers, and not merely a filter or stepping stone to section 4. By the logic of the section 3/section 4 divide, it is always the first issue in any case – and likely to be the only one in many – where it is at least 'reasonably possible' to fulfil the mandatory duty and give the statute a meaning consistent with the relevant right. Certainly, although hardly conclusive, the government argued during enactment of the HRA that most rights claims would be resolved by section 3, and resort to section 4 would rarely be necessary.[151] Moreover, the legal and political context in which statutory language is selected and approved in the first place now firmly includes section 3.

On the way section 3 has been used, I think it also overstates the case to view the practice of the courts as so aggressive and radical as to amount to rewriting legislation at will – thereby violating sections 3(2)(b)[152] and 6 by failing to give continuing effect to enacted statutes. It is certainly true that overall, the UK courts have treated the interpretative obligation as a strong one, stronger than New Zealand courts with essentially the same textual power, and have advanced beyond even the broadest conception of their pre-HRA common law, rights-protective interpretative powers. This is usefully illustrated by comparing *Fitzpatrick*, a 2001 pre-HRA case, with the post-HRA decision in *Ghaidan*, interpreting the very same provision of the 1988 amendment to the Rent Act 1977 in opposite ways.[153] Indeed, it is probably accurate and candid to describe the judicial function under section 3 as including limited modifications of statutes to protect rights rather than merely interpretation.[154] At the same time, however, (1) different judges take different views of the appropriate strength of the interpretative obligation so, as one commentator puts it, '[t]o distil or elicit any working principles or rules of guidance from

---

[151] One reason this is inconclusive is that governments would be expected to want to avoid declarations of incompatibility, and their associated political costs, like the plague.

[152] For an analysis of this textual constraint on the scope of the interpretive obligation under section 3, see C. Gearty, 'Reconciling Parliamentary Democracy and Human Rights' (2002) *Law Quarterly Review* 118, 249.

[153] For a detailed comparison of the two cases, see Kavanagh, *Constitutional Review*, pp. 108–14. Kavanagh argues, however, that the difference in outcomes of the two cases was at least as much due to the HRA's creation of a new substantive right against discrimination as to new or stronger interpretive powers. More generally, she argues that the courts do not have radically new interpretive powers under the HRA, the difference is that the courts have used their powers more frequently and with a greater sense of legitimacy, *ibid.*, pp. 115–17.

[154] Kavanagh, *ibid.*, p. 114.

the cases is not easy';[155] (2) undoubtedly there are still limits beyond which a Convention-compatible interpretation is not possible; and (3) overall, the courts have used section 3 in only a relatively small number of cases.[156]

Moreover, as we have seen, a strong case can be made that the general approach of the courts to section 3 has slightly weakened over time since the 2002 high point of interpretative power in *R. v. A*, given the additional limits set out in *Ghaidan*. And arguably, *Wilkinson*, decided the following year, rolled back the standard of impossibility a little further still.[157] Here, Lord Hoffman's leading opinion rejected the notion that section 3 required courts to give the language of statutes 'a contextual meanings',[158] again as perhaps implied in *R. v. A*,[159] and stated that 'the question is still one of *interpretation*, i.e., the ascertainment of what, taking into account the presumption [that Parliament did not intend a statute to mean something which would be incompatible with those rights] created by section 3, Parliament would reasonably be understood to have meant by using the actual language of the statute'.[160]

Indeed, if one looks at the *applications* of the stated section 3 principles in these three cases, the impression of a slight weakening over time is further confirmed. Thus, even though Parliament had not expressly limited the Article 6 ECHR right to a fair hearing, it seems hard to conclude that the section 3 interpretation of the rape shield law at issue in *R. v. A* – reading in a fair trial limitation – did not fly in the face of a 'fundamental feature' or the 'underlying thrust' of the statute as manifested in its unambiguous blanket exclusion of evidence of prior sexual history between the defendant and complainant. Accordingly, by *Ghaidan* standards, arguably such a reading-in would not be justified. By

---

[155] A. Samuels, 'Human Rights Act 1998 Section 3: A New Dimension to Statutory Interpretation?', (2008) 29 *Statute Law Review* 130, 138.

[156] Kavanagh, *Constitutional Review*, p. 117; Sedley, 'No Ordinary Law'.

[157] *R. v. Her Majesty's Commissioners of Inland Revenue ex parte Wilkinson* [2005] UKHL 30. This argument has also been made by van Zyl Smit, 'The New Purposive Interpretation of Statutes: HRA Section 3 after *Ghaidan* v. *Godin-Mendoza*' and Geiringer, 'The Principle of Legality and the Bill of Rights Act: a Critical Examination of *R. v. Hansen*', p. 81. For an argument against this view, see Kavanagh, *Constitutional Review*, pp. 91–7.

[158] *Wilkinson* at [17].

[159] 'Under ordinary methods of interpretation . . . [u]ndoubtedly, a court must always look for a contextual and purposive interpretation: section 3 is more radical in its effect.' *R. v. A (No. 2)* at [44].

[160] *Wilkinson* at [17] (emphasis in original).

contrast, in *Ghaidan* itself, it does not seem an unreasonable contextual reading of a statute extending tenure protection, absent other clear language to the contrary, to interpret the words 'living together as his or her wife or husband' to refer to a general relationship of sexual intimacy exemplified by but not limited to the heterosexual relationship of husband and wife. Indeed, Lord Nicholls argued that the 'social policy' underlying the statutory extension of tenure to the survivor of couples living together as husband and wife 'is equally applicable' to the survivor of homosexual couples living together in a close and stable relationship.[161] And in *Wilkinson*, because there were such clear contrary indications elsewhere in the statute, the court found that no 'reasonable reader could understand the word "widow" to refer to the more general concept of a surviving spouse',[162] so that a compatible, non-discriminatory interpretation of a tax provision granting a bereavement allowance only to widows was not possible.

Finally, in focusing almost exclusively on judicial powers, this second strand of commentary also tends to overlook the practical impact and distinctiveness of other components of the HRA, especially mandatory pre-enactment political rights review. While for the reasons just given, I question the conclusion that this is what 'most distinguishes' the HRA from US-style constitutionalism in practical terms,[163] I of course agree, indeed insist, that it is among its distinguishing and appealing features.

IV   Overall assessment of the HRA from the new model perspective

Looking at the HRA exclusively as an instance of the new model, its strengths lie in aspects of the first two stages. Although far from perfect, as discussed above, the HRA has in practice exhibited a more successful version of pre-enactment political rights review than in Canada and New Zealand. This is mostly due to the greater role of Parliament in scrutinizing government bills and specifically the work of the JCHR as a specialized, dedicated and high-quality select committee to which government ministers are politically obligated to respond. The JCHR has worked tirelessly to probe the evidence for the government's compatibility statements, inform Parliament of its rights concerns, educate members and generally increase Parliament's engagement with human rights issues.

---

[161] *Ghaidan* at [35].   [162] *Wilkinson* at [17].
[163] Hiebert, 'New Constitutional Ideas', p. 1985.

Although it has perhaps had a disappointingly small direct or quantifiable impact on legislative outputs, its less tangible influence in general, and its role in the successful oppositions to several of the most controversial government proposals in particular, should not be minimized. And, as we have seen, the frequency of references to JCHR reports in subsequent parliamentary debates increased substantially during the HRA's second five years. In addition, as in Canada and New Zealand, executive/bureaucratic rights review at the pre-legislative stage has been firmly established and routinized as a formal part of the policy development process. There have also been a handful of important government bills where the overall quality of parliamentary rights-conscious scrutiny has been very high.[164]

At the second stage of judicial rights review, courts have generally exercised their powers and responsibilities reasonably well and as required. It is my view that, following a few early teething problems, the courts' interpretation and application of the division between their section 3 and section 4 powers has for the most part properly reflected the statutory language and intent, and in particular the mandatory language attaching to the former. Notwithstanding the mixed rights record of the courts discussed above and the series of cases in which the ECtHR subsequently found a violation of an ECHR right where the domestic courts did not,[165] final judgments finding approximately forty pieces of primary legislation incompatible with Convention rights (via both sections 3 and 4) in ten years belies the argument that the courts have been so deferential as to revert de facto to traditional parliamentary sovereignty. As does their willingness, as part of this record, to end the previous practice of treating governmental national security claims as raising non-justiciable issues.[166] Moreover, the courts have generally followed the desired approach of a respectful attitude towards parliamentary rights deliberation at stage one, where it has occurred, but without being overly deferential towards it – although, of course, opinions differ on this latter point, as we have seen. A good example of the respectful judicial attitude towards political rights review is *Animal Defenders*, in which Lord Bingham's opinion praised the detailed and serious parliamentary consideration of the rights issue raised by the

---

[164] See text accompanying nn. 42–3 above.

[165] These include *Hirst* (fair elections); *Gillan* [2009] ECHR 28 (stop and search); *Al-Jedda* [2011] ECHR 1092 (right to life); *Al-Skeini* [2011] ECHR 1093 (liberty); *RB* [2012] ECHR 56 (fair trial).

[166] Kavanagh, 'Constitutionalism, Counterterrorism, and the Courts'.

continued blanket ban on political advertisements before enactment of the Communications Act 2003.[167] More generally, there have been sixty-four references to JCHR reports by UK courts, of which sixteen have been by the House of Lords/Supreme Court.[168]

The overarching weakness of the HRA as a practical experiment in the working of the new model has been the dominance over it of the ECHR system of what is often effectively supranational strong-form judicial review.[169] Courts, Parliament and government frequently have their 'hands tied' by the external constraint of actual or potential ECtHR judgments, so that there is relatively little sense of the HRA as an autonomous or self-contained rights regime in practice and relatively little evidence of how its component parts would play out but for the ECtHR. As we have seen, several of the leading HRA cases involved primary legislation that had already been the subject of adverse ECtHR judgments in cases against the UK which, regardless of sections 2, 3 and 4 of the HRA, bind both courts and Parliament under international legal obligation as the final word on the subject.[170] Other ECtHR cases directly on point, while not strictly binding domestically or internationally, are likely to be followed in a subsequent case brought by the disappointed HRA litigant, should the UK depart from them. Given the relatively narrow window for independent judgment that this leaves either courts or Parliament in the UK, the HRA very often seems to work in practice as a system for granting domestic remedies for violations of international human rights rather than a domestic bill of rights, whatever the theoretical merits of the argument for the latter characterization. Rather than a two-horse contest for balance of power over rights issues between domestic courts and Parliament, the race has significantly been pre-empted by a third. As Mark Elliott puts it, 'control over the meaning and application of human rights in the United Kingdom rests ultimately with the European Court'.[171]

At the more micro-level, after the previous changes in government practice and JCHR strategy, the major remaining weakness in the system of pre-enactment political rights review from the ideal perspective is the

---

[167] *Animal Defenders* at [13]–[21].

[168] Hunt *et al.*, 'Parliaments and Human Rights' pp. 46–8.

[169] That is, unlike under the HRA with respect to domestic courts, a legal obligation (albeit an international one) to respond follows from an ECtHR judgment that a UK statute violates an ECHR right. This impact of the ECHR on the operation of the HRA was predicted by Michael Perry in 'Protecting Human Rights in a Democracy'.

[170] See text accompanying n. 87 above. [171] Elliott, 'Interpretative Bills of Rights', p. 8.

still seemingly insufficient impact of the JCHR's activities on subsequent parliamentary debate and work product, especially in the House of Commons.[172] One additional problem it has occasionally faced is that where judges have issued weak rights decisions, the government has been able to counter expressed JCHR concerns by pointing out that the courts do not share them.[173] A more minor weakness is that although the JCHR now attempts to express its own views about compatibility rather than to predict what the courts will say, primarily through focusing on proportionality analysis, this analysis still tends to start with and centre around what the ECtHR has said in previous cases rather than take a fully independent and less legalistic position. The dominance of legal opinion remains even more marked at the executive vetting stage, despite the changes in the Cabinet Office guidelines aimed at counteracting it.

At stage two, although (as just noted) I think that courts have in recent years for the most part properly interpreted and applied the statutory division between section 3 and section 4, one structural weakness is the distorting effect of the different remedial implications of the two powers, as commentators have suggested.[174] In certain situations, courts face strong pressure to use section 3 under which they can grant a remedy to the aggrieved individual rather than the declaratory power, under which they cannot.[175] In this way, the judicial choice between sections 3 and 4 may become somewhat skewed or distorted. Similar remedial pressures also perhaps push the courts into assessing specific executive action under section 6, which they generally have the power to quash,[176] rather than the underlying statutes, which they do not.

In terms of political responses to judicial rights review at stage three, overall these have perhaps been a little court-centric and lacking in independence – although generally focused as much on ECtHR judgments than those of domestic courts. As far as the new model is concerned, the key test

---

[172] See Hiebert, 'Governing Under the Human Rights Act'.

[173] See Tomkins, 'Parliament, Human Rights, and Counter-Terrorism'.

[174] A. Kavanagh, 'Choosing between Sections 3 and 4 of the Human Rights Act 1998: Judicial Reasoning after *Ghaidan* v. *Mendoza*' in H. Fenwick, G. Phillipson and R. Masterman (eds.), *Judicial Reasoning Under the UK Human Rights Act* (Cambridge University Press, 2007) (remedial concerns have been central to the courts' use of section 3 versus section 4); R. Dixon, 'A Minimalist Charter of Rights for Australia: The UK or Canada as a Model?' (2009) 37 *Federal Law Review*, 335.

[175] That is, by interpreting the relevant statute in the rights-protective way requested by the claimant.

[176] For the exception under the HRA, see section 6(2).

of whether the legally limited nature of the declaratory power makes a difference in practice arises (1) where the government and Parliament do not have their hands tied by a prior ECtHR judgment against the UK, and (2) where there is room for reasonable disagreement with the domestic court's decision on a rights issue about which people care. Thus far, this scenario has arisen on far too few occasions to draw any reliable conclusions. Were the government to defy the ECtHR on the blanket ban on voting by prisoners, there seems little doubt that the declaration of incompatibility in *Smith* v. *Scott* would also be ignored.

As the future of the HRA remains very much on the political agenda, what alterations or reforms might address these identified weaknesses and shift the UK's new model experiment into more, or more obviously, intermediate territory and so enhance its distinctiveness as a form of constitutionalism in practice?

Taking the more 'micro-level' weaknesses first and in order, to the extent that the insufficient impact of the JCHR's scrutiny is due to lack of time in an often hectic legislative timetable, a requirement that Parliament consider JCHR reports on specific bills might help to remedy the problem. To the extent it is due to more general structural features of Westminster-style parliamentary systems, including government domination of Parliament and the highly partisan, two-sided nature of most House of Commons proceedings,[177] the problem is obviously more deeply rooted, although there are some signs that it has been acknowledged and that the situation is generally improving rather worsening.[178] Clearly the more that pre-enactment political rights review is intended to provide the major constraint on legislative outputs as compared to judicial rights review, the greater the importance of the political independence of Parliament from the government. Where judicial review is not envisaged or relied on at all, then the need for parliamentary independence is the greatest to prevent political review from becoming only a form of self-checking subject, of course, to ultimate electoral accountability. Exhibit A for this proposition is the JCHR, the relative success of which is widely perceived to stem from its independence and relatively non-partisan nature. Accordingly, political constitutionalists have tended to focus on the need to strengthen parliamentary independence from the government if its role as protector of the people's rights is to be realised, starting at

[177] Hiebert, 'Governing Under the Human Rights Act'.
[178] Tomkins, *Our Republican Constitution*, p. 137.

the top with such major reforms as introducing proportional representation and an elected second chamber.[179] Proponents of the new model should support such reforms for the same reasons, as well as smaller steps towards greater independence, even though for them parliamentary and judicial protection are nor alternatives but supplements.

In terms of the problem of remedial distortion mentioned above, the political branches have not done all they can to alleviate it and reduce the pressure on the courts. They should in future be encouraged to do so, thereby bringing sections 3 and 4 into more of a 'natural' or undistorted balance with each other. Under the currently politically endangered 'fast-track' procedure of HRA section 10,[180] there is express provision for the amending order to have retrospective effect and therefore to grant a legislative remedy to the individual (and those similarly situated) whose rights the court has declared have been violated.[181] However, this power has not been used,[182] primarily because all but three of the government's responses to final declarations of incompatibility have employed amending legislation through the ordinary parliamentary process rather than section 10 – a procedural record perhaps otherwise to be approved of. So where the government intends to comply with a declaration, it could and should either (1) use the express section 10 power to make orders retroactive, if this power survives, or (2) otherwise ensure that, wherever possible, along with the amending legislation – whether or not it is given retroactive effect – provision is made to afford a remedy to individuals affected by the incompatibility.[183] Indeed, Ireland has expressly included a discretionary governmental power to award an

---

[179] See, e.g., Ewing, *The Bonfire of the Liberties*; Adam Tomkins, while supporting an elected second chamber, also proposes a series of even more radical reforms to increase parliamentary independence, such as excluding party whips from the House of Commons. Tomkins, *Our Republican Constitution*, pp. 131–40.

[180] As the then Conservative shadow justice secretary, Dominic Grieve made criticisms of section 10 in a number of public speeches prior to the 2010 general election.

[181] HRA, Schedule 2, section 10, para. 1(1)(b): 'A remedial order may be made so as to have effect from a date earlier than that on which it is made.'

[182] So far, 'no amendments [to legislation in response to a declaration of incompatibility] have been given retrospective effect so as to afford rights to the individual at whose suit the declaration was obtained'. J. Beatson, S. Grosz, T. Hickman and R. Singh, *Human Rights: Judicial Protection in the United Kingdom* (London: Sweet and Maxwell, 2008), p. 37.

[183] This has also been proposed by the JCHR as the last of five recommended steps the government should take to try and persuade the ECtHR that the declaration of incompatibility is or has become an effective remedy. See JCHR, *Monitoring the*

ex gratia payment of compensation to the successful litigant following a declaration of incompatibility under its statute incorporating the ECHR into domestic law, although not to others affected by the rights violation.[184] The duty to repair the damage caused to individuals and to return them to their ex ante position is already a legal obligation of the UK under the ECHR whenever the ECtHR finds a violation.[185] Moreover, where national law permits only partial reparation to be made, the ECtHR itself is empowered to award any necessary 'just satisfaction' to the injured party against the member-state under Article 41 of the ECHR.[186]

I do not see any basis for thinking there might be a legal problem for a legislative remedy of compensating individuals affected by a law following a declaration of incompatibility. As for the separate issue of retroactive remedial orders or amending legislation, neither do I believe there is likely to be any general bar to this second or supplementary type of legislative remedy under section 4.[187] First, the traditional common law presumption of the non-retroactivity of statutes in the name of rule of law principles is just that: a presumption that has always been deemed rebuttable by clear legislative wording.[188] Secondly, there is nothing in

---

Government's Response to Court Judgments Finding Breaches of Human Rights, Sixteenth Report of Session 2006–07, HL 128, HC 728, para. 119 ('[These steps should include] ensuring that any legislative solution makes the necessary provision to afford a remedy to the applicants affected by the identified incompatibility'.)

[184] European Convention on Human Rights Act 2003 (Ireland), §5(4)(c). In addition, Canadian legislatures have occasionally given legislation responding to Supreme Court of Canada decisions retroactive effect. For an article discussing this phenomenon in Canada and advocating that the courts adopt a general interpretive presumption that such legislation have retroactive effect, see S. Choudhry and K. Roach, 'Putting the Past Behind Us? Prospective Judicial and Legislative Constitutional Remedies' (2003) 21 *Supreme Court Law Review* (second series) 205.

[185] JCHR, *Monitoring the Government's Response,* p. 10 (citing the relevant ECtHR judgments to this effect).

[186] HRA, section 8(3) and (4) adopt the language and approach of ECHR Article 41 in empowering courts to award damages against a 'public authority' where necessary to afford 'just satisfaction'. In only a handful of cases have courts awarded damages under section 8.

[187] Neither of two works focusing on retroactivity addresses this precise point (as distinct from the issue of to which events and causes of action pre-dating 2 October 2000 does the HRA apply). B. Juratowitch, *Retroactivity and the Common Law* (Oxford: Hart, 2008); D. Mead, 'Rights, Relationships and Retrospectivity: The Impact of Convention Rights on Pre-Existing Private Relationships Following *Wilson* and *Ghaidan*' (2005) *Public Law* 459.

[188] Recent examples of retroactive legislation include the Terrorist Asset-Freezing (Temporary Provisions) Act 2010 and the Terrorist Asset-Freezing etc. Act 2010.

the HRA itself to suggest that retroactive remedial legislation would violate any of the convention rights; to the contrary, as just mentioned, it grants express power to the minister to introduce remedial orders with retroactive effect under section 10.[189] Thirdly, the identical issue of retroactivity arises under sections 3 and 4. If common law rule of law principles (or any others) do not prevent changed and retroactive statutory interpretation altering 'vested' private rights under section 3 – as, for example, in *Ghaidan* – it is unclear how or why they could prevent precisely the same outcome via retroactive legislative amendment. The section 3 decision in *Ghaidan* meant, of course, that in 2004 the landlord was bound by an interpretation of the 1977 Rent Act that differed from the one on which he could reasonably have relied when entering into the lease with Godin-Mendoza's same-sex partner in 1983. Fourthly, the ECtHR has held that a declaration of incompatibility under section 4 does not constitute an 'effective remedy' for the purposes of the ECHR procedural requirement of exhausting domestic remedies[190] – and so might also find that it does not satisfy the ECHR right to an effective remedy before a national authority under Article 13, a right deliberately omitted from those incorporated under the HRA. Accordingly, action to strengthen this 'weak remedy' along either of the suggested lines is, I think, unlikely to face general obstacles from this source. Finally, one member of the House of Lords Judicial Committee opined that there is no such bar. In the course of his dissenting speech in *Ghaidan* arguing that section 4 should have been used because the non-discriminatory interpretation of the Rent Act was not 'possible', Lord Millett stated that: 'It [incompatible legislation] continues in full force and effect unless and until it is repealed or amended by Parliament, which can decide whether to change the law and if so from what date and whether retrospectively or not.'[191]

For these reasons, I do not believe there would be significant legal problems in implementing this proposal. As far as practical problems are concerned, some combination of the two legislative remedies would seem to be possible and reasonably effective in all types of cases. In criminal law, compensation could be paid for costs suffered in the time

---

[189] There is some language in HRA relevant to the entirely different issue of whether and when the HRA applies to events occurring or causes of action brought before it came into effect on 1 October 2000. On this issue, and not without a good deal of controversy, the courts have so far generally held that the HRA does not apply.

[190] *Burden and Burden* v. *United Kingdom* 44 EHRR 51 (2007).   [191] *Ghaidan* at [64].

between the judicial finding of incompatibility and the legislative response. Even in a case like *Ghaidan*, although practically the losing tenant would either have been evicted from the flat or paid more rent under a section 4 treatment of the case, there is no reason why the government could and should not compensate such tenants for their pecuniary loss resulting from the existence of a law on the statute books that both it and the courts agree violates their rights.[192] As mentioned above, a limited version of this approach has been taken by Ireland in its statute domesticating the ECHR. Moreover, the possibility of ultimately obtaining legislative or executive compensation may help to counter any 'plaintiff-disincentivising'[193] effects of the declaration of incompatibility, although the facts that (1) there is generally uncertainty as to whether judges will currently employ sections 3 or 4 in any given case, and (2) claimants can seek both remedies in the alternative suggests that these effects are small. Accordingly, the development of such a norm or legal rule should end or substantially reduce any artificial distortion in the interplay between the interpretive duty and the declaratory power caused by courts' remedial concerns.

Turning to the third stage, if and when – after a fair test period – parliamentarians prove to be overly reluctant to depart from judicial rights decisions with which they reasonably disagree, then a third reform would seek to enhance the perceived legitimacy of exercise of the legislative final word along the lines set out in Chapter 4, thereby recalibrating judicial-legislative power in practice. The goal here, once again, is that use of this power should have the primary connotation of overriding a judicial interpretation or decision on rights and not overriding the rights themselves – it should in Jeremy Waldron's terms be understood to be about 'rights disagreements', and not 'rights misgivings'.[194] To the extent the latter understanding has (or will) come to prevail, it threatens to render the political cost of using the power too high, and such a change would help to reduce it in a principled way. For the reasonableness of disagreements about the scope, application and limits of rights – between Parliament and the courts, no less than among judges themselves – in many, though not all, contexts is one of the basic reasons

---

[192] This would have been the remedy afforded by the ECtHR in *Karner* v. *Austria* [2003] ECHR 295, an essentially identical case to *Ghaidan* decided a year earlier, had the complainant survived or left beneficiaries of his estate.

[193] Butler and Butler, *The New Zealand Bill of Rights Act*, p. 1116.

[194] Waldron, 'Some Models of Dialogue', pp. 39–46; Hiebert, 'Is it Too Late to Rehabilitate Canada's Notwithstanding Clause?'.

for resisting judicial supremacy and granting the legislative power in the first place. In terms of how to achieve this goal, if understandings cannot now be easily changed, then text more likely can, especially if we end up with a replacement statute. Here, as both the Evanses and Roger Masterman have suggested,[195] the Victorian Charter's formula of a judicial declaration of 'inconsistent interpretation'[196] may well be an improvement, although an even more explicit textual statement is preferable in my view.

This change to the section 4 power could be further enhanced by reconsidering the parameters of that under section 3. To the extent that either the original statutory language or its judicial interpretation is now deemed to create too strong a power, this could be weakened in more or less radical fashion. The strongest option would be to omit the interpretative duty altogether and so reinstate only 'ordinary' modes of statutory interpretation.[197] A middle position would be to make the existing power discretionary rather than mandatory, like the declaration of incompatibility. The least radical change would be a textual attempt to limit the power by requiring interpretations that are consistent with legislative purposes, as in the Victorian and ACT examples,[198] or that are 'reasonably possible', as in New Zealand under *Hansen*. Any of these would likely result in greater reliance on judicial declarations, which in turn may reduce or 'normalise' the political costs associated with not responding to them and so create space for more independent and principled reconsideration by Parliament. And if this were to happen more frequently after judicial declarations, it might also happen more frequently before them, during pre-enactment rights review.

Finally, is there anything that can be done to eliminate or reduce the 'overarching' limitation of the HRA as a practical experiment in the working of the new model caused by its operating in the large shadow of the ECHR system? The short answer is that this limitation cannot altogether be eliminated while the ECtHR remains as the final interpreter of the UK's international legal obligations under the ECHR. It could be

---

[195] Evans and Evans, *Australian Bills of Rights: The Law of the Victorian Charter and ACT Human Rights Act*; R. Masterman, 'Interpretations, Declarations and Dialogue: Rights Protection under the Human Rights Act and Victorian Charter of Human Rights and Responsibilities' (2009) *Public Law* 112.

[196] VCHRR, section 31.

[197] As we shall see, this is effectively what has happened in the two Australian new model jurisdictions.

[198] ACT HRA, section 30; VCHRR, section 31(1).

reduced, at least on a temporary basis, if courts were to exercise greater independence from the ECtHR in interpreting HRA rights, as they are legally permitted to do under section 2,[199] although this would likely result in a greater numbers of applications to, and effective reversals by, the Strasbourg Court that it was the original point of the HRA to reduce. It could also be reduced if and to the extent that domestic rights are unhitched, and made to differ, from those under the ECHR, so that UK courts and Parliament would have greater autonomy, especially with any such rights that have no equivalent under the ECHR. Here, there would be a little more room for the relatively free working of the interpretative bill of rights version of the new model to play out, as in New Zealand. Ultimately, however, the ECHR would still act as a set of supra-national minimum rights, like most national bills of rights within a federal political system. Accordingly, a suitably drafted 'British bill of rights' might provide a somewhat better practical test of the new model than the HRA. Although this reason overlaps with the purely political desire to escape from the straitjacket of the ECtHR that appears to be fuelling this option's growing appeal, it is of course different.

---

[199] See Lord Irvine of Lairg, 'A British Interpretation of Convention Rights' (2012) *Public Law* 237.

8

Australia

In one way, Australia is the odd man out among the Commonwealth jurisdictions that have experimented with the new model, because it alone has a long and continuous history of legal constitutionalism, having had for more than a century the same single-document, entrenched, supreme law constitution granting courts the power of judicial review.[1] In another way, however, it most epitomizes the model of political constitutionalism with respect to rights, in that it remains today the rare country without a general charter or bill of rights at the national level. The Australian Constitution, of course, lacks one, and no statutory bill has been enacted. Accordingly, Australia already is – and has long been – a hybrid system of a different type from the new model, with judicial supremacy on the structural issues of federalism and separation of powers, and mostly parliamentary sovereignty on matters of rights.

Despite the rejection by the federal government of a recommendation for a national human rights act in April 2010, Australia has nonetheless taken significant and interesting steps in the direction of the new model. At the national level, legislation adopting only its purely political components has recently been enacted by the federal Parliament. At the sub-national level, the whole package – in its general UK/New Zealand form – was enacted by the Australian Capital Territory (ACT) in its 2004 Human Rights Act, and by the state of Victoria in its 2006 Charter of Human Rights and Responsibilities Act.

I Central features of the three Australian versions

At the federal level, on 10 December 2008, the Labor Government of Kevin Rudd launched the National Human Rights Consultation in conformity with its 2007 election commitment. A National Human Rights Consultation Committee was appointed, chaired by Father Frank Brennan, to consult the

---

[1] Constitution of the Commonwealth of Australia, 1900.

community on three primary questions: which human rights should be protected and promoted, are they currently sufficiently protected and promoted, and how could Australia better promote human rights? The government then rejected the committee's recommendation[2] that a statutory bill of rights along the general lines of the New Zealand and UK models be introduced.[3] Instead, five months later, in September 2010, the Attorney-General introduced into Parliament the Human Rights (Parliamentary Scrutiny) Bill, which adopted only the political rights review component of the model, without either a bill of rights or any new judicial powers. The bill, which received the Royal Assent in December 2011, contains two main elements. First, it establishes a ten-member Parliamentary Joint Committee on Human Rights (JCHR) based largely on the UK version, although its functions are somewhat narrower, limited to examining bills and legislative instruments for compatibility with human rights and reporting its findings to Parliament.[4] Secondly, it provides that a statement of compatibility or incompatibility with human rights must be presented to the House of Parliament in which a bill is introduced.[5] Although it does not contain a bill of rights, the political review that the statute mandates on the part of the executive and Parliament is also not limited to a specified set of enacted rights, as in the other jurisdictions, but can at least in principle take into account the full range and broader scope of human rights from the common law to all international treaties.[6]

Legally, too, the prospects for eventual adoption of a national human rights act have arguably suffered a significant setback as the result of the recent High Court of Australia (HCA) decision on the issue of the constitutionality of the declaration of incompatibility mechanism under Chapter III of the Commonwealth Constitution. In the much-awaited *Momcilovic* case,[7] the HCA was given its first opportunity to rule on the constitutional validity of a declaratory power, here the one contained in section 36 of the VCHRR.[8] The underlying constitutional issue is whether

---

[2] National Human Rights Consultation Report, 30 September 2009.
[3] Robert McClelland, 'Launch of Australia's Human Rights Framework' (speech delivered at the National Press Club of Australia, Canberra, 21 April 2010).
[4] Clause 4, Human Rights (Parliamentary Scrutiny) Bill.   [5] *Ibid.*, clauses 8 and 9.
[6] For more on the bill, see D. Kinley and C. Ernst, 'Exile on Main Street: Australia's Legislative Agenda for Human Rights' available at ssrn.com/abstract=1931915.
[7] *Momcilovic v. The Queen & Ors* [2011] HCA 34.
[8] VCHRR, section 36(2): 'Subject to any relevant override declaration, if in a proceeding the Supreme Court is of the opinion that a statutory provision cannot be interpreted consistently with a human right, the Court may make a declaration to that effect in accordance with this section.'

any courts, and if so which, can validly exercise the declaratory power given the limitations on federal judicial power contained in sections 73–7 of the Commonwealth Constitution. These limit the original jurisdiction of the HCA and the jurisdiction of other federal courts, as well as state courts exercising federal jurisdiction, to 'matters' – previously defined to mean the conclusive determination by a court of a legal right, duty or liability – and the appellate jurisdiction of the HCA to appeals from 'judgments, decrees, orders, and sentences'. In short, is the declaratory power sufficiently definitive of legal rights to constitute a 'matter' or 'judgment'? Although the HCA held by 4–3 that section 36 of the VCHRR was valid vis-à-vis the Victorian Supreme Court as a state court, five justices appeared to find that the exercise of a declaratory power would be unconstitutional for federal courts.[9] Since these are the courts that would presumably exercise the power (at least some of the time) under a national human rights act, this part of the *Momcilovic* decision seems to cast serious doubt on the constitutional permissibility of the UK model at the federal level.[10]

At the sub-national level, the ACTHRA was enacted in 2004, followed by a series of important amendments in 2007, some of which came into effect in 2008 and the remainder in 2009.[11] The state of Victoria followed suit by enacting the VCHRR in 2006. In their current forms, these two statutory bills of rights are broadly similar to each and other and the general structures of both are substantially modelled on the New Zealand and UK versions, especially the latter as they include an express judicial declaratory power in addition to a rights-friendly interpretative duty. Nonetheless, with the benefit of a few years' experience of the UK's HRA, the texts of both Australian statutes have been tweaked in certain interesting ways to try and address some of the criticisms of its practice or contextual differences in its operation. But tweaked rather than introducing fundamentally novel departures. This trial-and-error approach is both sensible, in my view, and also confirms the sense in

---

[9] Only Justices Crennan and Kiefel disagreed with this point. The decision in *Momcilovic* is extremely long, complex and divided, and several of the individual judgments on the multiple issues raised are open to various interpretations. In short, as Jeremy Gans put it in a comment to me: 'No one currently knows how these things might play out in a future constitutional challenge.' See H. Irving, 'The High Court of Australia kills dialogue model of human rights', *The Australian*, 16 September 2011; S. Zhou, *Momcilovic v. The Queen*: Implications for a Federal Human Rights Charter, available at ssrn.com/abstract=2128005.

[10] Irving, *ibid.*   [11] Human Rights Amendment Act 2007 (ACT).

which this really is, and is perceived as, a new Commonwealth model, rather than either a purely generic one or a series of entirely separate and independent, self-contained endeavours.[12]

Both the ACTHRA and the VCHRR adhere to the New Zealand and UK examples by taking most of the content of the protected rights (selectively) from an international treaty to which the country is a party, rather than creating a separate 'local' bill of rights, as in Canada – hence the justification of the term 'human rights'. In both Australian cases (as with New Zealand) that treaty is the ICCPR, which is expressly stated to be the primary source of the rights in the ACTHRA.[13] On the other hand, as sub-national entities formally lacking international human rights obligations, the operation of the two Australian statutes is freer and less accountable to international standards and supervision than even New Zealand, and certainly than the UK. Moreover the two statutes follow the New Zealand rather than UK example of generally deriving the rights from the international treaty rather than duplicating the exact content.

Turning from the content of the rights to general provisions or structure, there are ten specific differences between both the ACTHRA and the VCHRR on the one hand, and the UK and New Zealand versions of the new model on the other.[14] These are:

1. Unlike the UK's HRA, which incorporates the special limitations provisions attaching to certain of the rights under the ECHR, both Australian statutes have a general limitations clause applying to all rights – which largely borrows its language from section 1 of the Canadian Charter.[15] Unlike section 1 of the Charter and the similar section 5 of the NZBORA, however, both Australian statutes now go on in addition to adopt the language of section 36 of the South African Constitution's general limitations clause that sets out the various more specific factors that determine whether a limit is justified.[16] This arguably provides more textual guidance for courts in applying the limits.

---

[12] That is, it is evidence of my claim to this effect made in Chapter 1 above.

[13] ACTHRA, Part 3 Civil and political rights. Note: the primary source of these rights is the International Covenant on Civil and Political Rights.

[14] Many of these textual differences are identified and described in Evans and Evans, *Australian Bills of Right* and also, as between the UK's HRA and the VCHRR, in Masterman, 'Interpretations, Declarations and Dialogue'.

[15] ACTHRA section 28(2); VCHRR section 7(2).

[16] The original version of the ACTHRA was amended to this effect in 2007.

2. Whereas the NZBORA applies to acts done by the judiciary and the HRA includes courts as public authorities bound to act consistently with Convention rights, both the ACTHRA and the VCHRR expressly exclude courts from the list of public authorities bound to act compatibly with human rights.[17] This likely reduces the potential 'horizontal effect' of the statutes.

3. Both statutes expressly exclude damages as a remedy against public authorities for rights violations. By contrast, damages are expressly included as a remedy under section 8 of the HRA and have been implied under the NZBORA.

4. Both statutes create a duty on public authorities to 'give proper consideration to a relevant human right' in making decisions.[18] This adds a unique procedural obligation to the exclusively substantive one that outcomes must be consistent with human rights under the HRA and NZBORA.

5. In terms of mandatory political rights review, both statutes include requirements that compatibility statements address not only *whether* proposed legislation is compatible with rights, but also *how*. In the case of the ACTHRA, this duty to provide an explanation arises only where an incompatibility statement is made;[19] but under the VCHRR there is also a duty to explain how the bill is compatible – that is, a requirement of a reasoned statement of compatibility.[20]

6. Both statutes also mandate scrutiny of proposed legislation by the relevant parliamentary standing committee, requiring it to report to Parliament as to whether there are any incompatibilities with human rights. In the UK and New Zealand, such parliamentary scrutiny is not a statutory requirement, but has become part of the internal standing orders of the parliaments.

7. Importantly, both statutes qualify the rights-compatible interpretative duty that is otherwise phrased essentially identically to section 3 of the HRA by requiring such interpretations to be not merely 'possible', but possible consistently with legislative purpose.[21]

---

[17] ACTHRA section 40(2); VCHRR section 4(1)(j).

[18] ACTHRA section 40B(1)(b); VCHRR section 38(1).

[19] ACTHRA section 37(3)(b).   [20] VCHRR section 28(3)(a).

[21] VCHRR, section 32(1) reads: 'So far as it is possible to do so consistently with legislative purpose, all statutory provisions must be interpreted in a way that is compatible with human rights'. ACTHR, section 30 states: 'So far as it is possible to do so consistently with its purpose, a Territory law must be interpreted in a way that is compatible with human rights'.

8. Attorneys-General must both report judicial declarations of incompatibility to the legislature/responsible minister and prepare a written response to them within six months. No such duty or timetable applies in the UK.

9. Unlike under the NZBORA and HRA, human rights commissions are given roles in the rights regime by each statute, although that of the Victorian Commission is more extensive.

10. Finally, both statutes provide for mandatory reviews of their operation, after five years under the ACTHRA and both four and eight years under the VCHRR. The findings of these reviews will be discussed below.

In addition to these common innovations of the two Australian statutes, there are four general features that distinguish the VCHRR from both the ACTHRA and the other two earlier statutory bills of rights. First, it contains a legislative override power worded similarly to section 33 of the Canadian Charter in addition to – rather than instead of[22] – the default final word that comes from not having to accept a judicial declaration.[23] Unlike section 33 in Canada, section 31 VCHRR specifies that it is the legislature's understanding that this power is only to be used in 'exceptional circumstances', and the MP introducing a bill containing an override must make a statement explaining why this criterion is satisfied. The inclusion of the override provision has been widely viewed as redundant, something of a 'category mistake' in a statutory bill of rights without a judicial invalidation power, and the four-year review report recommended abolishing it.[24] The power has not so far been used, and the government of Victoria recently accepted this recommendation.

Secondly, although there is no apparent attempt in the wording of section 31 to adopt the 'reasonable interpretive disagreement' understanding of the legislative override power suggested by some for Canada,[25] interestingly such an attempt has arguably been made with the judicial declaration of incompatibility. For here the wording, unlike that in the ACTHRA, which largely matches the UK HRA,[26] is that 'if . . .

---

[22] The 'instead of' refers to the proposal for reform of the NZBORA suggested by Andrew and Petra Butler, see Chapter 6 above.

[23] VCHRR, section 31.

[24] The ACT Human Rights Act Research Project, *The Human Rights Act 2004 (ACT): The First Five Years of Operation* (Australian National University, 2009).

[25] VCHRR, section 31 states: 'Parliament may expressly declare . . . that the Act has effect despite being incompatible with one or more of the human rights'.

[26] Namely, 'if the court is satisfied that the statute is not consistent'.

the Supreme Court is of the opinion that a statutory provision cannot be interpreted consistently with a human right, the Court may make a declaration to that effect'.[27] The declaration is also termed a 'declaration of inconsistent interpretation' versus the 'declaration of incompatibility' in the ACT and UK HRAs. Use of the terms 'opinion' and 'interpretation' perhaps suggests greater room for reasonable disagreement.

Thirdly, section 32 of the VCHRR establishing the interpretative duty expressly permits 'international law and the judgments of . . . foreign and international courts and tribunals relevant to a human right' to be considered in interpreting a statutory provision.[28] This is a more general invocation of external jurisprudence, and for a more specific task, than under section 2 of the HRA. The four-year review report also recommended repealing this provision. Finally, the VCHRR alone does not create a new cause of action for violation of its rights; under section 39, claimants must rely on existing actions available to them. Both the UK HRA and the (amended) ACTHRA establish an independent cause of action for violation of a protected right, and this was implied in *Baigent's Case* in New Zealand.

II   The Australian bills of rights in operation

The mandatory review of the ACTHRA after its first five years concluded that 'one of the clearest effects of the HRA has been to improve the quality of law-making in the Territory, to ensure that human rights concerns are given due consideration in the framing of new legislation and policy'.[29] Indeed, the report stated that 'its impact on policy-making and legislative processes has been more extensive and arguably more important than its impact in the courts. Its main effects have been on the legislative and executive, fostering a lively, if sometimes fragile, human rights culture within government.'[30] The twin mechanisms of this political rights review are the statutory requirements that the Attorney-General prepare a compatibility statement for each new bill presented to the Legislative Assembly by a minister stating whether it is consistent with human rights and, if not, how,[31] and that the designated standing

---

[27] VCHRR, section 36(2).   [28] VCHRR, section 32(2).
[29] The ACT Human Rights Project, *The First Five Years*, p. 6. The ACT review was prepared by the ACT Human Rights Act Project of the Australian National University.
[30] *Ibid.*   [31] ACTHRA section 37(2) and (3).

committee report to the Legislative Assembly on any human rights issues raised in them.[32]

Compatibility statements are drafted by the specialist Human Rights Unit (HRU) within the ACT's Department of Justice and Community Safety (JACS) in consultation with the sponsoring government department. Where the Attorney-General concludes that a bill is compatible with the protected rights, there is no requirement to explain why (unlike with a conclusion of incompatibility) and the general practice has been not to include a statement of reasons but for human rights issues to be addressed in the separate explanatory statement prepared by the department responsible for the bill.[33] Both the five-year review report and the parliamentary scrutiny committee have been critical of the often inadequate detail and factual bases in these statements, and the former recommended that a statement of reasons including a clear proportionality/limitations analysis under section 28 should accompany each compatibility statement. Thus far, Attorneys-General have issued no statements of incompatibility under the ACTHRA.

Under section 38(2) of the statute, the speaker of the Legislative Assembly nominated the existing Standing Committee on Legal Affairs to undertake human rights scrutiny as an additional task. A broadly nonpartisan body, the committee has adopted the general policy of not taking definitive positions in its reports on whether limitations of rights are justified under section 28, although occasionally it has stated a strong view on the issue.[34] The five-year review concluded that the government gives serious consideration to the views of the committee, citing two bills that were amended in light of criticisms in committee reports, additional justifications provided by the government in the course of ongoing communications and dialogue over committee concerns, and a high formal response rate to committee reports.[35] Finally, the report listed a series of eight government bills that produced 'serious human rights debate' in the Legislative Assembly in the two-year period from 2005 to 2007.[36] Overall, the report concludes that: 'The development of new laws by the executive has clearly been shaped by the requirement to issue a statement of compatibility for each new bill, and the approach of

---

[32] ACTHRA section 38(1).
[33] Statements of reasons have been provided in a few high-profile cases, such as the Mental Health (Treatment and Care) Amendment Bill 2005 and the Terrorism (Extraordinary Temporary Powers) Bill 2006.
[34] *The First Five Years*, p. 30.   [35] *Ibid.*, pp. 31–2.   [36] *Ibid.*, p. 28.

government has been influenced by a robust dialogue with the legislature, the Scrutiny Committee and the Human Rights Commissioner.'[37]

Under the VCHRR, it is the Member of Parliament proposing to introduce a bill who is required to make a statement of compatibility, which must state not only whether it is compatible but, if so, 'how' (i.e., it must contain a statement of reasons).[38] There is little publicly available information about the process by which the Victorian government prepares statements of compatibility or ensures compliance with the protected rights, although James Kelly reports the results of interviews with senior officials disclosing that statements are created in collaboration between the Victorian Government Solicitor's Office, the Department of Justice and the sponsoring minister.[39] In its submission to the four-year review of the VCHRR conducted by Parliament's Scrutiny of Acts and Regulations Committee (SARC), the government stated that it had audited all existing legislation for charter compatibility, prepared guidelines for legislation and policy officers,[40] and established a human rights unit in the department of justice to assist departments in the development of legislation.[41] The audit resulted in the Statute Law Revision (Charter of Human Rights and Responsibilities) Act 2009, which amended eleven provisions in seven statutes. Since the VCHRR came into effect, there have been two statements of incompatibility concerning government bills, both dealing with expanded police powers to conduct random weapons searches, and both bills were enacted with the acknowledged incompatibilities intact.[42] In 2010, the average length of compatibility statements was 3,000 words.[43] As specified in section 30, SARC, whose current governing statute was enacted in 2003, has the obligation to consider and report on human rights concerns in proposed legislation. Of its 195

---

[37] *Ibid.*, p. 27.   [38] VCHRR section 28.

[39] J. B. Kelly, 'A Difficult Dialogue: Statements of Compatibility and the Victorian Charter of Human Rights and Responsibilities Act' (2011) 46 *Australian Journal of Political Science* 257.

[40] Human Rights Unit, Department of Justice, *Charter of Human Rights and Responsibilities: Guidelines for Legislation and Policy Officers in Victoria* (Melbourne, Victoria: Department of Justice, 2008), available at the Victorian Government Solicitor's Office (VGSO) website.

[41] Scrutiny of Acts and Regulations Committee, *Review of the Charter of Human Rights and Responsibilities Act 2006* (Melbourne, Victoria: Victorian Government Printer, 2011) ('SARC report'), pp. 78–9.

[42] *Ibid.*, p. 84. These were the Summary Offences and Control of Weapons Amendment Act 2009 and the Control of Weapons Amendment Act 2010.

[43] *Ibid.* Although the length of statements has dropped dramatically under the new government elected at the end of 2010.

total reports on introduced bills thus far, seventeen have concluded that the legislation may be incompatible with Charter rights, including the second of the two government bills on weapons searches attracting statements of incompatibility.[44] In its four-year review, SARC states that 'nearly all' of these seventeen bills were enacted, the one exception being the Judicial Commission of Victoria Bill 2010, although two of the reports prompted amendments during parliamentary debates.[45] According to the Victorian Equal Opportunity and Human Rights Commission's submission, thirty-seven out of 109 bills in 2009 and forty-two out of ninety in 2010 were the subject of 'parliamentary comment relating to human rights issues'.[46] SARC's conclusion as to the effect of political rights review on the substance of legislation was that 'the Charter has had some impact on a number of statutory provisions and may have had a significant impact in a number of instances. However, it is not possible to identify the actual effect of these processes [for human rights assessment] on any particular statutory provision.' The report stated there was a range of effects, from the Statute Law Revision Act to the weapons searches bills.[47]

As for judicial rights review, we have seen that the five-year review report for the ACTHRA contained the general conclusion that its impact on policy-making and legislation had been 'more extensive and arguably more important' than its impact on the courts, which the report also stated had generally used the ACTHRA 'cautiously'.[48] As of May 2009, the date of the report, the ACTHRA had been referred to in ninety-one cases in the ACT courts,[49] although often perfunctorily, of which over 60 per cent concerned the criminal law.[50] No declarations of incompatibility had been issued and only very rarely had one been sought, also reflecting the report's conclusion that 'the legal profession has displayed a relatively low level of interest in the HRA'.[51] The first declaration by an ACT court was made subsequently, by the ACT Supreme Court in November 2010, finding the presumption against bail for charges of murder or certain serious drug offences contained in section 9C of the Bail Act 1992 incompatible with the 'general rule' in favour of bail under section 18(5) of the ACTHRA.[52] In its required response to the declaration within six months, in June 2011, the government reiterated that the ACTHRA's 'dialogue' model was designed to protect the role of the legislature as the 'final law-maker' and stated that it

---

[44] Scrutiny of Acts and Regulations Committee, Alert No. 8 of 2010, pp. 7–11.
[45] *Ibid.*   [46] Quoted in SARC report, p. 86.   [47] *Ibid.*   [48] *The First Five Years*, p. 48.
[49] *Ibid.*, p. 47,   [50] *Ibid.*   [51] *Ibid.*, p. 61.
[52] *In the matter of an application for bail by Isa Islam* [2010] ACTSC 147.

was awaiting the outcome of an appeal to the ACT Court of Appeal.[53] The appeal was later withdrawn and the government issued a 'final' response in May 2012, in which it canvassed options for reform that do not squarely address the court's concerns and announced a consultation period preceding any formal proposals.[54]

Following the recommendation of the previous twelve-month review, the wording of the interpretative duty in section 30 was amended and simplified as of 2008 from its more convoluted original form to more or less match that of the VCHRR; that is, section 3 of the UK HRA plus the 'consistently with its purpose' language. Although the highest ACT court, the Court of Appeal, had previously suggested that section 30 should be interpreted and applied along the lines of *Ghaidan* in the UK,[55] it subsequently expressly rejected this approach in favour of a narrower one, albeit also in dicta. In *Casey* v. *Alcock*,[56] decided in January 2009, Besanko J. stated that neither the pre-amended nor present form of section 30 authorised the court to take the *Ghaidan* approach.[57] A month later, he reiterated this view in *R.* v. *Fearnside:*[58]

> In its present form, s 30 appears to give the Court a broader power to adopt an interpretation of a Territory law which is consistent with a relevant human right. I am conscious of the fact that discussing the matter in the abstract is of limited assistance. Nevertheless, I think s 30 would enable a Court to adopt an interpretation of a legislative provision compatible with human rights which did not necessarily best achieve the purpose of that provision or promote that purpose, providing the interpretation was consistent with that purpose. On the other hand, I do not think s 30 authorises and requires the Court to take the type of approach taken by the House of Lords in *Ghaidan*. There is no reference to purpose in s 3(1) of the United Kingdom Act and the primary constraint in that subsection is stated in terms of what is or is not possible. By contrast, under s 30 in the HRA the purpose . . . of the legislative provision must be ascertained through well-established methods, and the interpretation adopted by the Court must be consistent with that purpose.[59]

In addition, in both cases the ACT Court of Appeal affirmed its adoption of the '*Hansen*' versus '*Moonen*' approach on the methodological issue of at what stage of the analysis the interpretive duty is applied, finding that

---

[53] www.legislation.act.gov.au/a/2004–5/relatedmaterials/government_response.pdf.
[54] www.legislation.act.gov.au/a/2004–5/relatedmaterials/government_response_for_legislation_register.pdf.
[55] *Kinsley's Chicken Pty Ltd* v. *Queensland Investment Corp.* [2006] ACTCA 9.
[56] [2009] ACTCA 1 (23 January 2009).   [57] *Ibid.* at [108].
[58] [2009] ACTCA 3 (24 February 2009).   [59] *Fearnside* at [89].

it should be employed only after a statute in its ordinary meaning has first been deemed an unreasonable limit on a right under section 28.[60]

The four-year review of the VCHRR also concluded that the Charter had had relatively limited impact on the courts. 'SARC considers that the Charter has only played a role in a small fraction of court and tribunal decisions and played no significant role in a majority of those', although it noted that three-and-a-half years of operation was likely 'too short to meaningfully assess the potential effect of the Charter on the courts … given timelines of litigation and the cumulative nature of jurisprudence'.[61] In this period, the report states there were 112 published reasons for judgment in the Supreme Court[62] referring to the Charter, fourteen judgments in which the interpretive duty under section 32 had a 'significant effect' on the courts' analysis (although only four of these expressed section 32 to have been 'determinative'), and six cases in which courts had found that a public authority had breached the Charter.[63] There was a single declaration of inconsistent interpretation, where the Court of Appeal held that the reverse onus provision of section 5 of the Drugs, Poisons and Controlled Substances Act 1981[64] cannot be interpreted consistently with the Charter's right to be presumed innocent until proved guilty according to law.[65] However, this single declaration was subsequently overturned on appeal by the High Court of Australia in Momcilovic.[66] In the course of its judgment in this case, the Court of Appeal rejected the broader understanding of the interpretive duty in section 32(1) of the Charter previously given by a lower Victoria court[67] and unanimously gave it a narrow reading, finding that it 'does not create a "special" rule of interpretation [in the Ghaidan sense]', but rather codifies traditional understandings of the process of interpretation, including the principle of legality.[68] The HCA affirmed this approach to section 32 on appeal in Momcilovic. As the SARC report states: 'a clear majority of the High Court held that the Charter's interpretation rule is limited to traditional methods of interpretation, rejecting the

---

[60] *Ibid.* at [98].   [61] SARC report, p. 114.

[62] The Supreme Court of Victoria is divided into two divisions: the Court of Appeal and the Trial Division.

[63] SARC report, p. 122.

[64] Section 5 deems a person to possess drugs that are in places he or she uses, enjoys or controls unless he or she 'satisfies the court to the contrary'.

[65] *R.* v. *Momcilovic* [2010] VSCA 50.

[66] *Momcilovic* v. *The Queen & Ors* [2011] HCA 34.   [67] *Momcilovic* [2010] at [35].

[68] *Ibid.*

significance of overseas approaches'.[69] In its decision, the Victoria Court of Appeal also adopted the *Moonen* over the *Hansen* methodological approach, applying section 32 at the first rather than the last stage of the analysis, thereby limiting its use as a remedial power; but the HCA produced no clear majority position on this issue.[70]

Given the existence of only one final declaration of incompatibility[71] and the narrow approach to the interpretive duty recently affirmed by the highest courts in the ACT and Victoria (and also by the HCA), there has not been a great deal in the judicial record for legislatures to respond to. The most interesting, and perhaps telling, legislative response to a judicial decision was one by the Parliament of Victoria that did not, at least for the majority of the Victoria Court of Appeal, involve any questions under the Charter. In 2005, the Victorian legislature had enacted the Serious Sex Offenders Monitoring Act, section 11(1) of which permitted a court to make an extended supervision order (ESO) in respect of an offender 'if it is satisfied, to a high degree of probability, that the offender is likely to commit a relevant offence if released in the community on completion of the service of any custodial sentence that he or she is serving'. In *TSL*,[72] decided in 2006 before the VCHRR came into operation, the Court of Appeal unanimously held that the key term 'likely to commit' in section 11(1) is capable of meaning less likely to commit than not. Although the Court stated that 'likely' was used in the sense of connoting a high degree of probability, there was no reason to think it must be more than 50 per cent.[73] In *RJE* v. *Secretary to the Department of Justice*,[74] decided on 18 December 2008, the Court of Appeal unanimously overruled *TSL*, holding that 'likely' means more likely than not; that is, a probability greater than 50 per cent. The leading judgment (for two of the justices) expressly held that in so doing, they were relying not on section 32 but on the ordinary meaning of the term 'likely', and ordinary principles of statutory construction – favouring that interpretation of an ambiguous provision which produces the least infringement

---

[69] SARC report, p. x. But *cf.* Debeljak, '*Momcilovic v The Queen and Ors*: From Definite Pessimism to Cautious Optimism in 273 pages!' (arguing that Justice Heydon provided the fourth and deciding vote in favour of a broad reading of section 32).

[70] Although Debeljak similarly argues that Justice Heydon supplied the fourth and decisive vote in favour of the *Hansen* approach to section 7. *Ibid*.

[71] As stated above, the government's appeal against the declaration issued by the ACT Supreme Court in November 2010 was subsequently withdrawn.

[72] *TSL* v. *Secretary to the Department of Justice* [2006] VSCA 1999.   [73] *Ibid*. at [9].

[74] [2008] VSCA 265.

of a common law right (here, the right to be at liberty) – and that in disposing of the appeal it was not necessary 'to decide any of the questions that were said to arise under the Charter'.[75] By contrast, the third justice, Nettle J., thought it was necessary to rely on the Charter and section 32 because, in light of the fact that *TSL* had in comity twice been followed by the New South Wales Court of Appeal, there must be a compelling reason to depart from it and the Charter provides that reason.[76] As a result of section 32, he stated:

> one is now compelled to construe section 11 of the Act, so far as it is possible to do so consistently with the purpose of the section, in a way that subjects the appellant's rights to freedom of movement, privacy and liberty only to such reasonable limits as can demonstrably be justified in a free and democratic society, etc. In my view, that requires a departure from the *TSL* interpretation of 'likely'.[77]

Less than two months after *RJE*, on 10 February 2009, the Parliament of Victoria enacted the Serious Sexual Offenders Monitoring Act 2009 amending the 2005 statute 'to clarify the test to be applied by the court in making an extended supervision order'.[78] Section 4 of the Act overrules *RJE* and reinstates the (rights-incompatible?) meaning in *TSL*: 'for the avoidance of doubt, subsection (1) permits a determination that an offender is likely to commit an offence on the basis of a lower threshold than the threshold of more likely than not'.[79] Although, therefore, not strictly speaking the overruling of a Charter interpretation under section 32, the majority in *RJE* had left little doubt that the same result would be reached under the Charter[80] and, indeed, might be viewed as effectively applying the *Hansen* approach; that is, section 32 is not reached because the ordinary meaning of section 11 was consistent with Charter rights. Would it likely have made any difference to the legislature had all three justices relied on section 32?

III   Assessment of the Australian versions

As we have seen, official reviews of the early workings of the ACTHRA and the VCHRR concluded that the main practical impact of both bills of rights was on the drafting and passage of legislation rather than in post-enactment

---

[75] *Ibid.* at [2].   [76] *Ibid.* at [103]–[104], per Nettle, J.   [77] *Ibid.* at [106].
[78] Statute, clause 1.   [79] Section 4.
[80] This was why they thought it unnecessary to rely on the Charter in the case. *RJE* at [2].

litigation. Although admittedly stated less forcefully than in the ACT review, this conclusion did not prevent a majority of SARC from recommending ending the role of the courts altogether, by repealing all of Part 3 except Division I on scrutiny of new legislation, thereby effectively bringing Victoria into line with the new federal regime of political rights review only (apart from the existence of a bill of rights).[81] This majority 'preference' on the part of the four MPs from the now governing, VCHRR-sceptical, Liberal/National coalition reflects and expresses the same continuing political controversy over new judicial powers that sunk the prospects for a national human rights act two years ago, although it remains to be seen whether the Baillieu Government will act on it.[82] It also suggests the limits of non-partisanship on SARC, given that the three Labor members on the committee stated the opposite preference of retaining the judicial role, albeit within a formally unanimous recommendation that both of these options be considered.[83]

The fact that courts have used their new powers so cautiously also confounds certain predictions about how the Australian bills would play out. Thus, shortly after enactment of the VCHRR, bill of rights opponent James Allan speculated that 'the key provisions of the Victorian Charter ... will empower the unelected judges to draw far more of the social policy lines (lines at present drawn by the elected legislature) than the proponents of the Victorian Charter of Rights pretend'.[84] He also stated, with reference to declarations of inconsistent interpretation under section 36, that 'the only dialogue likely to emerge is of the sort seen in Canada and the UK, the "ordering in a restaurant" variety of dialogue where the judges do the ordering and the legislators the serving'.[85] Writing in the context of a possible human rights act at the national level, Rosalind Dixon cautioned against adoption of a 'UK-style charter', as enacted in the ACT and Victoria, on the ground that, although seemingly more 'minimalist' than overriding charters like the constitutional Canadian Charter or statutory CBOR, UK-style charters have a tendency towards 'statutory distortion'. That is, an unduly aggressive or strained approach to the interpretative duty that undermines the

---

[81] SARC Report, Recommendation 35.

[82] In its response to the SARC report, dated 14 March 2012, the Baillieu Government stated that it will seek specific legal advice regarding the questions raised by the majority recommendation for ending the role of the courts. See www.parliament.vic.gov.au/ images/stories/committees/sarc/charter_review/report_response/20120314_sarc.gov-tresp.charterreview.pdf.

[83] Ibid.   [84] Allan, 'The Victorian Charter of Rights and Responsibilities', p. 908.

[85] Ibid., p. 916.

capacity of Parliament to engage in more 'ordinary forms of dialogue' (namely, legislative sequels) than the politically impossible exercise of the formal override power.[86] The unanimous decisions of the ACT and Victorian Courts of Appeal in *Fearnside* and *Momcilovic* strongly suggest that, at least for the present, the courts are successfully resisting any such tendencies – indeed, to the point where the latter decision states that the interpretive duty adds nothing to traditional modes of statutory interpretation.[87] That is, the overall structural concern is whether they are too 'minimalist', doing too little rather than too much.

This limitation in the scope of the interpretive duty poses – and perhaps even partially answers – an interesting question about the role of text under the new model. The attempt to prevent statutory distortion or 'interpretation on steroids'[88] by inserting the unique textual limit of consistency with legislative purpose has been noted by some as an interesting experiment[89] and derided by others as likely powerless.[90] No one, of course, would suggest that the addition of these words provides the full and exclusive explanation, but it seems unlikely to be entirely coincidental that the most textually constrained version of the power coincides with the narrowest interpretation of that power in practice. Moreover, the *Fearnside* and *Momcilovic* judgments expressly justify their narrower conception of the power based on this textual difference, just as UK judges have reasoned that the strength of the duty under section 3 is based in significant part on the mandatory nature of the text.[91]

Returning to political rights review, the slightly lesser emphasis on its impact in the VCHRR review many not only reflect the greater bill of rights scepticism of its majority authors but also the reality. Despite the

---

[86] Dixon, 'A Minimalist Charter of Rights for Australia: the UK or Canada as a Model?'.

[87] In *Fearnside*, as we have seen, Besanko J. opined that section 30 grants the courts the slightly broader power of giving interpretations that are consistent, if not necessarily the *most* consistent, with legislative purpose.

[88] See Allan, 'The Victorian Charter', p. 912.

[89] See Evans and Evans, *Australian Bills of Rights*, pp. 95–6; Masterman, 'Interpretations, Declarations and Dialogue', pp. 119–21.

[90] See Allan, 'The Victorian Charter', p. 912 ('All that proponents of the Victorian Charter ... can point to as potentially vitiating this "interpretation on steroids" power and the resulting judicial activism is the s 32(1) phrase "consistently with their purpose" – a phrase absent in the New Zealand and UK reading down provisions. But that seems to be a fairly slight bulwark to constrain the judges, especially given Lon L Fuller's 60-year-old dissection of the malleability of purposive interpretation.').

[91] See Bingham, 'The Human Rights Act', p. 571.

required, and sometimes detailed, reasons in compatibility statements, the process of executive vetting remains opaque and the subsequent parliamentary review seems weaker than it might be in some respects. Although this conforms with the perceived norms of technical, non-partisan scrutiny and avoidance of policy issues, SARC's common practice of 'referring to Parliament for its consideration' identified human rights concerns, especially issues of justified limits, and at most concluding that legislative provisions 'may be incompatible' with human rights provides less specific guidance to Parliament than it may find useful from its designated rights committee.[92] SARC's failure to render even such a conclusion with respect to a bill that the responsible government minister acknowledged to be incompatible with, and an unreasonable limit on, several human rights is noteworthy,[93] although it has frequently disagreed with ministers' *compatibility* statements and the episode is not quite unprecedented among new model jurisdictions, in which such acknowledgements are rare.[94] And the subsequent, lopsided, bipartisan parliamentary approval of both bills subject to a government statement of incompatibility similarly does not suggest that a judicial role is redundant.

In terms of legislative responses to that judicial role in Australia, there is very little to go on, given the rarity of declarations of incompatibility and the current narrow conception of the interpretive duty. Nonetheless, the *RJE* episode described above is the best evidence to date of the likely approach of legislators to judicial rights review and suggests that they will play a more active role than the servile one James Allan predicted for them, one more along the lines of the *Hansen*/BZP series of events in New Zealand.[95]

Overall, despite the short time period involved, it seems clear that in practice neither of the two Australian bills of rights, with essentially the same set of judicial and legislative powers as under the UK's HRA, has created a system of de facto judicial supremacy, or strong-form judicial review in all but name. As with New Zealand, the more plausible concern

---

[92] This criticism of the style and tone of reports is equally, if not more true, of the ACT scrutiny committee.

[93] That is, the Summary Offences and Control of Weapons Amendment Act 2009.

[94] As we saw, the UK's JCHR eventually approved the clause of the Communications Bill 2003 that the government had stated was incompatible with an ECtHR precedent.

[95] As perhaps also does the government's response noted above (text accompanying n. 53) to the first declaration of incompatibility in the ACT, emphasizing that the dialogue model is designed to preserve legislative finality.

is whether they are, and (if they survive) will remain, distinct from traditional parliamentary sovereignty. Unlike in the UK or Canada, this issue of distinctness will turn on whether the courts – rather than legislatures – shed their reluctance to use their new model powers, interpretive and declaratory. If not, the Australian bills will end up duplicating the experience in Canada under the CBOR. Undoubtedly, this reluctance is partly explained by the pull of longstanding political culture,[96] but other new model jurisdictions with similar cultures show that it can be sufficiently transcended for these powers to take root. In addition to their interesting differences in text, the Australian bills operate in somewhat different contexts from the others, and this may also help to explain their early workings. First, whilst, as we have seen, the UK's HRA operates in the most heavily constraining environment of international legal obligations and oversight, the Australian bills are at the opposite end of the spectrum, uniquely free of both as sub-national entities with no such de jure obligations. Secondly, at least for the moment, both bills – and, more pointedly, the judges applying them – are operating in the shadow of scepticism following rejection of a statutory bill of rights at the national level.

---

[96] It may also be explained in part by the lack of a public consultation process, see Allan, 'The Victorian Charter'.

9

General assessment and conclusions

The initial and primary task of this final chapter is to assess the analytical and normative claims made for the new model in Part I of this book in light of its operational experience as presented over the course of the last four chapters. This experience inevitably forms part of the full case for or against the new model. In short, is practice living up to theory? To the extent it is not, or there is room for improvement on this score, the penultimate section will then consider if there are any general or specific reforms that might help to close the gap.

In Chapter 2 I argued that the new model is a distinct, intermediate form of constitutionalism consisting of two novel institutional features and techniques of rights protection: mandatory pre-enactment political rights review and non-final or weak-form judicial review. In Chapter 3, I claimed that in addition to being distinct, the new model is also a normatively appealing form of constitutionalism. This is because, by combining many of the strengths of both traditional polar models whilst avoiding their major characteristic weaknesses, it promises to effectively enforce constitutionalism's signature (though not exclusive) mandate of constraining governmental power in a way that gives maximum recognition to the principle of democratically accountable decision-making and political equality.

Accordingly, the two critical questions to be addressed respectively in the first two sections of this chapter are the following. First, taken as a whole, does the evidence indicate that the new model is operating in the distinct, intermediate manner that its twin novel features and constitutive allocation of powers and duties suggest? Is it in practice working anywhere close to the ideal case set out in Chapter 4? Or, by contrast, is it proving to be an unstable model in the real world, reverting to one or other of the traditional poles or even (in different jurisdictions) both, as has been variously claimed or predicted.[1] In

---

[1] Kavanagh, *Constitutional Review* (*de facto* judicial supremacy in the UK); Geddis 'Comparative Irrelevance' (reversion to parliamentary sovereignty in New Zealand; Tushnet, 'Weak-Form Judicial Review' (prediction of both).

particular, is mandatory pre-enactment political rights review having an impact on legislative processes and outputs? Is weak-form judicial review operating so that courts have a greater role in rights issues raised by legislation than under traditional parliamentary sovereignty but, at the same time, a less powerful or conclusive role than under judicial supremacy? Or does experience rather suggest that in practice there is no such thing as weak-form judicial review, no meaningful difference between it and the strong-form version?[2]

The second question is whether the new model is in practice fulfilling the normative promise I claimed for it. Is it functioning like the constitutionalist analogue to the mixed economy, combining the main strengths of the two polar models whilst avoiding their main weaknesses? Is the result a more optimal and proportionate combination of rights protection and political legitimacy than under the 'winner-take-all' approach of either traditional model? Although perhaps unlikely, it is possible that the new model could be operating in a distinct way but not in manner that secures the net benefits identified in Chapter 3. This would be the case, for example, if pre-enactment political rights review was triggering robust rights deliberation, courts were taking their role seriously and legislatures exercising their power of the final word in good faith, but all in a way that ultimately resulted in the systematic under-enforcement of rights. The converse, however, does not seem possible: that, in spite of operating in a way that is little different from one or both traditional models, the normative case for the new model has been made out in the crucible of practice. Accordingly, although these two questions are distinct, the answers to them are likely to overlap significantly.

I   Is the new model operating in a distinct, intermediate manner?

Let us begin to address this question by first considering the two more specific issues just identified regarding political and judicial rights review. What is the impact of the former, and is the weak-form version of the latter operating differently than either the strong-form version or no judicial review at all? As discussed in detail in the previous four chapters, it seems clear that the new model's constitutive mandatory pre-enactment political rights review is having an impact on legislative

---

[2] Kavanagh and Huscroft, see Chapters 5 and 7 above, effectively make this no difference claim focusing on the UK and Canada respectively.

processes in every jurisdiction, especially prior to a bill's introduction. At this stage of executive right-vetting, new procedures, guidelines and institutions have been created to advise both the relevant minister responsible for making a statement to Parliament and the Cabinet in devising and prioritizing its legislative agenda. Although, as we have seen, the results of this stage vary widely among the jurisdictions in terms of the number of incompatibility statements actually made – from zero to fifty-nine – the extent of executive review that the responsibility triggers and the seriousness with which it is taken are far more uniform and appear to be significant everywhere. And whilst, for the most part, the advice given has been more legal in content than the ideal working of the new model suggests, it still contributes significantly to the overall product of a distinctive, politically conducted *ex ante* rights review. After a bill's introduction, the procedural impact of political rights review has been greatest in the UK, where a powerful new specialized and non-partisan rights committee has helped to increase meaningful parliamentary oversight of the executive on rights issues and whose influential reports have informed several subsequent high-quality parliamentary debates.[3] Notwithstanding its undoubted current limitations,[4] the perceived relative success of the JCHR is increasingly leading to its being considered the gold standard under the new model generally, with calls for changes in its direction elsewhere.[5]

The impact of political rights review on legislative *outputs* is less clear. How often proposed bills are withdrawn or amended at the executive vetting stage is not generally public knowledge and hard to estimate. There appears to be a strong convention in Canada that bills deemed incompatible will not be introduced,[6] and a general sense that governments are most amenable to rights arguments at this point of the process, before they have committed themselves politically to its enactment. Post-introductory amendments based on perceived rights concerns of either the relevant legislative committee or other Members of Parliament have been relatively rare, in part due to the predictable reluctance of governments to reopen what they deem a done deal by this stage, although there have been a few notable examples in the UK. These include the Asylum

---

[3] See Chapter 7 above and the following paragraph below.
[4] See Hiebert, 'Governing under the Human Rights Act'.
[5] As noted in Chapter 8 above, the federal system in Australia has recently enacted legislation to create a parliamentary rights committee modelled on the JCHR, albeit without a bill of rights or increased judicial powers.
[6] See Chapter 5.

and Immigration Act 2004 and the Terrorism Act 2008, where the government was forced to withdraw the centrepiece of each bill following hostile
reception in Parliament and elsewhere.[7] These two pieces of legislation,
and others such as the Communication Act 2003, also elicited extended
and high-quality parliamentary debate on the relevant rights issues,
although with respect to both amendments and debate, the counterfactual
of showing they would not have occurred but for the HRA is, of course,
impossible to prove. There is evidence of generally increased parliamentary
oversight of the executive in the UK in recent years that roughly coincides
with enactment of the HRA, of which the JCHR is one important piece and
the inability of a government with a large majority to steer controversial
legislation through the parliamentary process intact on a few occasions is
another.[8] Overall, I may quibble with Janet Hiebert's use of the superlative
in characterizing political rights review as the most distinctive feature of
the new model in practice,[9] but not with the adjective. The role of this
co-equal, ex ante technique of rights protection has tended to be over-
looked by critics in favour of exclusive focus on the ex post mechanism of
weak-form judicial review.

Turning to the latter, in Chapter 4 I argued that the stability and
distinctness of the new model is threatened by non-use or misuse of the
powers granted rather than where these powers are placed at the outset or
their 'inherent' nature. Specifically, the new model risks collapsing in
practice into traditional parliamentary sovereignty where courts do not
use their powers of constitutional review or where legislatures too routinely
use theirs, and into judicial supremacy where either legislatures do not use
their power of the final word to the extent it becomes irrelevant or where
courts misuse their new powers. As far as the courts are concerned, it is
clear that they have been using their new powers of constitutional review, to
a greater or lesser degree, in all of the jurisdictions except the two
Australian ones. Here, as we have seen, the courts appear set on handing
back the powers their parliaments bestowed on them,[10] as evidenced first

---

[7] These were the ouster of judicial review from certain decisions of the Immigration and
Asylum Tribunal and the extension of the power to detain terror suspects to forty-two days,
respectively.

[8] See Tomkins, 'The Role of the Courts in Political Constitutionalism'.

[9] See Chapter 7, n. 101 above.

[10] This references the title of an article on the lower court (Victoria Court of Appeal)
decision in *Momcilovic*. J. Debeljak, 'Who is Sovereign Now? The *Momcilovic* Court
Hands Back Power Over Human Rights That Parliament Intended It To Have' (2011)
22(1) *Public Law Review* 15.

by the near absence of declarations of incompatibility and then in the decisions narrowing the scope of the interpretative duty to the traditional norms of statutory interpretation.[11] Elsewhere, however, this has not been the case. With the exception of Keith Ewing in the case of the UK, to the best of my knowledge no one from any part of the spectrum of commentary has accused either Canadian or British courts of generally and systematically failing to exercise their new powers of constitutional review, as distinct from in certain specific cases or subject-matter areas. In New Zealand, although the *Hansen* decision undoubtedly resolved for the time being the previous disagreements and uncertainty about the strength of the interpretative duty under section 6 of the NZBORA in favour of the weaker view, this view is still closer to the prevailing one in the UK than in Australia.[12] The NZSC has in no way suggested that section 6 simply codifies pre-existing, traditional norms of statutory interpretation and adds nothing to them, as the Australian courts have done. With respect to the judicial power to indicate a rights incompatibility that the NZCA seemed to imply into the NZBORA in 2000 but has never been exercised, it is certainly true that the New Zealand courts can plausibly be accused of tentativeness or feint-heartedness on this score,[13] but not of failing to exercise a power that has clearly and expressly been granted to them. Should the courts be formally empowered to issue declarations by Parliament and still not use them, as mostly in Australia, this would then be a different matter.

Are courts not only using, but also systematically misusing – in the sense of over-stepping or illegitimately expanding – their new but limited powers, so as to unduly minimize the legislative role and effectively create judicial exclusivity or supremacy? Although claims to this effect have been made with respect to both the UK and New Zealand,[14] the only plausible target is the former. As just mentioned, whatever the legitimate criticisms of the NZSC decision in *Hansen*, it cannot reasonably be said that it amounts to judicial overreaching – given the mandate in section 6. More generally, this case exemplifies the relatively cautious approach of New Zealand courts over the past decade, including the reluctance to employ the implied power to indicate legislative

---

[11] These decisions were *Fearnside* (ACT) and *Momcilovic* (Victoria). See Chapter 8.

[12] As the post-*Hansen* examples of *Brooker* and *Morse* illustrate. See Chapter 6 above.

[13] As, e.g., Claudia Geiringer does. See Geiringer, 'The Road to Nowhere'.

[14] As noted, James Allen had made this claim with respect to both jurisdictions. See Chapter 8 above.

inconsistencies with rights. The constitutional review powers of Canadian courts are not formally or internally limited in the way they are under the four other statutory bills of rights. Their powers are the same as under judicial supremacy; the limit is external, it comes from the outside as it were, via exercise of the legislative power under section 33. And, as we have seen, the opposite problem characterizes courts in the ACT and Victoria.

So, are UK courts misusing their powers under HRA sections 3 and/or 4, in a way that oversteps their limits and undermines the intended balance between them and also with Parliament on the resolution of rights issues? One major type of such misuse would be employing section 3(1) in a way that effectively violates section 3(2)(b) on the 'validity, continuing operation or enforcement of any incompatible primary legislation' and section 6(3) excluding Parliament from the public authorities bound to act consistently with Convention rights. This would, in practice, largely eliminate the declaration of incompatibility mechanism and its default rule in favour of Parliament, and amount to judicial lawmaking in the guise of interpretation (albeit statutory) just as often claimed under judicial supremacy. As we have seen, the evidence of such systematic misuse is slim and largely outdated. It is widely considered that the courts have scaled back from the strongest reading of section 3,[15] and that whilst the current standard is still more robust than courts in New Zealand and certainly Australia think legitimate for them, it contains the sorts of limits that maintain a non-negligible legislative role in resolving rights issues. In recent years, there have been few cases in which a substantial body of opinion believes the court used section 3 when it should have used section 4,[16] or indeed vice versa, and overall each has been used on roughly the same number of occasions.[17] Given the clear sense that section 3 is the primary HRA remedy and section 4 the exceptional one, this approximate equality effectively rebuts any such claim of abuse. A second major type of misuse would be systematic overuse of the declaratory power to find incompatibilities where none reasonably exist, but there is no plausible basis for such a claim. Finally, I explained in Chapter 7 my reasons for rejecting the line of criticism that even if UK courts are not misusing their powers,

---

[15] That is, in R. v. A. See, e.g., C. Gearty, 'The Human Rights Act – an academic sceptic changes his mind but not his heart' (2011) *European Human Rights Law Review* 582; Debeljuk, '*Momcilovic v The Queen and Ors*'; Geiringer, 'The Principle of Legality'.

[16] Gearty, *ibid.*   [17] See Chapter 7 above.

these powers themselves inherently amount in practice to a system of de facto judicial supremacy.[18]

And what about legislatures? Are they either failing to use their power of the final word so that the judicial view effectively becomes as conclusive as under judicial supremacy, or using it too routinely so that the judicial role in evaluating legislation for rights consistency becomes as minor and irrelevant, with as little impact, as under traditional parliamentary sovereignty? As we have seen at the jurisdiction-specific level, this is a major point of contention in both directions. In Canada, the recent non-use of section 33 as the distinctive mechanism for the legislative power of the final word, either pre-emptively or reactively, means that at best the SCC's view has become only marginally less conclusive than under judicial supremacy – even if this final judicial word is occasionally used at the court's discretion to uphold reasonable legislative disagreements enacted in sequels. Were use, or even serious consideration, of section 33 to be revived, as the current Harper Government periodically suggests, then this practical verdict would of course be open to revision.

In the UK, as discussed, it is still too early in the life of the HRA to draw definitive conclusions on this score, other than that (1) the ECHR has in practice placed a substantial constraint on the ability of both courts and legislatures to take independent positions, and (2) use of the legislative power in either the interpretative or declaratory context has certainly not been, and is very unlikely to become, routine. The prisoners' voting rights issue is the first one to be the subject of a declaration of incompatibility about which it can said both that there is room for reasonable disagreement on the substantive and interpretative merits, and ordinary citizens care.[19] Although the current stand-off is far more between the government and Parliament on the one side and the ECtHR, rather than the UK court issuing the declaration, on the other, this is still the most testing and telling scenario to have arisen thus far.[20]

---

[18] *Ibid.*, pp. 185–9.

[19] See the Angus Reid pubic opinion poll cited in Chapter 7, n. 101 above.

[20] As discussed above, because unlike the specific basis for the declaration of incompatibility in *A and others*, there is room for reasonable disagreement on the issue of whether a blanket ban on prison inmate voting interferes with the obligation 'to hold free elections at reasonable intervals by secret ballot, under conditions which will ensure the free expression of the opinion of the people in the choice of the legislature' under the First Protocol to the ECHR or is a justifiable limit on any individual right to vote that it contains.

In New Zealand, as we have seen, the legislature has almost always responded to judicial rights decisions in one way or another, with a mixed record of both accepting and not accepting these decisions.[21] The most obvious rejection of a conclusive judicial role and exercise of the legislative final word has been the recent BZP/Misuse of Drugs Act episode, in which Parliament not only failed to amend or repeal the reverse onus provision on possession that the NZSC had effectively found incompatible with the right to be presumed innocent in *Hansen*, but twice extended it to new drugs after this decision. This mixed record suggests that overall, the legislature is using its power and still has a significant voice in the ultimate resolution of rights issues raised by legislation, but not in the sort of automatic or routine way that denies or ignores a voice for the courts. Despite the statutory extensions of the reverse onus provision, the *Hansen* decision resulted in the establishment of a Law Commission inquiry which ultimately recommended its repeal, and the final outcome remains uncertain. However Parliament ultimately decides to resolve the issue – and it is Parliament that will decide – the NZSC decision did serve to identify and flag it, if admittedly not with the desired degree of visibility and priority. Although certainly not ideal, especially in terms of the quality of legislative rights deliberation, this still seems to be a fairly good example of how the new model is supposed to work.

In Australia, the general failure of the courts to use their powers means there has been little occasion for the parliaments to respond by using use theirs. Nonetheless, the Victorian Parliament's override of the Court of Appeal's statutory interpretation in *RJE*, albeit on formally non-Charter grounds, strongly suggests that legislatures will not shy away from acting on their disagreements.[22] If the courts' powers survive to be used, the main question is whether legislatures will override them too routinely.

What conclusions may be drawn from the above? It is not the case that the new model is generally operating indistinctly from judicial supremacy, as the instances of New Zealand and Australia illustrate. Here the record fairly clearly rebuts the claim that there is in practice no difference between strong-form and weak-form judicial review. At the same time, Canada and the UK demonstrate it is also not the case that the new model is generally operating indistinctly from legislative supremacy. More affirmatively and most importantly, the versions in New Zealand and the UK are operating in ways that are most distinct from either

---

[21] See Chapter 6, pp. 141–4 above.   [22] See Chapter 8, pp. 215–16 above.

traditional model, in that order. In three of the four countries, the new model is clearly working in a way that differs from the pre-existing regime of traditional parliamentary sovereignty, whereas in the fourth, Australia, the only major practical change thus far is the impact of political rights review during the legislative process. The experience of the ACT and Victoria also clearly shows that HRA sections 3 and 4-type interpretative and declaratory powers may operate in a very dissimilar way from US-style judicial review. They do not inherently amount to or result in de facto judicial supremacy, or indeed have any particular fixed 'strength'; rather, this varies with context.

Accordingly, taking both constitutive parts of the new model – political rights review and weak-form judicial review – into account, nowhere is there complete reversion to one or other of the two traditional models, and there is a range of distinctness in how the various versions of the new model are working. Superimposed on the general spectrum of forms of constitutionalism discussed in Chapter 2[23] and within the new model's intermediate portion of it, overall the Canadian Charter is operating closest to the judicial supremacy pole, with the HRA occupying the space next to it, a little further from the pole, the NZBORA the space after this, and the ACTHRA and the VCHRR operating closest to the legislative supremacy pole. This placement, it will be noted, matches that based on textual allocations of power alone noted above,[24] except for New Zealand and the Australian jurisdictions where it might be argued that the absence of a formal declaratory power in the NZBORA is more important in securing the near-polar slot than the latters' textual constraints on the interpretative power. Despite this general correspondence, however, the four statutory bills of rights exhibit only fairly small or relatively minor textual differences, which seem insufficient in themselves to explain the varying degrees of distinctness among them in practice. It is contextual differences that provide this fuller explanation.

Of the various bills of rights, the Canadian Charter was clearly designed and intended to introduce the most radical change from the pre-existing status quo of parliamentary sovereignty, and as such its popularity among the general population has remained stable and high.[25] As between the four statutory bills of rights, the HRA operates in the context and shadow of the supranational strong-form ECHR regime, which significantly limits the

---

[23] But putting aside the polar pure legal or total constitutionalism part of it for the purposes of this discussion.

[24] See Chapter 2 above.   [25] See public opinion poll numbers in Chapter 1, n. 56 above.

autonomy of both Parliament and the domestic courts. Although, unlike in Canada, there is much continuing discussion of the principle of parliamentary sovereignty, the reality is that there has been far greater erosion in what that sovereignty consists in, practically speaking, than in New Zealand and Australia, as well as more direct hostility to it in academic and judicial circles.[26] The two Australian bills of rights are, in turn, the least affected of the four by international human rights norms and accountability, to which as sub-national entities they are of course not legally bound. Moreover, not only have they both recently been operating in the shadow of a rejection of the new model at the national level, but the VCHRR has been subject to considerable partisan political pressure for its repeal since the change in government in 2010. The NZBORA is facing no such immediate political threats.

II Normative promise fulfilled?

As we have seen, the debate between proponents of the two traditional institutional forms of constitutionalism has significantly focused on the issue of the merits of judicial/constitutional review and, until recently, mostly consisted in essence of arguments about the proper resolution of the conflict between rights protection and democratic legitimacy. With the exception of the trade-off denying theories of Ely and Marshall/Hamilton/Ackerman discussed in Chapter 3,[27] the basic argument for political constitutionalism has been the argument from democracy (legal protection of rights beyond that afforded by, or subject to, politically accountable decision-making is an impermissible restriction of the principle of political equality and democratic legitimacy), and for legal constitutionalism the argument from rights (constitutional democracy requires a legal limit on the scope of majoritarian decision-making in order to properly protect individual rights).[28] In the past few years, however, the debate between legal and political constitutionalists has

---

[26] On the continued interest in the principle, see the amount of space devoted to it in a recent symposium on 'The Changing Landscape of British Constitutionalism', (2011) 9 *International Journal of Constitutional Law* 79–273. On the hostility, see e.g. the work of legal constitutionalists cited in Chapter 2 above. On the comparative point, see Geddis and Fenton, '"Which is to be Master?"', pp. 770–6 ('New Zealand's constitutional culture remains more deeply wedded to the orthodox idea of absolute parliamentary sovereignty than does the United Kingdom').

[27] See Chapter 3, section IV above.

[28] This basic argument for legal constitutionalism can be made in terms of redefining democracy to require that individual rights are legally protected against majoritarian

become more complex and also more of a direct colloquy, as each side has introduced a new dimension to its arguments leading it to claim the superiority (or deny the inferiority) of its position on *both* issues of rights protection and legitimacy. Thus, political constitutionalists have argued that by being able to focus more directly and fully on the underlying moral issues involved, legislative reasoning about rights is or may be superior to judicial reasoning, and legal constitutionalists that the overall political legitimacy of a constitutional democracy is enhanced and not diminished by judicial review. As argued in Chapter 3, the case for the new model is that, by blending and combining the various strengths of both models without their characteristic weaknesses, it promises to provide a more optimal and proportionate, less 'winner-takes-all', resolution of the two key issues of rights protection and legitimacy than either traditional model alone. That is, greater institutional protection of rights and no lesser legitimacy than political constitutionalism; greater legitimacy within a democracy and no lesser protection of rights than legal constitutionalism. Has this case been made out in practice?

Let us begin with the question of whether the new model jurisdictions have managed to combine the strengths of both traditional models with fewer of their weaknesses. Have they institutionalized the constitutionalist equivalent of the mixed economy? Recall that in concrete terms this combination means: (1) gaining the benefits of legislative rights reasoning but not to the exclusion of judicial reasoning; (2) gaining the benefits of judicial review to counter possible legislative under-enforcement of rights but without a judicial veto which creates its own risks of under- and over-enforcement of rights; and (3) maintaining specifically democratic legitimacy with a legislative power of the final word whilst acknowledging and accommodating the insight that other factors – protecting against rights under-enforcement and providing an adequate forum for individuals to challenge the reasonableness of legislative burdens imposed on them – are also jointly necessary for the full legitimacy of law in a constitutional democracy.[29]

As it occupies the space nearest the judicial supremacy pole,[30] practice under the Canadian Charter unsurprisingly combines several of the

---

decision-making, as with Dworkin's argument that a thick conception of equal concern and respect is necessary for a true democracy. R. Dworkin, *Freedom's Law: The Moral Reading of the Constitution* (Cambridge, MA: Harvard University Press, 1996). See Waldron, 'Constitutionalism – A Skeptical View', p. 31.

[29] See Chapter 3 above.

[30] Or the conventional legal constitutionalism space on the fuller spectrum discussed in Chapter 2, section III above.

strengths of legal constitutionalism but also several of its weaknesses, and has fewer of both the strengths and weaknesses of political constitutionalism. Thus, judicial review may help to counter legislative under-enforcement of rights and enable individuals to put the government to the burden of providing reasonable public justifications for limiting their rights, thereby contributing to overall political legitimacy. But the non-use of section 33 means that the various rights-relevant risks associated with a judicial veto are largely unmitigated. And, although the existence of section 33 does arguably mitigate part of the democratic legitimacy cost, its non-use also unnecessarily adds to this cost by accommodating the countervailing political legitimacy concerns in practically the same, disproportionate way as legal constitutionalism. The Charter regime also derives some of the political constitutionalist strength of political and legislative rights reasoning before and during a bill's introduction into Parliament, and occasionally a little afterwards in response to a judicial decision – as with *Daviault* and *O'Connor*. As we have seen, however, these two instances of legislative disagreement with the courts were not voiced as of right through the distinctive mechanism of section 33,[31] but were rather consented to by the SCC.

I have just argued that, all things considered, the NZBORA is operating in the most distinctly new model way, although still far from the ideal described in Chapter 4. How does this play out in terms of combining the strengths minus the weaknesses of the other two models? Legislative and judicial reasoning are both brought to bear on rights issues and have played important roles in several areas, with the courts helping to prompt Parliament to reform the law in the area of civil unions and its acceptance of the court's decision holding that public law damages are available for executive violations of the NZBORA.[32] In other areas, such as the reverse onus provision, Parliament has rejected the judicial view, although whether it ultimately accepts the similar position of the Law Commission remains to be seen.[33] Overall, therefore, legislative reasoning has tended to be final but non-exclusive, as the new model proposes, and is neither entirely unconstrained by the courts' view nor so constrained by it to amount in essence to a formality. From the ideal perspective, derived in turn from the normative case for the new model, the concern is whether this legislative final word is sufficiently reasonable or deliberative. In terms of specifically legislative rights

---

[31] That is, final for five years unless renewed.
[32] In *Baigent's Case*, see Chapter 6 above.   [33] *Ibid.*

reasoning versus executive, there is undoubtedly room for more in the pre-enactment review process. Arguably the contribution and benefit of non-final judicial review to both rights protection and broader political legitimacy would be further enhanced with the greater visibility and alerting power that formal indications of incompatibility might bring.

In the UK, the strength of political constitutionalism's focus on legislative and political rights reasoning as institutionalized in the new model has been a prominent feature of the HRA, although so far it has mostly been exhibited at the pre-enactment rather than post-enactment stage. At the same time, it is clearly not exclusive vis-à-vis the courts. The strengths of legal constitutionalism in terms of the role of the courts in identifying rights issues and critically examining government justifications has also been evident, if not always consistent. Whether the power of the final word has become a purely formal one that in practice cannot be exercised in disagreement with the courts is the key practical issue determining whether the HRA is avoiding the major weaknesses of legal constitutionalism whilst benefiting from its strengths. Once again, the resolution of the prisoners' voting rights issue may be illuminating here, although possibly only to underscore the dependence of the HRA on the de facto strong-form ECHR regime. Similarly key here is whether in practice the judicial contribution to broader political legitimacy is unnecessarily and disproportionately restrictive of specifically democratic legitimacy.

Operating nearest to the legislative supremacy pole, the two Australian jurisdictions are mostly experiencing the strengths and weaknesses of political constitutionalism, mitigated only a little by one of the strengths of legal constitutionalism. This latter is primarily the benefits of a fairly comprehensive bill of rights – namely, greater visibility and consciousness of rights – and an authoritative text and language of rights claims upon which political rights review can focus.[34] Otherwise, given the rarity of declarations of incompatibility thus far and the downgrading of the interpretative duty to nothing more than traditional, common law statutory interpretation, legislative rights reasoning effectively becomes exclusive and whilst this preserves democratic legitimacy, it is unnecessarily restrictive of other sources of overall political legitimacy.

---

[34] That is, political rights review is arguably easier and more effective where government lawyers, officials, ministers and Members of Parliament have an authoritative (if indeterminate) text and language to focus on rather than a mix of moral, common law, statutory and international rights, as under the new federal regime.

Accordingly, because Canada and the Australian jurisdictions are operating closer to the traditional poles of judicial and legislative supremacy respectively, they are experiencing more of the strengths and weaknesses of each with fewer of the countervailing net benefits of the other. By contrast, New Zealand and, to a lesser extent, the United Kingdom are operating closer to the middle of the spectrum, and so are reaping more of the net strengths of both in the way that the case for the new model suggests.

Let us now turn to the question of whether and to what extent the results of the attempted combination of the strengths minus the weaknesses of both models have matched the claims for it, in terms of the two key issues of rights and legitimacy. First, is the new model providing greater institutional protection of rights than traditional legislative supremacy, and no worse protection than under judicial supremacy? As discussed in Chapter 7, 9/11 and its aftermath have undoubtedly complicated the historical or internal comparisons by changing the political and regulatory context so that the types of national security responses and resulting civil liberties concerns had no immediate parallel before. Moreover, it is extremely difficult to assess the complex counterfactual of what protection of rights/civil liberties would now look like in the various jurisdictions absent their bills of rights. Nonetheless, overall it seems hard to argue that rights are not now better protected in Canada, the UK and New Zealand than before the Charter, the HRA and the NZBORA. The two Australian jurisdictions are another matter. The combination of (1) greater visibility, transparency and consciousness of rights that has come with a bills of rights, (2) the greater number of legally recognized rights, (3) the impact of pre-enactment political rights review on legislative processes and outputs, (4) the exercise of weak-form judicial review of legislation in its various modes, and (5) enhanced, full-blooded rights-based judicial review of administrative actions has resulted, to varying degrees in the different jurisdictions, in affording more rights protection than under the pre-existing regimes of parliamentary sovereignty. Although there are undoubtedly several instances in each country where, despite these changes, rights have been violated, there are many cases of rights being recognized and protected where they were not previously, or more recognized and protected, and essentially none the other way around.

On external or cross-regime comparison, one limited but concrete example of somewhat greater protection in new model jurisdictions than in a (continuing) parliamentary sovereignty one is the evidence mentioned above of more frequent and draconian terrorism legislation – especially relative to the official level of threat – at the federal level in Australia than in both Canada and the UK.[35] As to whether rights are as well, or even better, protected than under judicial supremacy, it is again difficult to make a systematic and rigorous comparison. Nonetheless, in terms of political rights review, Parliament's forcing the withdrawal of the proposed extension in pre-trial detention to 42 days under the UK's 2008 Terrorism Act compares favourably with the recent passage by the US Congress of the National Defense Authorization Act for Fiscal Year 2012, permitting indefinite detention of terrorism suspects without trial or charge.[36] And in terms of judicial review, despite other less rights-protective decisions in the national security context both before and since, the leading UK case of *A and others* also compares favourably with the facts that the United States Supreme Court (1) would likely not have decided a similar case in the same way, and (2) has not yet clearly and unequivocally held that any constitutional rights have been violated by post-9/11 government action – executive or legislative.[37]

On the second issue of legitimacy, it seems incontrovertible that exercises of judicial review under the statutory bills of rights – and even perhaps also under the Charter – have greater specifically democratic legitimacy than under mainstream strong-form review because of the existence of the legislative power to respond by ordinary majority vote. And to the extent the evidence just discussed suggests there is generally no lesser institutional protection of rights than under judicial supremacy, combined with the multiple forums – political and judicial – that the new model provides for putting governments to the task of providing a reasonable justification for limiting rights, it appears to be doing no worse on other sources of political legitimacy. Accordingly, the net claim of greater overall legitimacy than judicial supremacy remains a highly plausibly one after practice has been taken into account. So, too, does the converse case of no lesser overall legitimacy than traditional parliamentary sovereignty. The legal power of the final word maintains the democratic legitimacy of the new model as long as it does not become a pure and complete formality, which I have argued is not the case even in Canada, and very clearly not in New Zealand and Australia. And to the extent the two other sources of overall political legitimacy are enhanced

---

[35] See Chapter 7, text accompanying nn. 116–17 above.
[36] 112th Congress, 1st session, H1540CR.HSE, Title X, subtitle D, sections 1021–2.
[37] See Chapter 7, text accompanying nn. 127–8 above.

by the new model, as I have argued the evidence suggests, the net claim of at least no lesser legitimacy also remains highly plausible.

III   Reforms

I have argued that the new model is working in at least a minimally distinct way everywhere, if only because of the practice of pre-enactment political rights review, and more than minimally in New Zealand and the UK. Correspondingly, I have also explained how and to what extent the normative case for the new model is being realized in practice. It is clear, however, that nowhere is the new model operating close to the ideal version sketched in Chapter 4. Although this is hardly surprising, as neither legal nor political constitutionalism operates in the ideal way proponents tend to suggest in making their cases, it does raise the issue of what types of reforms might move the new model, either generally or in its specific versions, into more clearly intermediate territory. As an experiment in a novel institutional form of constitutionalism, it is entirely fitting that the trial and error approach based on experience and comparative observation should be used. Indeed, the ACT example of mandatory review followed by a series of amendments and practical reforms to address identified problems could usefully be copied everywhere.

Starting with the general, the experience and common aims of mandatory pre-enactment political rights review in the various jurisdictions suggests a standard model that should become the norm.[38] In every jurisdiction there have been two tendencies that depart from the ideal working of this initial stage of the new model. The first is too great a focus on legal and judicial rights reasoning, at the expense of more independent political judgment that takes a broader and more direct approach to the moral and policy issues involved. This latter is one of the major insights of political constitutionalism and is designed to be insti-tutionalized within the new model at both this first stage and the last. The second tendency has been for too little of the political rights review and deliberation to be undertaken by the legislature rather than the executive. Again, as many of the arguments for the new model focus specifically on the practical and normative merits of legislative rights reasoning, there needs to be a greater parliamentary role in this process.

[38] Although this model is premised on a parliamentary system of government and would have to be adjusted should a presidential system ever adopt the new Commonwealth model as a whole, these adjustments do not appear to pose an insuperable problem.

To these ends, and based on the experiences of the various jurisdictions, the standard model of first stage political rights review should incorporate the following features. Compatibility statements should be made by the responsible minister or Member of Parliament rather than the Attorney General or other senior law officer to reduce the perception that this is fundamentally a legal issue. They should also be required whether or not the minister is of the opinion that the bill is compatible with the bill of rights, as this ensures both that significant executive rights-vetting occurs and is taken seriously with every bill and that Parliament is always given at least some information and material to work with. In any event, the evidence produced during executive rights review should always be made available to Parliament. Incompatibility statements should not be made simply because legal concerns have been identified, or even deemed conclusive, but only where the minister, in the exercise of independent political judgment, is of the opinion that there is an incompatibility and yet still believes on behalf of the government that it is justified in proposing the legislation. Of course, sometimes the result of such political judgment will be to disagree with the legal advice received and find the proposed bill consistent with rights (including as a justified limitation) so that no such incompatibility statement is required.

In terms of enhancing Parliament's role, the JCHR should be viewed as the gold standard for a rights committee – specialized, non-partisan and with a full-time, high-quality legal advisor. It should be made clear, however, that the role of the latter is to assist the committee in giving it legal advice with the understanding that it is the task of the committee members to supply the independent political judgment in reaching their overall conclusions. In so doing, the committee should directly address proportionality issues, which, because they include assessments of alternative policy options, have an obviously political component at the very least. These conclusions on rights issues and concerns, including proportionality, should be stated clearly and forthrightly in the resulting reports, as it is more helpful to Parliament to have the views of its expert committee before it during subsequent debate than in effect merely to have issues flagged and identified. Finally, Parliament must have time to consider the committee's report and to debate the merits of the conclusions reached in it, as well as rights information from other sources, before a final vote on the bill. If and where necessary, this consideration of the committee report must be mandated. In the ways and to the extent each jurisdiction departs from this standard model, as discussed in

Chapters 5 to 8, a first set of country-specific reforms is to work towards achieving greater adherence to the norm.

With respect to stages two and three, a dilemma has emerged from the experience of the new model jurisdictions as a whole with weak-form judicial review and the legislative response to it. If courts are granted the power to invalidate rights-incompatible statutes (as under the Charter), there is a serious risk that the political costs will generally be too high for the legislature to exercise its override power, leading to a *de facto* judicial final word. If, on the other hand, courts are not granted the power of invalidation (as in the other four jurisdictions), then the risk that the individual whose rights they deem violated will not receive a remedy creates pressure on the courts to rely too much on their interpretative power/duty, again at the potential cost of ousting legislative judgment and creating a de facto judicial final word. In each case, the risk is that the legislative power is made too hard to exercise where the default rests with a court decision, as under both the invalidation and interpretative powers. Although New Zealand and Australian courts have seemed better able than those of the UK to resist the pressure under the second horn of this dilemma, the general solution, I believe, lies in reducing it by instituting a rule or norm of a legislative remedy to the individuals concerned where Parliament subsequently decides to amend or repeal a statute that was the subject of an express or implied judicial declaration of incompatibility, as discussed in Chapter 7 on the UK.

Finally, in terms of general reforms, there is the issue of judicial appointments. Judges exercising their new model powers of constitutional review remain largely free from the forms of direct and indirect political accountability typical of constitutional courts around the world. In most legal constitutionalist regimes, legislatures play a significant role in the appointment of constitutional judges and the political affiliation of judges is taken into account in almost all. Additionally, among civil law jurisdictions (and South Africa), nine- or twelve-year non-renewable fixed terms are the norm, rather than unlimited terms with or without mandatory retirement. As I argued in Chapter 3, one of the benefits of the new model, as compared with judicial supremacy, is that it has the resources to resist the call for the indirect accountability of constitutional court judges so that there is no necessity for high judicial offices to become political appointments. Nonetheless, increasing the political, and especially the legislative role, in judicial appointments to courts exercising the new powers of constitutional review is – along with adjusting tenure – a tool that is available for recalibrating judicial and legislative power where and to the extent it is thought the balance has moved too far in the direction of the former. Indeed, for those who advance or agree with the de facto judicial supremacy thesis, this continuing exceptionalism ought to be viewed as a serious anomaly.

Turning now from general to country-specific reforms, let us start with Canada. In terms of political rights review, there are several major shortfalls from the standard model. The Attorney General is responsible for incompatibility statements, and none are required where legislation is deemed compatible, which has been the case on every occasion. As the process and outcome of bureaucratic/executive rights vetting is far from transparent, this record raises obvious concerns about its integrity and/ or seriousness. Part of this opaqueness is manifested in the frequent denials of requests for access to the government's evidence of compatibility by the parliamentary committees, which hinders their own ability to assess Charter consistency. These two standing committees are semi-specialized only, have no legal advisers of their own, and often have too little time to conduct hearings and write reports, for which there is in turn frequently too little opportunity for parliamentary debate in the government-controlled legislative timetable.

Within stages two and three, as discussed above, the major issue is the practical status of section 33. Here, although expressed for opportunistic or partisan reasons, the position of the governing Conservative Party, that section 33 remains part of the Charter and is fair game to be used, is preferable to the principled opposition of the Liberal Party. If the politics of the Charter alone do not result in such a change, and the development of a theory of legitimate use does not succeed in altering citizens' generally negative connotation of section 33 as a legislative override of their rights, then efforts should be focused on amending its wording to try and clarify its legitimate and distinctive role as a vehicle for reasonable legislative disagreement with the courts.[39] Even then, there would still be the question of whether the political costs of the necessary affirmative exercise of the power – pre-emptive use aside – where the default position rests with the courts would likely be too high. And this problem would still be compounded, as it is now, by the sense that use of section 33 is unnecessary to the extent the same goal can be achieved via section 1, if courts exercise their strong-form power by choosing to defer (strategically or otherwise) to reasonable legislative disagreements enacted in sequels.

---

[39] Although, to be sure, the Charter is extremely difficult to amend. See Chapter 5, text accompanying n. 12.

The common problems of overly legal and executive dominated political rights review are evident under the NZBORA and should be addressed in the ways suggested above. The more singular problems are the comparatively large number of incompatibility statements, which may reduce the gravity with which both government and Parliament view rights-incompatible legislation, as Huscroft suggests,[40] and the absence of a parliamentary rights committee. As for the second and third stages, the main weakness in practice is the insufficient visibility, and therefore alerting power, of what are inevitably judicial findings of incompatibility once the court has held that a rights-consistent interpretation of a statute is not possible under section 6, as in *Hansen*. As Geiringer puts it, the NZSC found, but did not declare, the incompatibility.[41] This effective burying of the incompatibility results in too low a political cost on the legislature to retain the statute. As discussed, for reasons of judicial-legislative balance, the best solution may be for the courts to start exercising the implied power to declare an inconsistency in appropriate cases, but if the NZSC continues to back away from this due to cultural reluctance to challenge or criticize Parliament, it may be necessary to amend the NZBORA to include a formal declaratory power – or even a duty.

Despite the fact that political rights review comes closest to the standard model in the UK, there is certainly room for both more political judgment rather than legal advice in the process, and a greater parliamentary role. As discussed above and in Chapter 7, the establishment of a norm or rule of a legislative remedy where Parliament amends or repeals a statute declared incompatible with Convention rights by the courts should help to counter any remaining concerns about judicial skewing in favour of section 3 over section 4 for remedial reasons, although these concerns are perhaps less urgent in the light of more recent practice. Alternatively, section 3 could be weakened textually, along the lines of the Australian examples, with little prospect of this having the same over-compensating practical result as there. Finally, the Strasbourg handcuffs might be loosened a little, permitting the UK version to operate slightly more autonomously, by the establishment of a separately worded set of rights not identical to the ECHR.

Under the VCHRR, the process of political rights review at stage one needs to become more transparent and less secretive, and SARC reports should take a more clear-cut view on perceived incompatibilities, giving Parliament the benefit of its expert judgment in resolving rather than

---

[40] Huscroft, 'Reconciling Duty and Discretion'.   [41] Geiringer, 'On the Road to Nowhere'.

mostly identifying rights issues. The latter also applies to the ACTHRA. SARC also operates on a more politically partisan basis than is helpful for the model to work successfully in a parliamentary context. Here, at least, perhaps the new federal regime under the Human Rights (Parliamentary Scrutiny) Act might become something of a model. If Victoria is to remain a new model jurisdiction, it is obviously essential, first, that the majority recommendation of the parliamentary committee conducting the mandatory four-year review to abolish the new judicial powers be rejected and, second, that these powers are used. In particular, unless courts are willing to issue declarations of inconsistent interpretations whenever there is an apparent incompatibility, the *Momcilovic* decision narrowing the scope of the interpretative duty to the point of redundancy should be reversed. It must be affirmed and clarified that this is indeed a new power beyond traditional common law statutory interpretation, and the power broadened to somewhere close to the New Zealand one. Again, this second must also happen in the ACT, with respect to the similar decision in *Fearnside*. To the extent that the operation of these two experiments at the sub-national level has become affected by events at the federal level, obviously the enactment of a national human rights act might shift the momentum again in the direction of legal/political change and help to reverse the resulting drift back towards traditional parliamentary sovereignty.

IV   Conclusions

And so, finally, we return to the question with which this book began. Is ink or eraser the better response to the current pencilled-in status of the new model as a third institutional form of constitutionalism?

Practically, the new model is a politically endangered species in the UK and Victoria, and it may not survive a change of government in the ACT. This, of course, reflects not only the prevailing political climate, but also its formal legal status as an ordinarily repealable statute in four of the five jurisdictions. Normatively and analytically, however, *qua* model, its survival does not depend on a headcount of jurisdictions, as the increasingly elusive traditional model of parliamentary sovereignty demonstrates. Accordingly, in and of themselves, the political uncertainties surrounding the future of the new model are not directly relevant to our question. They become relevant only if they reflect net experiences under the new model that undermine its claimed distinctness or appeal, rather than opportunistic or purely political opposition.

So which way does the evidence point on these central issues? The first general conclusion to draw is that it is still too early in the short history of the new model to come to any definitive assessment. The best evidence of the still developing and maturing, in flux and unpredictable nature of the overall experiment is the current series of events, the outcomes of which are still uncertain, in all of the countries except Canada, where the overall contours of the new model are most stable and defined.[42] Bearing in mind the well-known claims and predictions of instability or indistinctness that have been made, what can be said with confidence is the following. There is clear evidence of reversion towards parliamentary sovereignty in the two Australian jurisdictions, and also of a slide towards judicial supremacy in Canada. At the same time, there is clear evidence of a more balanced, intermediate position taking hold in the UK and especially New Zealand, particularly when the impact of pre-enactment political rights review is taken into account alongside the practice of weak-form judicial review. In both countries, there is a significant, meaningful and complementary role in interpreting and applying the bill of rights (including its limitation provisions) for both the legislature and the courts, roles that vary with the context in which rights issues arise, and their political valences.

There is also clear evidence that essentially identical declaratory and interpretative judicial powers may in practice vary greatly in the extent to which they are similar or dissimilar to the powers of courts under US-style judicial review. The comparison of experiences in the UK and the Australian jurisdictions strongly suggests that these two new model judicial powers have no fixed or inherent 'weight', rather their relative strength or weakness depends on the context in which they are granted and exercised. So to the extent that these powers operate more similarly to strong-form ones in the UK, this is significantly because of the contingency (from the perspective of the new model) of the ECHR regime. But for the legal effect of the ECtHR decisions in *Hirst* and *Greens and MT*, affirmed in its recent *Scoppola* judgment, Parliament would almost certainly maintain section 3 of the Representation of the People Act despite the domestic judicial declaration of incompatibility, and may still do so anyway.[43] The interpretative power/duty operates differently in New

---

[42] I am referring here to the BPZ/*Hansen* episode in New Zealand, the prisoners' voting rights issues in the UK and the future of the new judicial powers under the VCHRR. See Chapters 6, 7 and 8 above.

[43] See Chapter 7 above.

Zealand than in both the UK and Australia, with a strength that is somewhere in between the latter two. Were New Zealand also to adopt a formal declaratory power, it seems quite likely that the combined effect of the two would also be more dissimilar from US-style judicial review than in the UK, but less dissimilar than in Australia.

The relatively early, incomplete and varied state of the evidence at this point also means that the core normative appeal of the new model, *qua* model, retains its promise. Given the modern circumstances of constitutionalism – a rights revolution alongside a democratic one, rights provisions that mostly trigger rights analysis rather than resolve it, and all filtered through the 'ultimate' principle of proportionality[44] – an overall mix of legislative and judicial, political and legal, rights reasoning and review seems preferable to, and more easily justifiable than, an essentially exclusive role for one or the other. Within this mix, the benefits of a more rights-conscious legislature and executive and of greater rights deliberation within the legislative process seem compelling, as does the claim of such a legislature to be granted the authority to ultimately resolve rights issues, where, informed by the judicial view, it reasonably disagrees with it in good faith and after serious consideration. Such promise is worth tinkering with in experimental mode for a while longer.

If it is not yet time to call for the ink, it is also too soon to employ the eraser.

---

[44] D. Beatty, *The Ultimate Rule of Law* (Oxford University Press, 2004).

BIBLIOGRAPHY

Ackerman, B., *We the People: Foundations* (Cambridge, MA: Harvard University Press, 1991).
'The Rise of World Constitutionalism' (1997) 83 *Virginia Law Review* 771.
Allan, J., 'Portia, Bassano or Dick the Butcher? Constraining Judges in the Twenty-first Century' (2006) 17 *King's College Law Journal* 1.
'The Victorian Charter of Rights and Responsibilities: Exegesis and Criticism' (2006) 30 *Melbourne University Law Review* 907.
'Statutory Bills of Rights: You Read Words In, You Read Words Out, You Take Parliament's Clear Intention and You Shake It All About – Doin' the Sanky Hanky Panky', in T. Campbell, K. Ewing and A. Tomkins (eds.), *Legal Protection of Human Rights: Sceptical Essays* (New York: Oxford University Press, 2011).
Allan, T. R. S., *Law, Liberty, and Justice: The Legal Foundations of British Constitutionalism* (Oxford University Press, 1993).
Constitutional Justice: A Liberal Theory of the Rule of Law (Oxford University Press, 2001).
Archer, C., 'Section 7 of the Bill of Rights Act' (2004) *New Zealand Law Journal* 320.
Bagehot, W., *The English Constitution*, The Fontana Library (London: Collins, 1963).
Barron, J. and Dienes, C. T., *Constitutional Law*, 4th edn (St Paul, MO: West, 1999).
Beatson, J., Grosz, S., Hickman, T. and Singh, R., *Human Rights: Judicial Protection in the United Kingdom* (London: Sweet & Maxwell, 2008).
Beatty, D., *The Ultimate Rule of Law* (Oxford University Press, 2004).
Bell, J., *French Constitutional Law* (Oxford: Clarendon Press, 1992).
Bellamy, R., *Political Constitutionalism: A Republican Defence of the Constitutionality of Democracy* (Cambridge University Press, 2007).
'Political Constitutionalism and the Human Rights Act' (2011) 9 *International Journal of Constitutional Law* 86.
Bickel, A., *The Least Dangerous Branch* (New Haven, CT: Yale University Press, 1962).

Bingham, T., 'The Human Rights Act' (2010) 6 *European Human Rights Law Review* 568.

Brewer-Carias, A., *Judicial Review in Comparative Law* (Cambridge University Press, 1989).

Bromwich, T., 'Parliamentary Rights-Vetting Under the NZBORA' (2009) *New Zealand Law Journal* 189.

Butler, A., 'The Bill of Rights Debate: Why the New Zealand Bill of Rights Act 1990 is a Bad Model for Britain' (1997) 17 *Oxford Journal of Legal Studies* 323.

Butler, A. and Butler, P., *The New Zealand Bill of Rights Act: A Commentary* (Wellington: LexisNexis, 2005).

Butler, P., 'It Takes Two to Tango – Have They Learned Their Steps?' available at ssrn.com/abstract=2022681.

Butler, P. and Butler, A., '16 Years of the New Zealand Bill of Rights', Paper presented at Southern Currents: Australian and New Zealand Law Librarians Conference, University of Melbourne Law School, 27–29 Sept. 2006

Cameron, J., 'The Charter's Legislative Override: Feat or Figment of the Constitutional Imagination' (2004) 23 *Supreme Court Law Review* (Second Series) 135.

Cappelletti, M. and Cohen, W., *Comparative Constitutional Law* (Indianapolis, IN: Bobbs-Merrill, 1979).

Cappelletti, M., Kollmer, P. J. and Olson, J. M., *The Judicial Process in Comparative Perspective* (Oxford: Clarendon Press, 1989).

Choper, J., *Judicial Review and the National Political Process* (University of Chicago Press, 1980).

Choudhry, S., 'The Lochner Era and Comparative Constitutionalism' (2004) 2 *International Journal of Constitutional Law* 1.

  'So What Is the Real Legacy of Oakes? Two Decades of Proportionality Analysis under the Canadian Charter's Section 1' (2006) 34 *Supreme Court Law Review* (second series) 501.

  'After the Rights Revolution: Bills of Rights in the Post-Conflict State' (2010) 6 *Annual Review of Law and Social Science* 301.

Choudhry, S. and Roach, K., 'Putting the Past Behind Us? Prospective Judicial and Legislative Constitutional Remedies' (2003) 21 *Supreme Court Law Review* (second series) 205.

Cole, D., 'English Lessons: A Comparative Analysis of UK and US Responses to Terrorism' (2009) 62 *Current Legal Problems* 136.

Comella, V. F., *Constitutional Courts and Democratic Values* (New Haven, CT: Yale University Press, 2009).

Debeljak, J., '*Momcilovic v. The Queen and Ors*: From Definite Pessimism to Cautious Optimism in 273 pages!', presented at the Public Law Weekend – 10 Years on from September 11: the Impact on Public Law, at the Centre for International and Public Law, Australian National University, Canberra, 9–10 September, 2011.

'Who is Sovereign Now? The Momcilovic Court Hands Back Power Over Human Rights That Parliament Intended It To Have' (2011) 22 *Public Law Review* 15.

Devins N. and Fisher, L., *The Democratic Constitution* (Oxford University Press, 2004).

Dixon, R., 'Creating Dialogue About Socio-Economic Rights: Strong v. Weak-Form Judicial Review Revisited' (2007) 5 *International Journal of Constitutional Law* 391.

'A Minimalist Charter of Rights for Australia: The UK or Canada as a Model?' (2009) 37 *Federal Law Review* 335.

'The Supreme Court of Canada, Charter Dialogue, and Deference' (2009) 47 *Osgoode Hall Law Journal* 235.

Dworkin, R., *Taking Rights Seriously* (Cambridge, MA: Harvard University Press, 1977).

Freedom's Law: The Moral Reading of the Constitution (Cambridge, MA: Harvard University Press, 1996).

Ellickson, R., *Order Without Law: How Neighbors Settle Disputes* (Cambridge, MA: Harvard University Press, 1991).

Elliott, M., 'Parliamentary Sovereignty and the New Constitutional Order: Legislative Freedom, Political Reality, and Convention' (2002) 22 *Legal Studies* 340.

'Interpretative Bills of Rights and the Mystery of the Unwritten Constitution' (2011) *New Zealand Law Review* 591.

Ely, J. H., *Democracy and Distrust* (Cambridge, MA: Harvard University Press, 1971).

Erdos, D., *Delegating Rights Protection: The Rise of Bills of Rights in the Westminster World* (Oxford University Press, 2010).

Evans, C. and Evans, S., *Australian Bills of Rights: The Law of the Victorian Charter and ACT Human Rights Act* (Chatswood: LexisNexis, 2008).

Ewing, K., 'The Futility of the Human Rights Act' (2004) *Public Law* 829.

The Bonfire of the Liberties (Oxford University Press, 2011).

Ewing, K. and Gearty, C., *Freedom Under Thatcher* (Oxford University Press, 1990).

Ewing, K. and Tham, J., 'The Continuing Futility of the Human Rights Act' (2008) *Public Law* 668.

Fallon, R., 'The Core of an Uneasy Case for Judicial Review' (2008) 121 *Harvard Law Review* 1693.

Favoreu, L., 'Constitutional Review in Europe', in L. Henkin and A. Rosenthal (eds.), *Constitutionalism and Rights: The Influence of the United States Constitution Abroad* (New York: Columbia University Press, 1990).

Feldman, D., 'Extending the Role of the Courts: The Human Rights Act 1998' (2011) 30 *Parliamentary History* 65.

Forsyth, C. (ed.), *Judicial Review and the Constitution* (Oxford: Hart Publishing, 2000).

Friedman, B., 'Dialogue and Judicial Review' (1993) 91 *Michigan Law Review* 577.

The Will of the People: How Public Opinion has Influenced the Supreme Court and Shaped the Meaning of the Constitution (New York: Farrar, Straus & Giroux, 2009).

Gardbaum, S., 'The New Commonwealth Model of Constitutionalism' (2001) 49 *American Journal of Comparative Law* 707.

'Limiting Constitutional Rights' (2007) 54 *UCLA Law Review* 789.

'The Myth and the Reality of American Constitutional Exceptionalism' (2008) 107 *Michigan Law Review* 391.

'Reassessing the New Commonwealth Model of Constitutionalism' (2010), 8 *International Journal of Constitutional Law* 167.

'The Place of Constitutional Law in the Legal System' in M. Rosenfeld, and A. Sajo (eds.), *The Oxford Handbook of Comparative Constitutional Law* (Oxford University Press, 2012).

Gearty, C. 'Reconciling Parliamentary Democracy and Human Rights', (2002) 118 *Law Quarterly Review* 249.

'The Human Rights Act – An Academic Sceptic Changes His Mind But Not His Heart' (2010) *European Human Rights Law Review* 582.

Geddis, A., 'The Comparative Irrelevance of the NZBORA to Legislative Practice' (2009) 23 *New Zealand Universities Law Review* 465.

Geddis, A. and Fenton, B., '"Which is to be Master?" – Rights-Friendly Statutory Interpretation in New Zealand and the United Kingdom' (2008) 25 *Arizona Journal of International & Comparative Law* 733.

Gee, G. and Webber, G., 'What is a Political Constitution?' (2010) 30 *Oxford Journal of Legal Studies* 273.

Geiringer, C., 'The Principle of Legality and the Bill of Rights Act: A Critical Examination of *R v. Hansen*' (2008) 6 *New Zealand Journal of Public and International Law* 59.

'On a Road to Nowhere: Implied Declarations of Inconsistency and the New Zealand Bill of Rights Act' (2009) 40 *Victoria University Wellington Law Review* 612.

Ginsburg, T., *Judicial Review in New Democracies: Constitutional Courts in Asian Cases* (Cambridge University Press, 2003).

Glendon, M. A., *Rights Talk: The Impoverishment of Political Discourse* (Cambridge, MA: Harvard University Press, 1991).

Goldsworthy, J., 'Homogenizing Constitutions' (2003) 23 *Oxford Journal of Legal Studies* 483.

'Judicial Review, Legislative Override, and Democracy' (2003) 38 *Wake Forest Law Review* 451.

Parliamentary Sovereignty: Contemporary Debates (Cambridge University Press, 2010).

Green, A., Johns, N. and Rix, M., 'Liberty, National Security and the Big Society' (2011) 16 *Sociological Research Online* 19.

Greschner, D. and Norman, K., 'The Courts and Section 33' (1987) 12 *Queen's Law Journal* 155.

Gunther, G., 'Congressional Power to Curtail Federal Court Jurisdiction: An Opinionated Guide to the Ongoing Debate' (1984) 36 *Stanford Law Review* 895.

Harel, A. and Kahana, T., 'The Easy Core Case for Judicial Review' (2010) 2 *Journal of Legal Analysis* 1.

Harel, A. and Shinar, A., 'Between Judicial and Legislative Supremacy: A Cautious Defense of Constrained Judicial Review' (forthcoming)

Hickman, T., 'In Defence of the Legal Constitution' (2005) 55 *University of Toronto Law Journal* 981.

Public Law After the Human Rights Act (Oxford: Hart Publishing, 2010).

Hiebert, J., *Limiting Rights: The Dilemmas of Judicial Review* (Montreal: McGill-Queen's University Press, 1996).

Charter Conflicts: What is Parliament's Role? (Montreal: McGill-Queen's University Press, 2002).

'Is it Too Late to Rehabilitate Canada's Notwithstanding Clause?' (2004) 23 *Supreme Court Law Review* (Second Series) 169.

'New Constitutional Ideas: Can New Parliamentary Models Resist Judicial Dominance when Interpreting Rights?' (2004) 82 *Texas Law Review* 1963.

'Rights-Vetting in New Zealand and Canada: Similar Idea, Different Outcomes' (2005) 3 *New Zealand Journal of Public and International Law* 63.

'Parliament and the HRA: Can the JCHR Facilitate a Culture of Human Rights?' (2006) 4 *International Journal of Constitutional Law* 1.

'Parliamentary Bills of Rights: An Alternative Model?' (2006) 69 *Modern Law Review* 7.

'Constitutional Experimentation: Rethinking How a Bill of Rights Functions' in T. Ginsburg, and R. Dixon (eds.), *Comparative Constitutional Law* (Cheltenham: Edward Elgar, 2011).

'Governing Under the Human Rights Act: The Limitations of Wishful Thinking' (2012) *Public Law* 27.

Hogg, P. W., *Constitutional Law of Canada* (Toronto: Thomson, 1977).

Constitutional Law of Canada, 5th edn, 2 vols. (Toronto: Thomson, 2007).

Hogg, P. W. and Bushell, A. A., 'The Charter Dialogue Between Courts and Legislatures (Or Perhaps The Charter of Rights Isn't Such A Bad Thing After All)' (1997) 35 *Osgoode Hall Law Journal* 75.

Hogg, P. W. Thornton, A. A. B., and Wright, W. K., 'Charter Dialogue Revisited – or "Much Ado About Metaphors"' (2007) 45 *Osgoode Hall Law Journal* 1.

'A Reply on "Charter Dialogue Revisited"' (2007) 45 *Osgoode Hall Law Journal* 193.

Holmes, S., 'Gag Rules, or the Politics of Omission' in J. Elster and R. Slagstad (eds.), *Constitutionalism and Democracy* (Cambridge University Press, 1988).

Hunt, M., 'The Impact of the Human Rights Act on the Legislature: A Diminution of Democracy or a New Voice for Parliament?' (2010) 6 *European Human Rights Law Review* 601.

Hunt, M., Hooper H. and Yowell, P., 'Parliaments and Human Rights: Redressing the Democratic Deficit' (2012) *Arts & Humanities Research Council* April, 19–22.

Husa, J., 'Guarding the Constitutionality of Laws in the Nordic Countries: A Comparative Perspective' (2000) 48 *American Journal of Comparative Law* 345.

Huscroft, G., 'The Attorney-General's Reporting Duty' in P. Rishworth, G. Huscroft, S. Optician and R. Mahoney (eds.), *The New Zealand Bill of Rights Act* (Melbourne: Oxford University Press, 2003).

'Constitutionalism from the Top Down' (2007) 45 *Osgoode Hall Law Journal* 91.

'Rationalizing Judicial Power: The Mischief of Dialogue Theory' in J. Kelly and C. Manfredi (eds.), *Contested Constitutionalism: Reflections on the Charter of Rights and Freedoms* (Vancouver: University of British Columbia Press, 2009).

'Reconciling Duty and Discretion: The Attorney General in the Charter Era' (2009) 34 *Queens' Law Journal* 773.

Huscroft, G. and Rishworth, P., '"You Say You Want a Revolution": Bills of Rights in the Age of Human Rights' in D. Dyzenhaus, M. Hunt, G. Huscroft (eds.), *A Simple Common Layer: Essays in Honour of Michael Taggart* (Oxford: Hart, 2009).

Ignatieff, M., *The Rights Revolution* (Toronto: House of Anansi Press, 2000).

Irvine of Lairg, Lord, 'A British Interpretation of Convention Rights' (2012) *Public Law* 237.

Joseph, P., 'Parliament, the Courts, and the Collaborative Enterprise' (2005) 15 *King's College Law Journal* 321.

Jowell, J., 'Of Vires and Vacuums: The Constitutional Context of Judicial Review' (1999) *Public Law* 448.

Juratowitch, B., *Retroactivity and the Common Law* (Oxford: Hart, 2008).

Kahana, T. 'The Notwithstanding Mechanism and Public Discussion: Lessons from the Ignored Practice of Section 33 of the Charter' (2001) 43 *Canadian Public Administration* 255.

'Understanding the Notwithstanding Mechanism' (2002) 52 *University of Toronto Law Journal* 221.

'What Makes for a Good Use of the Notwithstanding Mechanism?' (2004) 23 *Supreme Court Law Review* (second series) 191.

Kavanagh, A., 'Choosing between Sections 3 and 4 of the Human Rights Act 1998: Judicial Reasoning after *Ghaidan v. Mendoza*' in H. Fenwick, G. Phillipson, R. Masterman (eds), *Judicial Reasoning Under the UK Human Rights Act* (Cambridge University Press, 2007).

Constitutional Review under the UK Human Rights Act (Cambridge University Press, 2009).

'Judging the Judges under the Human Rights Act: Deference, Disillusionment and the "War on Terror"' (2009) *Public Law* 287.

'Constitutionalism, Counterterrorism, and the Courts: Changes in the British Constitutional Landscape' (2011) 9 *International Journal of Constitutional Law* 172.

Kelly, J. B., 'Bureaucratic Activism and the Charter of Rights and Freedoms: The Department of Justice and its Entry into the Centre of Government' (1999) 42 *Canadian Public Administration* 476.

'The Commonwealth Model and Bills of Rights: Comparing Legislative Activism in Canada and New Zealand' Paper presented at the conference on Parliamentary Protection of Human Rights, University of Melbourne, 20–22 July 2006.

'A Difficult Dialogue: Statements of Compatibility and the Victorian Charter of Human Rights and Responsibilities Act' (2011) 46 *Australian Journal of Political Science* 257.

'Judicial and Political Review as Limited Insurance: The Functioning of the New Zealand Bill of Rights Act in "Hard" Cases' (2011) 49 *Commonwealth & Comparative Politics* 295.

Kelly, J. B. and Hennigar, M. A., 'The Canadian Charter of Rights and the Minister of Justice: Weak-form Review within a Constitutional Charter of Rights' (2012) 10 *International Journal of Constitutional Law* 35.

Kelsen, H., 'La Garantie Juridictionnelle de la Constitution' (1928) 4 *Revue du Droit Public* 197.

Kinley, D. and Ernst, C., 'Exile on Main Street: Australia's Legislative Agenda for Human Rights' (2012) *European Human Rights Law Review* 58.

Klug, F. and Wildbore, H., 'Breaking New Ground: The Joint Committee on Human Rights and the Role of Parliament in Human Rights Compliance' (2007) *European Human Rights Law Review* 231.

Kolstad, C., Ulen, R. and Johnson, G., '*Ex Post* Liability for Harm vs. *Ex Ante* Safety Regulations: Substitutes or Complements?' (1990) 80 *American Economic Review* 888.

Kommers, D., *The Constitutional Jurisprudence of the Federal Republic of Germany*, 2nd edn (South Bend, IL: Notre Dame University Press, 1997).

Kramer, L., *The People Themselves: Popular Constitutionalism and Judicial Review* (New York: Oxford University Press, 2004).

Kumm, M., 'Who is Afraid of the Total Constitution? Constitutional Rights as Principles and the Constitutionalization of Private Law' (2006) 7 *German Law Journal* 341.

'Institutionalising Socratic Contestation: The Rationalist Human Rights Paradigm, Legitimate Authority and the Point of Judicial Review' (2007) 1 *European Journal of Legal Studies* No. 2.

'Political Liberalism and the Structure of Rights: On the Place and the Limits of the Proportionality Requirement' in S. Paulson and G. Pavlakos (eds.), *Law, Rights, Discourse: Themes of the Work of Robert Alexy* (Oxford: Hart Publishing, 2007).

'Democracy is Not Enough: Rights, Proportionality and the Point of Judicial Review' in M. Klatt (ed.), *The Legal Philosophy of Robert Alexy* (Oxford University Press, 2009).

Lakin, S., 'Debunking the Idea of Parliamentary Sovereignty: The Controlling Factor of Legality in the British Constitution' (2008) 28 *Oxford Journal of Legal Studies* 709.

Lasser, M., *Judicial Deliberations: A Comparative Analysis of Judicial Transparency and Legitimacy* (Oxford University Press, 2004).

Law, D., 'Why Has Judicial Review Failed in Japan?' (2011) 88 *Washington University Law Review* 1425.

Laws, J., 'Law and Democracy' (1995) *Public Law* 72.

'The Constitution, Morals and Rights' (1996) *Public Law* 622.

Legrand, P. and Munday, R. (eds.), *Comparative Legal Studies: Traditions and Transitions* (Cambridge University Press, 2003).

Leigh, I., 'Concluding Remarks', in H. Fenwick, G. Phillipson and R. Masterman, (eds.), *Judicial Reasoning under the UK Human Rights Act* (Cambridge University Press, 2007).

Leigh, I. and Masterman, R., *Making Rights Real: The Human Rights Act in its First Decade* (Oxford: Hart Publishing, 2008).

Lester, A. and Taylor, K., 'Parliamentary Scrutiny of Human Rights', in A. Lester and D. Pannick (eds.), *Human Rights Law and Practice*, 2nd edn (London: LexisNexis, 2004).

Lewis, J., 'The European Ceiling on Human Rights' (2007) *Public Law* 720.

de Londras, F. and Kelly, C., *European Convention on Human Rights Act: Operation, Impact and Analysis* (Dublin: Thomson Reuters, 2010).

McGarrity, N. and Williams, G., 'Counter-Terrorism Laws in a Nation without a Bill of Rights: The Australian Experience' (2010) 2 *City University of Hong Kong Law Review* 45.

Manfredi, C., *Judicial Power and the Charter*, 2nd edn (Toronto: Oxford University Press, 2001).

'The Day the Dialogue Died: A Comment on *Sauvé v. Canada*' (2007) 45 *Osgoode Hall Law Journal* 105.

Manfredi, C. and Kelly, J. B., 'Six Degrees of Dialogue: A Response to Hogg and Bushell' (1999) 37 *Osgoode Hall Law Journal* 513.

Masterman, R., 'Aspiration or Foundation? The Status of the Strasbourg Jurisprudence and the "Convention Rights" in Domestic Law', in H. Fenwick, G. Phillipson and R. Masterman, (eds.), *Judicial Reasoning under the UK Human Rights Act* (Cambridge University Press, 2007).

'Interpretations, Declarations and Dialogue: Rights Protection under the Human Rights Act and Victorian Charter of Human Rights and Responsibilities' (2009) *Public Law* 112.

Mead, D., 'Rights, Relationships and Retrospectivity: The Impact of Convention Rights on Pre-Existing Private Relationships Following Wilson and Ghaidan' (2005) *Public Law* 459.

Meese, E., 'The Law of the Constitution' (1987) 61 *Tulane Law Journal* 979.

Morton, F. L. (ed.), *Law, Politics and the Judicial Process in Canada*, 3rd edn (University of Calgary Press, 2002).

Nesbitt, K., 'Preventative Detention of Terrorist Suspects in Australia and the United States: A Comparative Constitutional Analysis (2007) 17 *Public Interest Law Journal* 39.

Nicol, D., 'The Human Rights Act and the Politicians' (2004) 24 *Legal Studies* 451.

'Law and Politics after the Human Rights Act' (2006) *Public Law* 722.

'Legitimacy of the Commons Debate on Prisoner Voting' (2011) *Public Law* 681.

Paulsen, M. S., 'The Most Dangerous Branch: Executive Power to Say What the Law Is' (1994) 83 *Georgetown Law Review* 217.

Perry, M., 'Protecting Human Rights in a Democracy: What Role for Courts?' (2003) 38 *Wake Forest Law Review* 635.

Petter, A., 'Taking Dialogue Theory Much Too Seriously (or Perhaps Charter Dialogue isn't Such a Good Thing After All)' (2007) 45 *Osgoode Hall Law Review* 147.

Phillipson, G., '(Mis-)Reading Section 3 of the Human Rights Act' (2003) 119 *Law Quarterly Review* 183.

'Deference, Discretion, and Democracy in the Human Rights Era' (2006) *Current Legal Problems* 40.

Pildes, R. 'Law and the President' (2012) 125 *Harvard Law Review* 1381.

Post, R. and Siegel, R., 'Popular Constitutionalism, Departmentalism, and Judicial Supremacy' (2004) 92 *California Law Review* 1027.

Reitz, D. and Richter, G., 'Current Changes in German Abortion Law' (2010) 19 *Cambridge Quarterly of Healthcare Ethics* 334.

Rishworth, P., 'Interpreting Enactments: Sections 4, 5, and 6' in P. Rishworth, G. Huscroft, S. Optician and R. Mahoney (eds.), *The New Zealand Bill of Rights Act* (Melbourne: Oxford University Press, 2003).

'The New Zealand Bill of Rights' in P. Rishworth, G. Huscroft, S. Optician and R. Mahoney (eds.), *The New Zealand Bill of Rights Act* (Melbourne: Oxford University Press, 2003).

'The Inevitability of Judicial Review under "Interpretive" Bills of Rights: Canada's Legacy to New Zealand and Commonwealth Constitutionalism?' (2004) 23 *Supreme Court Law Review* (second series) 233.

Roach, K., 'Editorial: When Should the Section 33 Override be Used?' (1999) 42 *Canada Law Quarterly* 1.

'Constitutional and Common Law Dialogues between the Supreme Court and Canadian Legislatures' (2001) 80 *Canadian Bar Review* 481.

'Dialogic Judicial Review and its Critics' (2004) 23 *Supreme Court Law Review* (second series) 49.

'A Comparison of Australian and Canadian Counter-Terrorism Laws', (2007) 30 *University of New South Wales Law Journal* 53.

Sadurski, W., 'Judicial Review and the Protection of Constitutional Rights' (2002) 22 *Oxford Journal of Legal Studies* 275.

Sager, L., 'Fair Measure: The Legal Status of Underenforced Constitutional Norms' (1978) 91 *Harvard Law Review* 1212.

Samuels, A., 'Human Rights Act 1998 Section 3: A New Dimension to Statutory Interpretation?' (2008) 29 *Statute Law Review* 130.

Schwartz, H., *The Struggle for Constitutional Justice in Post-Communist Europe* (University of Chicago Press, 2000).

Sedley, S., 'No Ordinary Law', 30 *London Review of Books*, 5 June 2008.

Sharpe, R. and Roach, K., *The Charter of Rights and Freedoms*, 4th edn (Toronto: Irwin Law, 2009).

Shavell, S., *Economic Analysis of Accident Law* (Cambridge, MA: Harvard University Press, 1987).

Slattery, B., 'A Theory of the Charter' (1987) 25 *Osgoode Hall Law Journal* 714.

Smillie, J., 'Who Wants Juristocracy?' (2006) 11 *Otago Law Review* 183.

de Smith, S. A., *The New Commonwealth and its Constitutions* (London: Stevens, 1964).

Sullivan, K., and G. Gunther, G., *Constitutional Law*, 17th edn (New York: Foundation Press, 2010).

Stone Sweet, A., 'Abstract Constitutional Review and Policy Making in Western Europe, in D. Jackson and C. N. Tate (eds.), *Comparative Judicial Review and Public Policy* (New York: Greenwood Press, 1992).

Governing with Judges: Constitutional Politics in Europe (Oxford University Press, 2000).

Stone Sweet, A. and Mathews, J., 'Proportionality, Balancing and Global Constitutionalism' (2008) 47 *Columbia Journal of Transnational Law* 68.

Tarnopolsky, W., 'The Historical and Constitutional Context of the Proposed Canadian Charter of Rights and Freedoms' (1981) 44 *Law & Contemporary Problems* 169.

Thayer, J. B., 'The Origin and Scope of the American Doctrine of Constitutional Law' (1893) 7 *Harvard Law Review* 17.

John Marshall (Cambridge University Press, 1901).

Tomkins, A., *Our Republican Constitution* (Oxford: Hart Publishing, 2005).

'The Rule of Law in Blair's Britain' (2007) 26 *University of Queensland Law Journal* 255.

'National Security, Counter-Terrorism and the Intensity of Review: A Changed Landscape?' (2010) 126 *Law Quarterly Review* 543.

'The Role of Courts in the Political Constitution' (2010) 60 *University of Toronto Law Journal* 1.

'Parliament, Human Rights, and Counter-Terrorism' in T. Campbell, K. Ewing and A. Tomkins (eds.), *The Legal Protection of Human Rights: Sceptical Essays* (Oxford University Press, 2011).

Tribe, L., 'Jurisdictional Gerrymandering: Zoning Disfavored Rights Out of the Federal Courts' (1981) 16 *Harvard Civil Rights-Civil Liberties Law Review* 129.

Tuori, K., 'Judicial Constitutional Review as a Last Resort' in T. Campbell, K. Ewing and A. Tomkins (eds.), *The Legal Protection of Human Rights: Sceptical Essays* (Oxford University Press, 2011).

Tushnet, M., 'Alternative Forms of Judicial Review' (2003) 101 *Michigan Law Review* 2781.

'New Forms of Judicial Review and the Persistence of Rights – and Democracy-Based Worries' (2003) 38 *Wake Forest Law Review* 813.

'Social Welfare Rights and the Forms of Judicial Review' (2004) 82 *Texas Law Review* 1895.

'Weak-Form Judicial Review: Its Implications for Legislatures' (2004) 23 *Supreme Court Law Review* (second series) 213.

Weak Courts, Strong Rights: Judicial Review and Social Welfare Rights in Comparative Constitutional Law (Princeton University Press, 2008).

'How Different are Waldron's and Fallon's Core Cases for and against Judicial Review' (2010) 30 *Oxford Journal of Legal Studies* 49.

Tushnet, M. and Jackson, V., *Comparative Constitutional Law*, 2nd edn (New York: Foundation Press, 2006).

Waldron, J., 'Participation: The Rights of Rights' (1998) 98 *Proceedings of the Aristotelian Society* 307.

'Some Models of Dialogue Between Judges and Legislators' (2004) 23 *Supreme Court Law Review* (second series) 7.

'The Core of the Case Against Judicial Review' (2006) 115 *Yale Law Journal* 1348.

'Constitutionalism – A Skeptical View' in T. Christiano and J. Christman (eds.), *Contemporary Debates in Political Philosophy* (London: Wiley-Blackwell, 2009).

'Judges as Moral Reasoners' (2009) 7 *International Journal of Constitutional Law* 2.

Walker, N., 'Constitutionalism and the Incompleteness of Democracy: An Iterative Relationship' (2010) 39 *Rechtsfilosofie & Rechtstheorie* 206.

Weiler, P. C., 'Rights and Judges in a Democracy: A New Canadian Version' (1984) 18 *University of Michigan Journal of Law Reform* 51.

Weiler, J. and Lockhart, N., '"Taking Rights Seriously" Seriously: The European Court and its Fundamental Rights Jurisprudence' (1995) 32 *Common Market Law Review* 51 and 579.

Weinrib, L., 'Learning to Live with the Override' (1990) 35 *McGill Law Journal* 542.

'The Postwar Paradigm and American Exceptionalism' in S. Choudhry (ed.), *The Migration of Constitutional Ideas* (Cambridge University Press, 2005).

Wintermute, R., 'The Human Rights Act's First Five Years: Too Strong, Too Weak, or Just Right?' (2006) 17 *King's College Law Journal* 209.

Young, A. L., *Parliamentary Sovereignty and the Human Rights Act* (Oxford: Hart Publishing, 2009).

'Is Dialogue Working Under the Human Rights Act 1998?' (2011) *Public Law* 773, 774–8.

van Zyl Smit, J. 'The New Purposive Interpretation of Statutes: HRA Section 3 after *Ghaidan* v. *Godin-Mendoza*' (2007) *Modern Law Review* 294.

INDEX